I0200525

Dedicated

To my mom, Lorene Hopkins Barrett

SOS SELF IMPROVEMENT

ASSESSMENTS I, II, III, IV

Dr. John C. Barrett Jr. is the coordinator of Support Outreach Services = SOS LLC. Dr. Barrett is dedicated to publishing books on helping you help yourself. It is our hope that this book will help you discover truths for your own life and help you meet the needs of others.

All Scripture quotations, unless otherwise noted, are taken from the taken from the Holy Bible, King James Version, copyright © 1979, 1980, 1982 by Thomas Nelson, Inc. Used by permission.

Support Outreach Services SOS LLC West Plains, MO 65775
(417) 204-8022 – drbarrettphd@yahoo.com
www.sosselfhelpbooks.info

ISBN-10 0692573968
ISBN-13 978-0692573969

Cover Design: Lisa Narodowski – WiredNDesign Book Design: Lisa Narodowski – Wired

Dr. John Barrett
Clinical Psychologist
Counselor / Analysis
Group Sessions

Support Outreach Services =
SOS Publications
Author: John C. Barrett Jr. B.S/ M.A/PH-D

To participate in any of our services are free. When you order our books, and the study materials and DVD's, there is an expense:
One book $15.00
Two Books $25.00
Three Books $35.00
Study materials$10.00
Shipping costs $ 10.00
What you do will enable us to carry out some of these programs and services.

Our information network will give you a list of study guides, newsletters are on the link, and some booklets are free. There is so much information out there and there are all kinds of help.

Check out our Support Outreach Services and Processing Center.

Support Outreach Services is not supported by any government agency, church or denomination. Support Outreach Services SOS is supported by our directory, conferences, donations, and book sales. When you help us I will share the results of our surveys and studies, and keep you up to date with our newsletters. I hope you will want to help, but if you can't I will be glad to help you if I can. Only what you feel in your heart is all that is expected from you.

Our processing center is an independent processing center. One of the links is called: "Gems for Jams." This is a community service bulletin board, but really it is much more than that. Here you can share those special thoughts, poems, or words of wisdom that have helped you. This could be something you have written yourself, or someone else may have written. The main idea is to get people to share something personal out of their life. This will give us a chance to access a wealth of information, and this information will be shared with others. There are lots of DVD's, books, and studies out there.

SOS SELF IMPROVEMENT

SELF IMAGE

SELF ESTEEM

SELF WORTH

Profiles, Charts / Axioms, & Questionnaires

CHAPTER 1 - Introduction

Meeting Your Basic Needs

CHAPTER 2 - Dealing with SELF-IM HIERARCHY NEEDS by ADLER & MASLOW

Negative thoughts Block Creative or Critical Positive Thinking & Problem Solving

CHAPTER 3 - What Does Intelligence Have To Do With The Thinking Process?

Cognitive Behaviors & Cognition feelings lead to Meta Cognition Self-Awareness

CHAPTER 4 - Look At The Reflections In Your Life

CHAPTER 5 - Introduction To Self-Esteem

Applying SELF HELP PRINCIPLES used in SELF-ESTEEM In Conjunction with the Mind & Heart

CHAPTER 6 - Low Self-Esteem, Gloom, Doom, Despair, And Depression

CHAPTER 7 - Explanation For Saying "We Have Two Minds" What Does This Mean

CHAPTER 8 - Resourceful Thinking & Problem Solving

CHAPTER 9 – Assessment I

Life Is About The RESPONSIBILITY In A Person's Life

CHAPTER 10 - Assessment II

In Meeting The Demands Of Interpersonal Conflicts Life Is About ACCOUNTABILITY In A Person's Life

CHAPTER 11 - Self Controlling Techniques

CHAPTER 12 - Developing Your Strengths While Managing Your Weaknesses

Control Management Means Controlling the Uncontrollable

CHAPTER 13 - Resiliency & Coping-Skills

We are going to teach some

- Methods
- Use the tools you have and
- Use analytical skills of motivation
- Chapter 14 – CONCLUSION Are You Happy? Meeting Your Needs Self-Esteem!

- Applying SELF HELP PRINCIPLES used in SELF-ESTEEM!

ASSESSMENT I - Life Is About The RESPONSIBILITY In A Person's Life

ASSESSMENT II - Life Is About The ACCOUNTABILITY In A Person's Life

ASSESSMENT III - Life Means Personal DISCIPLINE Such As In Self-Correction, Resiliency & Coping-Skills.

ASSESSMENT IV- Life Means Personal Motivation In How A Person Lives Their Life
DETERMINATION

    A. Recognition   B. Resiliency C. Recovery

    A. Life means personal RECOGNITION is understanding the need for changes

    B. Life means personal RESILIENCY is meeting the challenge

..... C. LIFE MEANS PERSONAL RECOVERY IS OVERCOMING THE POSSIBILITIES

LIGHTHOUSE ON THE HILL SIDE POEM
HERE IS A LIGHT HOUSE ON THE HILLSIDE
THAT OVER LOOKS LIFE'S SEA
AND WHEN MY SOUL IS TOSSED,
IT SENDS OUT A LIGHT, SO THAT I MIGHT SEE

AND THE LIGHT THAT SHINES IN DARKNESS
NOW SAFELY LEADS ME HOME
AND IF IT WASN'T FOR THE LIGHTHOUSE
THIS SHIP WOULD BE NO MORE.
HERE IS A LIGHT HOUSE ON THE HILLSIDE
THAT OVER LOOKS LIFE'S SEA
AND WHEN MY SOUL IS TOSSED,
IT SENDS OUT A LIGHT, SO THAT I MIGHT SEE

AND THE LIGHT THAT SHINES IN DARKNESS
NOW SAFELY LEADS ME HOME
AND IF IT WASN'T FOR THE LIGHTHOUSE
THIS SHIP WOULD BE NO MORE.
EVERYBODY THAT LIVES AROUND US
SAYS TEAR THAT LIGHT HOUSE DOWN

CAUSE THE BIG SHIPS DON'T PASS THIS WAY ANYMORE
THERE'S NO USE OF IT HANGING ROUND.
EVERYBODY THAT LIVES AROUND US
SAYS TEAR THAT LIGHT HOUSE DOWN

BUT MY MIND GOES BACK TO ONE STORMY NIGHT
WHEN JUST IN TIME, I SAW THE LIGHT
IT WAS THE LIGHT FROM THAT OLD LIGHTHOUSE
THERE UP ON THE HILL.
I THANK GOD FOR THE LIGHT HOUSE
I OWE MY LIFE TO HIM
FOR JESUS IS THE LIGHTHOUSE
AND FROM THE ROCKS OF SIN
HE HAS SHOWN A LIGHT AROUND ME
SO THAT I MIGHT CLEARLY SEE
AND IF IT WASN'T FOR THAT LIGHTHOUSE
WHERE WOULD THIS SHIP BE.

PREFACE

Self-Help Books Have Value Because:

We Never Know What Will Happen or When!

Take Time To Let These Four Assessments Work!

There is the second in a series of self-help studies where I use other methods to evaluate and make 4 assessments on these self-control concepts and deal with how you feel about yourself and life.

I want people who read any of my books to take time to stop at any point; because you need to let the information help you, come back when you feel the need for more information about the study. You may not need this book now, but likely, there is someone in your family who will need the information in this study. Some may wait until they feel the need to take a look at one's self.

I recommend all of our books; SOS LIFE ENHANCEMENT, I believe everyone needs a doctor's check-up at some time in their life or when you feel the need for encouragement, or something to inspire you, or when you want to know more about yourself. You will find that SOS SELF IMPROVEMENT goes to the core of a person and who they are.

SOS NEW BEGINNINGS analytical profiles on premarital marriage, marriage, family and children, divorce & single parenting, blended families, & treatments and profiles on addictions.

This book takes a view of one's self and it is based on three self-concepts as we deal with a person's intelligence, two **Meta cognition** *awareness and the* **intelligence of a person**, *and* **three how they fit into the psychology** *of one's self, the satisfaction of self-improvement in a person throughout this study.*

Chapter 1 – Introduction: We will focus on four basic areas: "self-image, self-esteem, self-worth and self-discipline." I believe it is important to understand our own self-concepts in relation to self-improvement, and the concepts of how others see you.

These are the views held by some contemporary philosophers in relation to Self-Image:

- Altruism or Egoism?
- Then Egoism verses Altruism?
- Egoism and Altruism in Early Psychology
- The Altruism Question in Contemporary Psychology
- The Altruism and Egoism of the Greek philosophy, based on Plato and Aristotle's perception of life.

In Chapters, 2 - 5, each person has their own values and that has to do with their ego and their validation as a person, self-image is how a person feels about him or herself.

Chapters 6 - 9 the bottom line self-esteem is to describe those who seem more concerned with themselves than with others. It is important to distinguish between those who have some narcissistic personality traits and other traits comes from a person's personality disorders rather than behaviors in the previous chapters and how a person feels about themselves. Let me explain those with a control personality are often seen as arrogant, confident, prideful, and self-centered they are people who accomplish things, but on the other hand we have people who are just as affective they have a view of their own abilities that characterizes their intellectual assists. However, we believe some people have some or both of these characteristics and only need to identify and reshape their view of themselves and I believe there is a need to have a more humble approach, in summation a person needs determination to accomplish things as they see (him or her) SELF.

Chapters 10 - 11 Self-Worth is another part of the study dealing with self-extension, because it is how a person incorporates actualization principles of the thinking process along with their self-discipline and analyses of one's self.

Chapters 12 we finish with the conclusion on the value of happiness and sum-up the 4 premises in this study.

I have been the coordinator of Support Outreach Services = SOS LLC; since 1997. Link to www.sosselfhelpbooks.info for more self-help books and information. There are other self-help manuals 1. Is on Mentoring and Coaching, 2. Is on Leadership Training, and how to set up group sessions.

Self Help Books

Book: "SOS LIFE ENHANCEMENT - Opens the doors to who are you, behavior identification and behavior modification; Evaluations "now that you have made a decision, what are the next steps in your life."

Book:"SOS NEW BEGINNINGS" Analytical Study Guide Dating, Marriage and Family Divorce, Single Parenting, Blended Families, & Treatments for Addictions. A preview of our Health Awareness & Fitness Program.

Books in the future:

These are Christian Self-help "Studies & Methods, Skills & Tools, Values, and Biblical Principles" include: (Reconciliation) - (Restoration) (Prayer & Spiritual Warfare) - (Rehabilitation & Forgiveness)

Book: Christian Fundamentals in Psychology & the Modern Techniques of Psychology (Reconciliation) The Basic Fundamentals of Christian Psychology Studies & Methods, in understanding how the Bible describes your heart, mind, body & soul.

Book: (Restoration) Knowing The Old You & Creating a New Life in you!

Book: How I got answers to my Prayer & Spiritual Warfare in Prayer!
   1. Standing in the GAP for others, (God Answers Prayer).
   2. Co support & Co-prayer-support for others.

Booklet: (Free) (Rehabilitation & Forgiveness) My Testimony: Life can cast a "Shadow of doubt in a person's life?" & falling by the way (backsliding as a Christian)! We discuss my testimony and what happens and the changes in my life.

Questions I had to answer, Christian Methods, Values, & Biblical Principles.

(Booklets)

What are some Secrets for a Happy Christian Life? Secrets to Happiness.

Common Enemies in a Christian's life.

How Can Christian's "Develop Control & Balance while Maintaining a Disciplined Life.

Understanding & Creating a New Life in You!

Comparing the modern age of psychology and the

Self-image has to do with the character of a man or women.

Scriptural view of Self-image.

The modern age of methodology in terms of the Scriptural view of the person

A down-hill-spiral exposes the weaknesses in man-kind/Christian.

Burnout - Depression - Anxiety in Christian's,

Why is the New Reformation Wrong?

Biblical out looks on divorce. Or (Booklets & Video)

Applying CHRISTIAN PRINCIPLES that will help & heal Relationships!

Standing in the <u>GAP</u> for others, (<u>G</u>od <u>A</u>nswers <u>P</u>rayer). Co support & Co-prayer- support.

Dr. John C Barrett Jr. B.S / M.A / in Counseling, & PH-D in Psychology

Lighthouse on the Hill Side Poem by the Hinsons
A lighthouse guides,
A lighthouse warns of rocks,
reefs, and currents.
A lighthouse serves as a beacon,
A beacon to guide others safely into port.
A lighthouse is built from strong material,
And reinforced with even stronger materials,
So that it may stand up to the all that may happen to it.
A lighthouse may vary in size, shape, or color.
A lighthouse gives off a light for all,
A light that will be bent by a lens into a powerful central beam,
So that it may shine a bright light to all things around it.

There is a keeper lives in the lighthouse,
To keep it clean and maintain it,
So that it may be tall and strong.
For a lighthouse is built high,
So that it may shine the light to as much as possible.

A coast needs to be lined with lighthouses,
So that the four corners of the world shall be safe,
And there may be light where there is only dark.
For God tells us to be a lighthouse for him,
So that we may shine the light to all,
And bring everyone into his harbor.

Submitted by John Raedeke

Self-Image

Meta Cognition = Self-Awareness

Chapter 1

SELF-IMAGE

Introduction

I want to start by saying a person can do anything if they put their mind into gear and want to do it bad enough. That largely depends on the amount of effort, another component depends on how bad a person wants to accomplish anything and in some cases the situation dictates the amount of success.

I like the book display of a "light house" to show a personal insight and the way to enlighten a personal perception of one's self, and I will use other references to point ways you can challenge you're life.

These are views held by some contemporary philosophers in relation to Self-Image:

- Altruism or Egoism?
- Then Egoism verses Altruism?
- Egoism and Altruism in Early Psychology
- The Altruism Question in Contemporary Psychology
- The Altruism and Egoism of the Greek philosophy, based on Plato and Aristotle's perception of life.

The Bible relates to man as an intelligent being which states "we are made in the image of God" of course that accounts for our intelligence. Man has come a long way in understanding what intelligence is as we see the progress of man in regards to the building of the Ark to men flying in space.

"I will deal with all three components of a (man and women) Self-Image, Self-Esteem, & Self-Worth"; we use the holistic approach to human concepts of the mental, psychical, and spiritual, I want to add a person needs to understand how the mind and heart works in solving problem.

Definition of Holistic: {1}
   relating to or concerned with wholes or with complete systems rather
   than with the analysis of, treatment of, or dissection into p
   <holistic medicine attempts to treat both the mind and the body>
   <holistic ecology views humans and the environment as a single
   system> of or relating to relating to or concerned with wholes or with
   complete systems rather
   than with the analysis of, treatment of, or dissection into parts
   <holistic medicine attempts to treat both the mind and the body>
   <holistic ecology views humans and the environment as a single
   system>
http://unabrided.merriam-webester   5/20/2014

I have two wonderful profiles of people that use all three concepts and how they deal with their handy caps who achieved great things. The first person is a contemporary story about Ray Charles the second is Fanny Crosby who wrote poems, songs, and hymns:

RAY CHARLES – Blues, Jas, R&B Music –corporate Entertainment Booking   Pages 1 of 6 [1]

"Ray the never-before-told story, a musical biographical drama of an American legend Ray Charles. Born in a poor town in Georgia, Ray Charles went blind at the age of seven shortly after witnessing his younger brother's accidental death. Inspired by a fiercely independent mother who insisted that he make his own way in the world, Charles found his calling and his gift behind a piano keyboard. (Spending his early years in church learning the old Gospel songs and Spirituals).
As a young man touring across the Southern musical circuit, the soulful singer gained a reputation and then exploded with worldwide fame when he pioneered and while incorporating gospel, country, and jazz orchestral influences into his inimitable style. As he revolutionized

the way people appreciated music, he simultaneously fought segregation in the very clubs that launched him and championed artists' rights within the corporate music business. 'Ray' provides an unflinching portrait of Charles' musical genius as he overcomes drug addiction while transforming into one of this country's most-beloved performers.

Ray Charles Robinson was not born blind, only poor. The first child of Aretha and Baily Robinson was born in Albany, Georgia, on September 23, 1930. He hit the road early, at about three months, when the Robinsons moved across the border to Greenville, Florida. It was the height of the Depression years and the Robinsons had started out poor. 'You hear folks talking about being poor,' Charles recounts. 'Even compared to other blacks'. We were on the bottom of the ladder looking up at everyone else. Nothing below us except the ground.

By the early 1960's Ray Charles had accomplished his dream. He had come of age musically. He had become a great musician, posting musical milestones along his route. He had made it to Carnegie Hall. The all-time hit records of ('Georgia,' & 'Born to Lose') successively kept climbing to the top of the charts.

'I knew being blind was suddenly an aid. I never learned to stop at the skin. If I looked at a man or a woman, I wanted to see inside. Being distracted by shading or coloring is stupid. It gets in the way. It's something I just can't see.'

'Ray Charles was never one to pay attention to musical boundaries. Born in the Deep South, raised on gospel, blues, country, jazz, and big band, he forged these disparate styles into something all his own he was one of the first to bring about' (Soul music as it is known today)."

1/10/05

The second is no less an admiral story of Fanny Crosby:

Fanny Crosby Biographies   **Pages 1-2** [2]

"Known as an American hymn writer and poetess, Fanny Crosby wrote over 9,000 hymns during her life. Many **stories** have been told about her.

She entered what was then known as the **New York Institution for the Blind** at the age of fifteen and afterward taught English and history (1847-58).

As a pupil and as a teacher, Fanny spent 35 years at the school. She was often asked to entertain visitors with her poems and she frequently met with presidents, generals and other dignitaries. She was asked to play at President Grant's Funeral. Her first book of poems was published in 1844 was called The Blind Girl and Other Poems.

After leaving the school, she dedicated her life to serving the poorest and the neediest. Supporting herself by her writing, she quickly gained fame for her hymns. It is said that publishers had so much of her work that they took to using them under pseudonyms. Her usual fee was a mere $2 which frequently went to her work with the poor. Her mission work is legendary, as is her devotion to serving others above herself.

When she was ninety years old, Fanny stated, 'In my quiet moments I say to myself, Fanny, there are many worse things than blindness that might have happened to you'.

'How in the world could I have lived such a helpful life as I have lived had I not been blind? I am very well satisfied. I never let anything trouble me, and to my implicit faith, and to my implicit trust in my heavenly Father's goodness, I attribute my good health and long life.'
Her unfailing joy and childlike faith enabled her to encourage and comfort others with songs like:
Blessed Assurance
Blessed as – sur – ance, Jesus is mine! Oh what a for taste of glory devine
'*God will take care of you, be not afraid, He is your safeguard through sunshine and shade*
Tenderly watching, and keeping His own, He will not leave you to wander alone.'

HOW RECOGNIZING THE UNSEEN BENEFITS OF PHYSICAL BLINDNESS ENABLED FANNY CROSBY TO REJOICE

A Scotch minister once remarked to her: 'I think it is a great pity that the Master, when He showered so many gifts upon you, did not give you sight.'

Fanny replied, 'Do you know that if I had been able to make only one petition to my Creator it would have been that I should remain blind?' The surprised minister.

'Because, when I go to heaven, the first face that shall ever gladden my sight will be that of my Savior,' she answered. Before she went home to see her Savior face to face, Fanny had given the world nearly eight thousand poems.

Because Fanny Crosby did not view her blindness as a handicap, it never became a root of bitterness in her life and she was able to live a life of mercy for others."

Quotations taken from S. Trevena Jackson. *Fanny Crosby's Story of Ninety-Four Years* (New York: Fleming H. Revell Company 29, 33).

Known as an American hymn writer and poetess, Fanny Crosby wrote over 9,000 hymns during her life. As a pupil and as a teacher, Fanny spent 35 years at the school. Her first book of poems was published in 1844 was called *The Blind Girl and Other Poems*.

It is collection of secular stories and poems filled with the same, emotional tone she gave her hymns. Her last book, *Memories of Eighty Years*, was published in 1906.

One biographer wrote of her, "...in her day, she was considered by most people to be the greatest in America. As Johann Strauss reigned in Vienna as the 'Waltz King', and John Phillip Sousa in Washington as the 'March King', so Fanny Crosby reigned in New York in the later nineteenth and early twentieth century as the 'Hymn Queen'.

One of Miss Crosby's hymns was so personal that for years she kept it to herself. Kenneth Osbeck, author of several books on hymnology, says its revelation to the public came about this way: 'One day at the Bible conference in Northfield, Massachusetts, Miss Crosby was asked by D.L. Moody to give a personal testimony. At first she hesitated, then quietly rose and said, 'There is one hymn I have written which has never been published. I call it my soul's poem. Sometimes when I am troubled, I repeat it to myself, for it brings comfort to my heart.' She then recited while many wept:

At the age of 95 Fanny Crosby passed on and on her grave in Bridgeport, Conn., there is a simple little headstone with the name 'Aunt Fanny,' and these words:

Blessed assurance, Jesus is mine. Oh, what a foretaste of glory divine.
http://www.nyise.org/fanny/bios.html   1/7/05

The smallest deeds are greater, when, knowing your intentions and fulfilling them.

We have two people who probable did not aspired to greatness, but it was probably a driving force as they used their talents to the fullest extent and that made them great. They did not let their handicap keep them from living a full life and that is what I want this study to do for you.

Defining the term KNOWLEDGE:

It is the science of the knowing what a person can learn, sometimes known as the science of learning about one's self in this case we're talking about knowing *who you are*. We are concerned about how people feel about themselves; an analogy that might fit, why do wolves howl at the moon and teen agers rebel against their parents. Why do birds sing, and moths fly into a flame; why does a person remember how to ride a bicycle after twenty years; why do people speak and gesture, love and at the same time go to war.

The Phenomena that deals with how a person takes on tasks with certain amount risk and there is an enormous range of activities involved what they think about themselves and some of the things a person's does relates to their personal make-up and choices. Some border on things like their **genetics, biological make-up** touches on **social sciences** such as **social background**. Some of the other concerns are developed **behaviors known as traits**; many others pertain to behaviors related to **heredity**. Some are about the **conscious experience**; we will focus on what people do regardless of what they may think or feel. Some of the other reasons involve, why people do things, because they just want to do things. Those kinds of **human traits;** people do all of this while dealing with other concerns. We will look at how a person reacts in different situations or in a personal relationship. These are a few initial glimpses into man's thinking:

1. Different parts of the brain have different physical functions.

2. When any part of the body and mind are activated, in that case more blood will flow from the brain and creates energy = it can also cause high blood pressure. The blood flow depends on what the person does and the amount of activity.
3. Social communications are based on built-in signals called "verbal signals."
4. Some human behaviors depend on the circumstances, like when people are in a crowd they behave differently depending on the type of group and its influences peoples behaviors and what they say, for instance yelling at a sporting event.
5. But when they are alone they may act and think entirely in a different way because no one sees or knows what they are thinking.

META COGNITION – AWARENESS

You need a **mental awareness** as it does with *self-awareness* and your mental state of mind is vital in knowing who you are. Stress-Factors also have vital links to your **mental well-being**.

Everybody has a different way of dealing with STRESS. Our main goal is for you to keep a STRESS BALANCE and have checkpoints be aware of your emotional needs I call this part of our life enhancement STRESS-FACTORS. I want you to have an idea of how stress-factors play role and how to deal with them.

This is another chance to see the other components of your emotional make-up I have a male sensitivity, I am very sensitive to others feels, a woman has their way of looking at life, then children and young people have their own way of looking at life. I am very aware of the different sensitivity levels in each and how emotions affect reactions and let you know how STRESS relates in your PERSONAL PROBLEMS, then how stress can affect your HEALTH. I have dealt with the personal side, stress is an interaction, all of these factors manifests it's self that affects a person's outward expression in some way. It is very visible when a person is hurt and emotions build; there are different ways to measure the amount of stress.

There are all kinds STRESS or STRESSES some are good, but we have to be careful some kinds of STRESS can bring about mental and physical damage. Be aware of the stress level in a situation or relationship look at the STRESS LEVEL:
1.   THESE ARE THE WARNING SIGNS
2.   THESE ARE THE ALARM SIGNALS.

These are the bases we use in our "self-help studies", I hope they will help you deal with your stress and understand the role it plays in your life how has stress affected a person in the past? It is an interaction and it involves every aspect of the stress point when there is too much stress a person needs to stop and look at why. When there is personal damage be careful watch for the breaking point or the point of no return.

I want to give you some ways to deal with stress, first take some timeout for yourself and share your life with someone else or by some kind of hobby or activity. This is one of the most important steps in dealing with the stress another is by being able to talk openly with someone. Sometimes you cannot always talk openly with your fiancé-spouse, family member or a friend because of an argument or fight you have had in the past.

A person needs to manage their thoughts and feelings and look at their emotions. We use the cognitive approach in our book "SOS LIFE ENHANCEMENT", now we are dealing with *personal intelligences* that are involved in a person's thinking and actions, especially when it comes to *intrapersonal intelligence*. That means *intelligence* is involved more on the line of *Meta cognition* the awareness of one's mental process "rather understand how a person's emotions are involved in their cogitative well-being".

Meeting Your Basic Needs

To set new guidelines in your life is very important, but a person has to deal with their emotional make-up. A person's love and the need to be loved brings' about different kinds of feelings and even different degrees of love. There are opposite ends of the spectrum when it comes to love and so can the emotions go from one extreme to another. It is as if we are at opposite ends of the world's polar system trying to meet and we know they can't, but they are tied to each other because they are a part of the universe.

How we love, even to the point of how much we care or to the point we don't like something and the feelings in between. How we relate to our love for each other will play a significant role in our lives. How we feel and love reflects on how we see others. This more than anything else our past will determine our prejudices, and the hurt involved in our situations and relationships. We need to get this part of our lives headed in the right direction or to some degree. However, there should be some joy in life and we will develop these basic premises as we deal with self-esteem; we want you to have more bounce and joy.

Personal Meta Cognition is Paying Attention to Your Self-Image and Self-Worth

This **self-improvement** study deals with **Self-Image** first and **Self-Worth** is another aspect of a person, the nerve center of a person is their attitude and emotional make-up, the center of activity is **Self-Image** to understanding your **Self-Esteem**. A person has to deal with their pride and how it affects their relationships and so on. We are intelligent and complex beings, that is why it is hard to define *who you are* and what is best for you. (**SOS**) self-help studies puts a major emphasis on the person; because you need to understand your own thoughts and to be able to understand how your **self-image** affects your circumstances and relationships. We use **self-esteem** principles in discipline, self-improvement and anger management.

Personal Influences Concerning Self-Image

This is where we deal with the persons inner feelings and how they deal with outside influences, and how to meet their own needs at the same time without destroying their relationships. The way to do this is by seeing how you deal with your own feelings and emotions, and see how they affect the way you get things done and how to help yourself at the same time. Your needs may vary from day to day, if you are (women or man) how do you meet those needs regardless of your sex.

The person has to relate to their inner thoughts and feelings what you think of yourself (**self-worth**) is important how you relate and get along with other people will determine your value and (**self-worth**). You may think of yourself in one way, but one of the guidelines may be what others think of you, they may not really know all of your inner feelings and how things are affecting you.

HIERARCHY NEEDS by ADLER & MASLOW

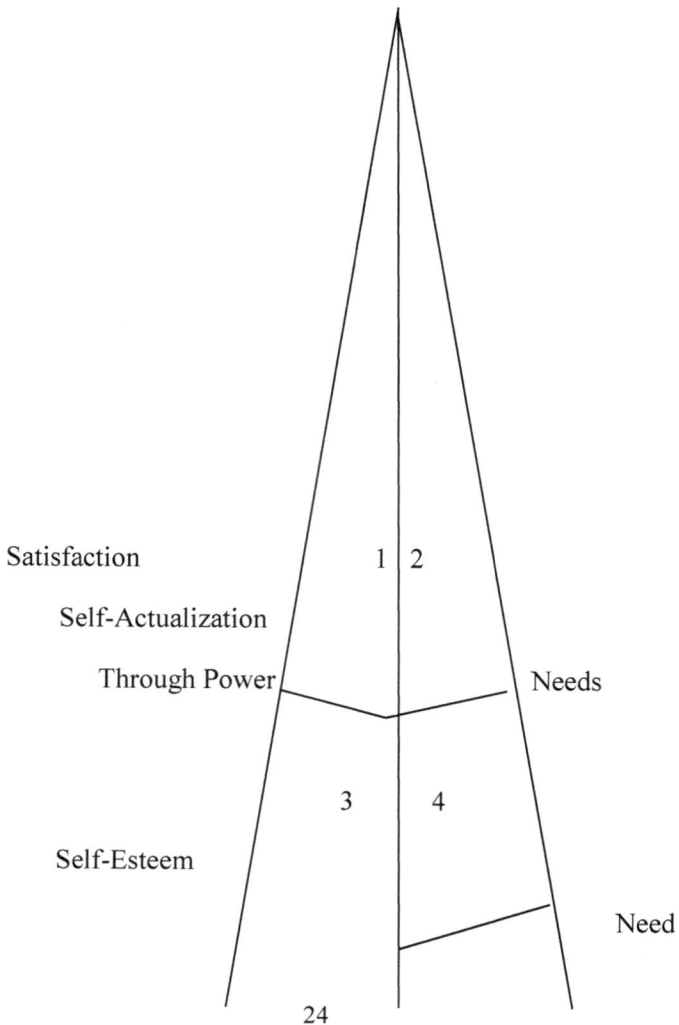

Satisfaction

1 2

Self-Actualization

Through Power

Needs

3 4

Self-Esteem

Need

24

Significance   5

Safety & Security

Belonging   Needs

Security   Needs

Physiological   Love needs

Adler & Maslows

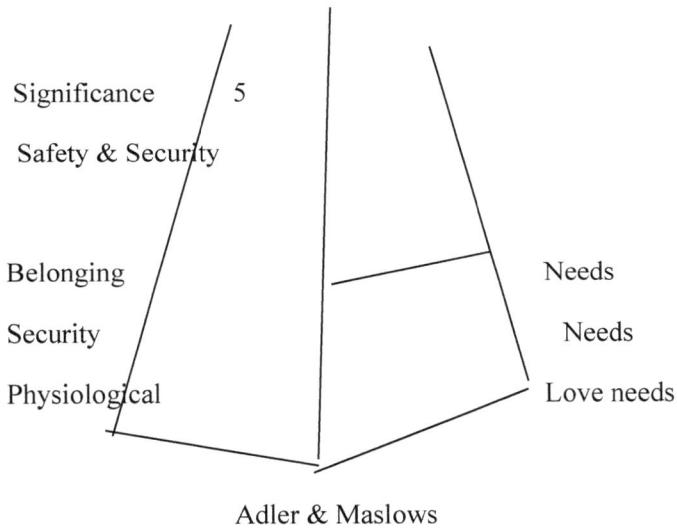

Now let's look at how Creative Thinking as it is involved in Problem solving?

What is Creative Thinking?

1. Negative Attitudes Block Creativity or Critical Thinking & Problem Solving
2. Mental Blocks to Creative or Critical Thinking and Problem Solving
3. Myths about Creative Thinking or Critical Thinking and Problem Solving

What is "ALTRUISM?"

It was Adler's fundamental view of a person realizing the need for fulfillment and satisfaction. This can only be done when (his or her) need for security and significance can be met. Maslow took this idea, reshaped and amplified it under the heading of "self-actualization."

Maslow was (right) about the fact that most theoreticians had developed their concepts of human functioning from cases they met in counseling. While there are probably some things wrong with their approach; Maslow thought that the study of man should not be based on studies of failures, or persons having great difficulties, etc. He set out to study those who were making it, really making it in life-self-actualized. "He determined that there were 30 or more characteristics that are common to such persons. He also noted that these self-actualized people reach out beyond themselves. Maslow concluded if we don't achieve self-actualization until their needs met or were lower because their expectations were either too low and did not perform well. Consequently those who sat their expectation too high were unable to meet their expectations and self-actualization."

Another reference to this kind of thinking comes as we, **"Open the three Doors to SOS Life Enhancement"** but this study deals with **ALTRUISM.**

Again let me make a connection between assessments as to how a person thinks as we go on in the connection to creative and critical thinking & problem solving. I hope you're going see how altruism and egoism relates to your life.

In some cases, it is a good idea to look at the definition of the words and terms we're going to be dealing with that will give us a clearer understanding of the meaning in light of the subjects we are covering.

We cannot discuss the study of physiology of man without including the actual working of the brain and its functions, and systems make-up of the inner thoughts of (men/woman). The adrenal glands produce energy, we know the Atom is made up of energy and mass, which is two-fold. The body is also made of energy and mass, its functions are in relation to the physiology we are three-fold body, soul, and spirit; the psychology of a person also has three-fold elements that relate to psychology Behaviors, and Created Traits, Characterized by feelings and emotions.

Then what are your feelings towards your relationships is very important, but more importantly is how you take on the challenges of the circumstances in your relationships how are they affecting you as a person? I know that there is an interaction within your relationships, but on the other hand, you may feel alone whether you are married or single. The outside influences are another thing you have to deal with.

I contend a person really does not understand all of their feelings as well as they think, it is hard for people to know themselves because they hide and cover up their problems. When looking at one's self the real truth lies in their subconscious and sometimes it is hidden so deep they can't accept the truth of what has happened. A person may pretend or think everything is alright when it is not I think some people may be right about themselves, but only to some degree don't count on it unless they are honest with themselves!

Definition of Physiology: *Noun*   {2}
Latin *physiologyia* **natural science**

> 1a: a branch of biology that deals with the functions and activities of life or of living matter (as organs, tissues, or cells) and of the physical and chemical phenomena involved – compare anatomy.
> 2: the organic process and phenomena of an organism or any of its parts or of a particular bodily process

Referenced from http://www.merriam-webstercollegiate.com/ Merriam-Webster's Collegiate Dictionary Eleventh Edition / (date 2/15/04)

There are three parts of the body system that interact with the psychology of a man & women.

1. The Adrenalin, Thyroid, and Pituitary Glands that Sucrets Chemicals into the body and they create energy and drive the nerve system.
2. The central nerve system reacts to these Chemicals usually by creating a balance or imbalance in a person's health, and mental well-being.
3. The Brain is the Head Quarter that interlocks these glands, systems, and they all go through the central nerve system and they should create emotional control and good well if not there are other problems to deal with.

Every person must be able to understand their own physical limitations in relation to how a (men & women) treat their bodies. We must be able distinguish between the physical aspects of **physiology** and the mental aspects of the **conscious** and **subconscious psychical phenomena** of **psychology** of a person. We deal with each person in relation to a problem, situation, in relation to what is happening in (his or her) relationships.

There may be imbalances that are created in the *psychogenesis,* such as patterns of hostility and anger from within as it is manifested in a person's outward expressions of emotion, such as hurt feelings and as the anger is expressed or because of what happened.

The opposite has to do with feelings that can lead to subdued inner-personal-introvertedness, **Low Self-worth** and depression. The inner-personal-aggressiveness in *these cases a person may consider counseling and support, or group sessions for themselves.* This is very important in the dynamics of being able to help themselves; what direction should they take and how they are going to deal with each situation.

In some cases, they are going to need more than counseling and support when a person cannot deal with their problems. They may need to be under the direct care of a Clinical Psychologist for Counseling or theorist for proper medication and guidance.

The psychology of a person also interacts with the heart and soul of a person, which is actually the make-up from the inner workings of a person. The proper understanding of one's self or at least working with someone who understands the inner workings of a person. There is that aspect of a man or woman which cannot be understood without proper knowledge of the inner man or women.

The spirit of a person is made of how well a person reacts to a situation, the human element shows up the spirit and will of person when it comes to overcoming something. The Psychic inner being links a person to God the connection of the human spirit to the Holy Spirit.

How a person sees things has a lot do with how they think the eyes of a person is their heart the second is how they deal with the different senses. Everything that happens can cause the triggering mechanisms in a person to respond, (shut down or excel) that triggers more reactions in some way, but not always. There are four inner locking senses that have to do with the body taste, smell, sight, and touch. The most important thing that happens is being conscience of the very inner being of a person. How do all of these interconnects work within a person, and how a person thinks and feels about themselves.

I don't think we can study the person without giving some credence to how they feel, nor without discussing what the five senses do; they do have a bearing on how a person sees things. On the other hand, we will focus on how a person thinks, and how they see the other influences in their life. All five senses play a role in every moment of your weakening day, but the eyes are the primary receptor that triggers other factors and functions.

I am interested in how a person responds to adversity. I have given two examples of people who were blind who used other senses in a unique way, the other senses kick in and activate other responses to help the body and mind react, but what about the mind and how it functions? As you can see, Ray Charles and Fanny Crosby had very productive lives with handicaps. I know of people in our own family with extreme handicaps who are able to live productive lives they are both cousins one has physical limits the other is handicapped and can't talk, but understands everything you say has and physically handy caped. They both live independently and run her own business one is dependent on her husband who has limited abilities neither can drive a car so they pay someone to drive them both of them travail all over the country.

The quickest way to make a handicap worse is by not letting a person learn for themselves, and it is like doing everything for a child. A person needs a certain amount of teaching or counseling, but more than that they need to do things for themselves. They need to reach goals that don't take away from their independence, this even works with people who are handicapped. If it is possible, let them do things for themselves that is what I want people to learn in this study.

Altruism and Egoism is based on the Greek philosophy, most notably Plato and Aristotle's Judeo-Christian beliefs.

Why do we send money to help famine victims halfway around the world? Why do we want to save the whales? Why do we stay up all night to comfort a friend who has just suffered a broken relationship? Why do we stop on a busy highway to help a stranded motorist change a flat?

Why would an intelligent self-assured young woman want to have a baby "just for the experience," no she is saying "I want a baby I would do anything for my baby; I would throw myself under an oncoming car to save my baby if it was in danger of being run over. I never dreamed that I could feel this way about anybody."

Why did Lenny Skutnik risk his life diving into the icy waters of the Potomac to save an airplane crash victim, and why did "the sixth man," Arland Williams, surrender his life by giving others his place in the rescue helicopter? Why did Mother Teresa reach out to the dying of Calcutta, the lowest of the low? Why did Miep Gies help hide Anne Frank and her family from the Nazis month after month, risking imprisonment, torture, and even death?

We have to ask ourselves why we help others. Often, the answer is easy because we care; sometimes, we help people because it is expected, or because it is in our own best interest.

We may help a friend because we do not want to lose their friendship or because we expect to see the favor come back in another way. But, we want to know if we are helping someone else will help them it is nice when we get a thank you. There are some who are exclusively motivated by the prospect that they will benefit from it personally or monetarily, however, subtle they are in their thinking.

We want to know if anyone ever helps someone without (him or her) feeling obligated; because of what someone has done for them, we believe that it is important to help others without them feeling guilt for what you've done. The potential for getting caught is one thing, it is one of the most fundamental questions we can ask ourselves, what is the motive behind your actions and why should I help them?

Egoism verses Altruism
Definition of altruism   {3}

Etymology: French *altruism,* from *autrui* other people, from Old French, oblique case form of *autre* other, from Latin *alter*

1. unselfish regard for or devotion to the welfare of others

2. behavior by an animal that is not beneficial to or may be harmful to itself but that benefits others of its species

- **al•tru•ist** /-tru-ist/ *noun*
- **al•tru•is•tic** /,al-tru-'is-tik/ *adjective*
- **al•tru•is•ti•cal•ly** /-ti-k(e-)le/ *adverb*
http://www.merriam-webstercollegiate.com/cgi-bin/Eleventh?book=Dictionary&altruism   1/6/2005

  Definition of egoism   {4}

  Pronunciation: 'e-ga-,wi-zam, -go-,i- *also* 'e-

  Function: *noun*

  Date: 1800

  1a: a doctrine that individual self-interest is the actual motive of action
  1b: a doctrine that individual self-interest is the valid end of all actions
  2: excessive concern for oneself with or without exaggerated feelings of self- importance --compare
  EGOTISM
  http://www.merriam-webstercollegiate.com/wgi-bin/Eleventh?book=Dictionary&egoism 1/07/05
  © 2005 by Merriam-Webster, Inc.   5/07/10

The economic theory and models of social and personal problems, if we drop the assumption that self-benefits should not stand-alone it does define duty to some degree rather than being responsible to others. Imagine the consequences for your feelings, and the conscientiousness of what happened and why without thinking of the moral and ethics implications.

Knowing whether we are capable of altruism will not tell us what is morally right or wrong, in either case it can be oversimplified by looking at the altruism-egoism debate. We can best describe it by what a person thinks of themselves, by Augusta Comte, who is credited with coining the term altruism. Before Comte, the question of why do people help others should not distort their feelings for others or an over simplification of the altruism-egoism debatable.

Before Comte, the question of why we help someone is employing the view of motivation, to be more specific I would suggest the following definition: *"Altruism is a motivational state with the ultimate goal of helping another's welfare."* There are three key phrases in this brief definition, and to avoid confusion we need to be explicit about each.

The Altruism Question in Contemporary Psychology

Some psychologists have defined *altruism* as requiring self-sacrifice when a person helps someone if they are motivated by a variety of egoistical motives, ranging from the desire for physical comfort, to the desire to be loved, and to succeed; to the desire to express one's self and be self-actualized at the same time.

The most important form of this discussion is whether it's altruistic or egoistical which motives a person to do something or is it the quest of a goal which is more important? Thus there is more than one motive involved both altruistic and egoistical motives both can exist simultaneously within a single individual situation, but not always.

If the altruistic and egoistical goals are equal, both behaviors are leading toward one goal in that case. They may also lead to self-motivation of the egocentric person to do it for alternative motives. These answers usually employ two strategies. One strategy is to argue for the logical necessity of having egoism, as a personal benefit or two is it altruism as self-serving.

Altruism and Egoism is based on Greek philosophy, most notably Plato, Aristotle's, and Judeo-Christian beliefs.

There are two major thoughts and views on egoism and altruism. One comes from a Greek Philosophers most notably Plato and Aristotle; the other comes from the Judeo-Christian religion.

It is common to contrast these two schools of thought, the Greek emphasis is on self-interests and a Judeo-Christian emphasis is on loving your neighbor as yourself. It is also common to call the former egoistic, the latter altruistic. This may be misleading neither ancient tradition confronts the altruism question directly; perhaps because each assumes that human interactions take place in the context of a larger metaphysical scheme. Human behavior is not judged in terms of the goals of the person, but whether it does or does not conform to some higher standard or idealism. Ideals set by Plato or Aristotle set the standard for the Greeks.

The Good Samaritan Christ's true example of altruism

I can't think of a better example of altruism. The setting is Christ's teachings of the "Seventy disciples sent out," he talked with His disciples in **Luke Chapter 10**:

V-23 "And he turned him unto *his* disciples, and said privately, blessed are the eyes which see the things that ye see:

V-24 For I tell you, that many prophets and kings have desired to see those things which I see, and have not seen *them;* and to hear those things which ye hear, and have not heard *them.*"

We have four good questions posed in this discourse V-25-29 "And, behold, a certain lawyer stood up, and tempted him, saying, Master, what shall I do to inherit eternal life?

V-26 He said unto him, What is written in the law? How readest thou?

V-27 And he answering said, Thou shalt love the Lord thy God with all thy heart, and with all thy soul, and with all thy mind: and thy neighbor as thy self.

V-28 And he said unto him, Thou hast answered right: this do, and thou shalt live.

V-29 But he, willing to justify himself, said unto Jesus, And who is my neighbor?"

In Verses-30-36

V-30 "And Jesus answering said, A certain *man* went down from Jerusalem to Jerico, and fell among thieves, which stripped him of his raiment, and wounded *him*, and departed, leaving *him* half dead.

V-31 And by chance there came down a certain priest that way; and when he saw *him* he passed by on the other side.

V-32 And likewise a Levite, when he saw at the place, came and looked on *him*, and passed by on the other side.

V-33 But a certain Sa-mar-i-tan, as he journeyed, came where he was: and when he saw him, he had compassion *on him*,

V-34 And went to *him* and bound up his wounds, pouring in oil and wine, and set him on his own beast, and brought him to an inn, and took care of him.

V-35 And on the morrow when he departed, he took out two pence, and gave *them* to the host, and said unto him, Take care of him; and whatsoever thou spendeth more, when I come again, I will repay thee.

V-36 Which now of these thee, thinkest thou, was neighbour unto him that fell among the thieves?"

The question was answered by "who is your neighbor?"

V-37 "And he said, He that shewed mercy on him. Then said Jesus unto him, Go, and do thou likewise."

This is also a Scriptural view of three different men's egoism

The question may be answered by the way they control their thinking of others (their nature shows up in how they treat others who need help this example shows in up the way they see the need to help others).

You will be able to detect those people by their **attitude, emotions/feelings, actions** and **reactions / pride/vanity /self-well/ego** and **self-image**. This can even happen in **exaggerations/ inconsistency / personal** and **intellectually honesty** and **self-worth**. All of these attribute and can affect your personal beliefs and conduct. It does not keep a person from being a Christian, even if they don't go to church, a bigger is when they don't face the problem.

Life can be like a beautiful rose the women thinks of its beauty, a man is more likely to think in terms of a beautiful car, but what happens when a women sees a withered rose, it could remind her of many things in her life, like her first prom.

In most cases, it depends on what she sees in that rose, it is the same way when a person is dealing with their life, looking to find the purpose for a person's life can be (beautiful) depending on what they see happening. A person may see a withered rose and think of a proem, it may remind them of heartache or a bad memory; a man can see a car and it reminds of his first car or maybe a bad accident.

Also, we are looking for the roses in life, family, friends, job, etc. All of us need to take some time to smell the roses, the good things in life, and "count our blessings" is another way of saying be happy with life and your relationships, those are the things that really count.

We also see that a rose has a stem with thorns and there are those occasional thorns in life. We have to deal with the thorns to observe the beauty of life, and sometimes we have to deal with the unpleasant things like sickness or even the death of a loved one.

This study is about building on personal experiences.

If we cannot deal with any aspects of a person without first understanding *who they are*, people do not have the same education or skill level, but a person should try to do their best in reaching their goal to be a better person. The way to do this is not always based on ability, but how a person uses those skills taught them. Here at **S**upport **o**utreach **S**ervices we provide programs / tools and try to teach a person how to use the knowledge and skills they have learned through their life experiences and if they don't work, how to go about making changes in their life.

The **human behaviors** are stored in the brain that pertains to a person's thinking, and what resides in (his or her) **brain** *can it control their thinking*. The **brain** uses prior information stored in the brain and is separated into the different functions of the **brain**. Another factor are the genetics passed on from one generation to another, the next influence is *your* environmental / cogitation is developed from the family history, and being able to understand the current physical structure of the human neurological system. We will study the cognitive aspects of **human behavior** within the person.

That is the overall goal of **Life Enhancement counseling study guide.** I want to help *you* understand the **brain** and why you do certain things and why things don't change. How the **brain** does not stand alone because the

brain is an important part of our study guide, I will use developmental chats, axioms and profiles in **human behavior identification steps** 5-8 on the bases of the nature of a person, and for the use in developing a life of happiness. To do this we must use the (educational, psychological, sociological) tools necessary for the formation and maintenance of the individual's behavior identity as a person.

Self-Image is what you think of yourself?
What is Creative & Critical Thinking?
How is Intelligence Related to Self-Esteem?
Why do some people fail or Achievements

CHARACTERISTICS IN CRITICAL THINKING

Dealing with SELF-IMAGE

There seems to be connections between the heart and soul, but also there is a connection between the heart and the way (man or women) think. The actual processing of information comes through in several different avenues of the mind and mind-set.

There are paths in life and in your way of thinking; the task is to convey a sense of what **self-image** relates in what you are dealing with and the way a person feels. Now you have a much larger job on your hands by leaning more about the way you think of yourself. The thought process can strongly be influenced by a person's needs and wants (rather than what they think they need or want). Up to this point we have emphasized caring for others, the honor of severing others is totally apart from whether a person has really met those needs in their own life or whether a person's needs are actually being met or you just think they have been met if not they may feel unworthy as a person.

Of course it is impossible to meet every need, how a person sees themselves in relation to their self-image; these are some of the insights that shows up in a personal self-worth. But, that would imply people are unable to solve their previous problems or the other issues they don't understand, thinking also has a lot to do with self-image all essential things in life gives every person an opportunity for life and being happy.

We don't always have to be creative to do things, but simply put your mind in to action the problem may simply be within **themselves** as simple as how they want to live; the world is full of opportunities. A person who commits suicide dies because they wanted to escape the problem; it is because they can't face life as they want it to be, we know that suicide is an act of self-centered thinking. At times people have to deal with bad things.

Love itself is the very essence of self, a self-concerned person is not necessarily a self-centered-person. That is why living for one's self is not enough to make them happy it is important to love others and to be loved points a person away from themselves.

Romans 12:3 "For I say, through the grace given unto me, to every man that is among you, not to think *of himself* more highly than he ought to think; but to think soberly, according as God hath dealt to every man the measure of faith." **(KJV)**

An important implication of the **self-worth** philosophy: on a personal level (his or her) own **self-esteem** "needs" are met, this means that the lower-level needs of satisfaction is held higher because a person needs to be responsible for their failures and their ability to love others. This is not done until (he or she) is confronted with their own **self-image** when a person realizes their **self-worth** is raised to a satisfactory level of their **self-esteem** for themselves I believe it is based on your ability to love others. A person needs to look at the truth about one's self, when a person is held responsible for (his or her) actions. I think it means we are not to do things to hurt or harm another person, take advantage of another person and if we do that is it wrong we should be responsible to make it right.

How the thinking process works as we explore the mind.

First, a person must analyze there is a problem; they must generate possible solutions next they must choose and implement the best solution; and finally, they must evaluate the effectiveness of the solution. As you can see, this process reveals alternatives between the two kinds of thinking creative and critical thinking. In practice, both kinds of thinking operate together most of the time and are not independent of each other.

There is another kind of thinking, when one focuses on exploring new ideas, generating possibilities, looking for answers rather than just accepting one answer. Both of these kinds of thinking are vital to success, yet the latter critical thinking tends to override a person's negative thinking in a situation. We might differentiate in these two kinds of thinking when a person is critical of another person or their point of view.

A person can think they can do something because of the way they feel a positive attitude about generating new and useful ideas when it comes to solving problems this is a larger part of the whole process.

Much can be done by thinking things through, by using their own skills in understanding others who have different opinions. They may have creative and logical arguments the object is to figure out the best answer, and eliminate the incorrect paths and focus on the correct one.

Everyone is creative to some extent most people are capable of very high levels of creativity; just look at young children when they play and imagine things. The problem may be their creativity has been suppressed by their parent's attitude. If you say something negative about another person and look at their attitude change, you may discover you are surprising their thinking about you and when someone does that to you what do you think of that person. I will use this illustration to make a husband or wife feel bad by suppressing (his or her) feelings about her dress or what he thinks of her by saying that won't work, or by saying why not try on a different dress?

Let me give you other ways to look at something. When I help a person with car trouble and they say I want to pay you, I say, "Pass it on to the next person in trouble because it was passed on to me."

How does the Thinking Preprocess Work in Solving Problems?

Next let's start with the assumption there is a solution to every problem, there may be several possible answers of cause a person has to choose and make a decision, but what happens when people does not use good judgment for some reason. A lot as to do with the way a person perceives the problem I want to take up the challenge of how to deal with "Creative thinking", "Critical thinking & a person's Attitudes", in relation to "Problem solving".

Chart layout on Critical Thinking & Creative Thinking

Critical Thinking	Creative Thinking
Analytic	Analytical
Logical	Analytical
Vertical	Lateral
Probability	Possibility
Judgment	Suspended judgment
Focused	Diffuse
Objective	Subjective
Answer	an answer
left brain	right brain
Verbal	Visual
Linear	Associative
Reasoning	
Richness, novelty	
Yes but	Yes and

We are trying to help people understand how to solve a problem there are other kinds of thinking besides creative and critical, which one is more important; we have discussed both at length don't dwell on the problem, but dwell on the solution.

What is critical thinking?

A simple definition of critical thinking Diffuse is the ability to think something through and create a new ways to look at the problem. As you can see from the chart lay out above, that creativity is the ability to create something or do something, the ability to generate new ideas by combining changes, or reapplying existing ideas. Some creative ideas are astonishing and brilliant while others are just simple in nature, some are good while others are practical ideas that no one seems to have thought of before.

Believe it or not, everyone has some creative abilities, just by forming new ideas starts the path to creativity, but too often, it has been suppressed by a leak of education or just a foolish idea, it is there in some form when a person puts their mind to it. A person can do things, all it takes is the need to get things done; it takes a commitment to be creative and to take the time to do it.

Creativity is the ability to accept the change and a willingness to give your ideas a chance to grow there are endless possibilities and when that happens you will need the flexibility to change things when things don't go the way you thought, learn to enjoy the good while looking for ways to make things better. We are socialized to except changes, even if they are small things or normal things, or something new like chocolate-covered strawberries for example. The creative person realizes that there are other possibilities like peanut butter and banana sandwiches, or chocolate-covered prunes.

Creative people think "outside box" work hard continually to improve ideas and solutions, by making gradual adjustments and refinements in dealing with situations. Contrary to the mythology surroundings of the past, people have always been creative, but we don't always see it that way. Very few things would have happened without creative people making things better, to produce things with a single stroke of brilliance or in frenzy to adapt to an activity. There are stories of people and companies who had their inventions taken away from them or stolen, many fail several times in order to improve ways to market their products better, some are inventors and others start new businesses, others by tweaking their ideas and finding new ways or trying to make them better.

The creative person knows that there is always room for improvement we have discussed several methods and ideas we have tried identify some them by producing new things and that creates positive results. How can we apply this to our personal problems?

What is Creativity?

This is the method of incremental improvements new ideas stem from other ideas, new solutions from previous ones in some cases it is improving the old ones. Many of the sophisticated changes we enjoy today were developed over a long period of constant changes. Making something a little better gradually makes something a lot better in some cases, or something entirely different from the original product.

For example, look at the history of the automobile or any product of technological progress. With each new model improvements are made each new models builds upon the collective creativity of previous models over time it has created more comfort and durable cars.

Here the creativity lies in the refinement step-by-step improvement rather than in something completely new. Another example would be the improvement of chemical products.

The evolutionary method of creativity thinking also reminds us of a critical principle: **Every problem that has been solved can be improved on by finding a better way.** Creative thinkers do not subscribe to the idea that once a problem has been solved "if it isn't broke don't fix it." Creative thinking is "there is no such thing as an insignificant improvement."

With this method two or more existing ideas are combined into a third, a new idea may be just as simple as improving it by combining two or more ideas, in the news media it is very useful for handy capped people they have closed captions now everybody enjoy the news through many devices.

For example, the best idea could be a completely different idea or product, a marked change from the previous ones.

The evolution of improvement in philosophy might cause a professor to ask?

"How can I make my lectures better or more interesting?" A revolutionary idea might be, "Why stop lecturing have the students use new technology, or working as teams in presenting reports?'

For example, the evolutionary technology in fighting termites eating away at houses has been to develop safer and faster pesticides and gasses to kill them.

Look at something old in a new way may go beyond labels as such maybe it's more important to remove the prejudices, expectations, and assumptions and discover how something or a person can be made different. Two people may look at the same thing and see two different ideas. The key is to see beyond the previous or stated applications for some new idea, solution, or thing to see what other applications are possible.

For example, paint can be used as a kind of glue to prevent screws from loosening in machinery; dish washing detergents can be used to remove the DNA from bacteria in a lab; general-purpose spray cleaners can be used to kill ants.

Many creative breakthroughs occur when attention is shifted from one idea to another. This is sometimes called creative insight.

These examples reveals a critical truth in problem solving when one solution path is not working, shift to another. If there is no commitment to a particular problem, there should be particular goal in mind. Path fixations can sometimes be a problem for those who do not understand why something went wrong; or know there is a problem, but when committed to a problem does not work and only frustration is the result of what do, you do give up when it becomes too hard or it is important to become more determined to find a solution.

I have used this example before, "Block Creative or Critical Thinking & Problem Solving

1. What is Creative & Critical Thinking?
2. Negative Attitudes Block Creativity or Critical Thinking & Problem Solving.
3. Mental Blocks to Creative or Critical Thinking and Problem Solving.
4. Myths about Creative Thinking or Critical Thinking and Problem Solving.
5. Mental Blocks to Creative or Critical Thinking and Problem Solving.
6. Positive Attitudes for Critical Thinking.
7. Motivation for Critical Thinking & Good Attitudes.
8. Characteristics of a person's Critical Thinking & Problem Solving.

The way a person reacts to a problem is often a bigger problem than the problem itself some people avoid or deny problems exists until it's too late. These people need to learn to anticipate how to deal with their emotions, psychology, and use practical responses. Look at a problem as an opportunity welcome the outcome and seek out ways to solve problems, meeting them as challenges and opportunities that will bring better results.

Looking at a problem

1. Seeing the difference between what you have and what you want,
2. An opportunity for a positive action in seeking problems aggressively will build confidence, increase happiness, and give you a better sense in solving your problem
   (Creative thinking)
3. Recognizing or believing that there is something better than the current situation
   (Critical thinking)

This is in effect surrendering before you go into battle by assuming that something cannot be done or a problem cannot be solved, a person gives the problem power over them and that strengthens the hold it has over a person giving up before they start of course that is self-defeating. Look at the different solutions by proving the skeptics wrong. Some said man will never fly, diseases will never be conquered, and rockets will never leave the atmosphere. Again, the appropriate summation is can it be done, the difficultly comes in not trying to take on the impossible tasks. Some people think the problem can be solved by an expert and some don't think of themselves as experts because they don't believe they can do it:

1. I am not smart enough,
2. I can't do it,
3. I'm not creative enough
4. I can' is the biggest excuse, I don't have enough education, or I'm not an expert, etc.

Well Known People in American History who succeeded

Again, look at the ways you can solve the problem we would have never known who the Wright brothers were if they had not invented an airplane, and believed that it could fly? They were not aviation engineers they were bicycle mechanics. The ballpoint pen was invented by a proofreader not a mechanical engineer. Major advances in submarine design were made by an English clergyman G. W. Garrett and by Irish schoolmaster John P. Holland. That well-known attorney and tutor, Eli Whitney, invented the cotton gin.

In a nutshell, a good mind with a positive attitude looks at a problem with their skills and motivation those that succeed will go farther in solving any problem. Interests and commitment to the problem are the keys, motivation / a willingness to expend a person's efforts is more important than laboratory apparatus and remember that you can always do something even if you don't know all the answers, you can learn from someone else or take classes there is always new ideas and ways to do something and to make the situation better.

In our effort to appear mature and sophisticated we often look at what is wrong first; others are usually marked by indecisions. For instance if you are able to solve a problem that saves your marriage, gets you a promotion, or keeps your friend from suicide, do you care whether the other person describes your solution as right or wrong? They look at the outcome, remember at times people may laugh at you when things are funny, but when something tragic happens some may laugh because they don't understand the way you met the situation.

There are strong social pressures that makes people conform to ordinary things and don't challenge your creative thinking.

The constant emphasis in society is to conform. People who have an instinctive nature and those who succeed don't let it get them down; others are like sheep following others and not being an individual who gets things done.

What will people think? Some are going to talk about you in unflattering ways; you might as well relax and let your creativity and individualism work for you.

Almost every famous person has to face those kinds of remarks by their critics they believe in themselves they ignore critics, some people ridicule others to make themselves feel important at the other person's expense and sometimes it makes them look bad because of what they have done to someone. Think about Galileo and look at what happened to Jesus. *Quotation: "Progress is made* only *by those who are strong enough to endure being laughed at."* Solutions are often new ideas greeted with laughter, contempt, or both from the scoffer. That is just an unpleasant fact, so make up your mind not to let it bother you. Ridicule should be viewed as a badge for the innovative thinker.

Thomas Edison, in his search for the perfect filament for the incandescent lamp, tried anything he could think of, including whiskers from a friend's beard. In all, he tried about 1800 things. After about 1000 attempts, someone asked him if he was frustrated at his lack of success. He said something like, "I've gained a lot of knowledge I now know a thousand things that won't work."

Fear of failure is one of the major obstacles to creativity and problem solving. The cure is being able to change your attitude about failure. Failures along the way should be expected and accepted; they are simply learning tools that help you focus the way toward success. Not only is there nothing wrong with failing, but failing is a sign of action and struggle, an attempt is much better than inaction. The go-with-the-flow types may never have any problems and they feel they have never failed, but they are essentially at a loss for new ideas, nor can they ever enjoy the feeling of accomplishment that comes after a long struggle.

Suppose you let your fear of failure hold you back and your risk taking, and if it doesn't bother you that you never fail. If you try three things in a year and you accomplish three things. At the end of the year the score is: 3 Successes, 0 Failures. Now suppose the next year you don't worry about failing, you try a hundred things, you fail at 70 of them. At the end of the year, the score is 30 successes, but most people are not able to deal with 70 failures. Which would you rather have three successes or 30 times as many? And just think what 70 failures will have taught you if you can look at the positive aspects in your life. A proverb: *Mistakes aren't fun, but they sure are educational.*

Myths about Creative Thinking – Critical Thinking and Problem Solving

The goal of problem solving is to solve the problem; most problems can be solved in any number of ways. If you discover a solution that works, is it the best solution, but others might have thought of a better solution; who is right in that instance? There may be other solutions, other people may have other ideas for a solution, but that doesn't make your solution wrong. What is the solution to putting words on paper? Use a pencil, marker, typewriter, printer, Xerox machine, or a printer all of them depend what works best for you? They don't work until you use them the same is true in finding solutions or it usually means taking some kind of action.

Look at the different solutions and how to make improvements, new solutions, look for the right answers for you.

On an everyday level many solutions are now seen or solved by technology sources. When things are done hastily without much thought, think of your drivers' licenses as an ID card or social security numbers for taxpayer ID numbers. These are obvious ID's, but in some cases, it is a matter of thinking outside the box.

Only a few problems require complex technological solutions most problems require a little more thought some solutions require little personal action and perhaps a few simple tools. There are problems that seem to require a technological solution that could be addressed in other ways.

There are many successful techniques for stimulating an idea we will be discussing how to apply them.

Mental Blocks to Creative Thinking and Problem Solving

The older we get the more some of our preconceived ideas set in and the way we think about things. These preconceptions often prevent people from seeing beyond what they already know or believe to be possible. They are bounded by old habits and not willing or wanting to accept changes.

Sometimes we begin to see an object only in terms of what it can do. Thus, we see a mop only as a device for cleaning a floor, and do not think that it might be useful for clearing cobwebs from the ceiling, washing the car, doing aerobic exercise, propping a door open, and so on.

Think a minute; how you reacted to certain situations, it is usually based on your past experiences. This is known as stereotyping it can even be a form of dysfunctional fixations on past arguments and disagreements. Too often people permit only a narrow range of thinking and behaviors based on bias, prejudice, hasty generalization, or limited past experience. Think of these statements, "I can't believe they said that," or "Imagine her doing that", "The goal in my life is not to live down my expectations, but live to my expectations."

There are some who feel they don't have the tools and skills, knowledge, materials, or the ability to do anything, "they might say why try?" Some rely on others to do it for them, people who think small and limit themselves.

HUMAN DEVELOPMENT

Psychological blocks to Self-Image

Some solutions are not considered or they reject them because people react before they think. People isolate themselves because they feel insecure in how they go about solving a problem or because they don't feel safe within their own thinking or they are afraid of what others might think of them. More importantly, something may seem to be a bad idea, but after looking at it again, it may lead to better solutions down the road.

The brain can block ideas and prevent you from doing certain things just because it doesn't sound good or right, which is a pretty good approach to most things, but there are exceptions.

Positive Attitudes for Critical Thinking & Problem Solving

Creative people want to know things because they want know the answer or want to try a new solution. Knowledge does not always require a reason, but why does a person need answers is the question that should be asked, this may seem strange to the creative person, who is likely to respond, "Because I don't know the answer." Knowledge is enjoyable and often useful in strange and unexpected ways.

Next, knowledge and understanding is necessary for creativity to flourish to its fullest creativity arises from variations of a known or combinations of two unknowns. The best ideas come from a well-equipped mind "nothing can come from nothing."

In addition to knowing and learning creative people want to know why? What are the reasons behind decisions, problems, solutions, and when events are based on the facts set forth? Why this way and why not another?

The curious person asks questions why didn't this work, or why didn't they take a positive approach, that can lead to a destructive reaction or response that reflects on skepticism, or negativism. People often feel threatened because there is no good reason behind why something has happened or take things for granted, to them there is no "why" they accept the status quo as acceptable.

Why ask questions when you know the answer? Why not ask the same question from a different point of view to help people understand what you really mean. Look into areas of knowledge about yourself never explored before, whether it's the way you think, weather exploring the foods you eat, budgeting, or the toxic things you take into your body.

Curious people like to identify and except challenges, proposals, problems, beliefs, and statements. Many assumptions turn out to be quite necessary, but many others may have come up with the same assumptions and taken them wrong in the wrong direction, breaking out of those assumptions often comes new ways to deal with and finding new solutions.

I hope my approach has not an over whelmed you and our approach has brought about a new ideas and the way you think, but your ability to see a need for improvement that is the purpose for our studies and then finding other method of making improvements in your life. Constructive discontent can be a positive force, enthusiastic discontent can also bring about a new way of thinking, and "I wanted to make my life better."

Constructive discontent is necessary for a creative problem solving, if you want to be happy, that does not mean you want to change things. Only when you become discontent with something can you see how a problem is causing more problems, now you may want to take on the problem and improve the situation.

One of the hallmarks of a discontented person is seeks a new solution to the problem and seek a new outlook. The more you find out about yourself, the more likely you are going to come up with good solutions and therefore improvements can be made. Even previous unsolved problems can be solved in a constructive way, but if there is discontent a person might think, there must be a better solution that works even better.

Another mark of constructive discontent is the enjoyment of the challenge. Creative people are eager to test their own limits and the limits in problems, willing to work hard and not give up too easily. Sometimes the discontent is good because you aren't really happy with the status quo or an area in your life, but a person should want to find something better consider the challenge as an opportunity to improve your own life and others around you.

The faith in one's self the creative thinker believes that something good can come out of something bad there is always something to be done to eliminate problems or help solve almost every problem. Problems are solved by commitment and energy, and where commitment is present, more things are possible.

The belief in the solvability of problems is essential and useful in attacking any problem, because many problems seem utterly impossible and scare off the faint at heart. Those who take on their problem with confidence will be the ones most likely to think it through and think the impossible is possible.

An idea may begin to look good only after it becomes a bit more familiar or it is seen in a slightly different context the wildest ideas can serve as a stepping-stone to an effective solution to a problem or idea. By being too quick in judgment before the situation plays out, you're thinking maybe fragile early on the first rule is brainstorming, the next suspend judgment until later so that your ideas generates power and you will be free to create before having a chance to work through your fears while other's will want to criticize. You can always go back later and examine your thoughts as critically as you want by going through the thought process.

Creative thinkers when faced with poor solutions, don't cast them away instead they ask, "What can I do to make them better?" There may be something useful in the worst of ideas; it might turn out better than you think if you don't give up on an idea.

We easily fall into a trap by thinking and believing that a solution is good or bad, in every aspect look at the facts you can borrow from other ideas by thinking of other solutions it may be inappropriate in some cases if it is worth doing give it best. A bad solution may have some redeeming features if changes are made that can help in the solution. The way you deal with the solution while keeping in mind the good points a person identifies with.

The attitude of constructive discontent in searching for a solution while looking for other possible areas of improvement many times the problems workout on their own don't expect this to happen every time. The unexpected in some cases can be a blessing perhaps some unwanted problems are not necessarily bad, because they often permit solutions never thought of before.

Many people confront every problem with the idea I don't want to deal with it or I don't care what happens which is a passive approach. Some don't want to admit that a problem exists, or if the results turns out bad they blame it on someone else, often the problem persists and drives them crazy, but when a crisis drives them to getting upset or angry.

Creative people see problems as challenges worth tackling. They think of problems and are not fearful or boost because they are not afraid; others are able to solve the problem and make light of the problem, thus rewarding their ego rather than finding a helpful solution to the situation.

Most people don't succeed because they don't spend enough time dealing with their problems. There is no quick and easy secrets to success, you need to acknowledge your problem. Our studies and research you must put your knowledge to work by positive approaches to thinking things through. You may have read of other difficulties and setbacks faced by famous people, how many aircraft designs failed in the attempt to break the sound barrier.

Creative people are comfortable with thinking of new ideas because there is a need for improvement just the stimulation of the mind by brainstorming ideas with others there are all kinds of thoughts and ideas entertained by giving an idea a chance to work before casting it a side. The mind will probably find something useful if the challenge is put to the test we will look at several examples of this later in this study.

Modern society has for some reason that nothing is wrong, and convened people of the idea it is unforgivable if things fail or they may have the mistaken idea failure can be an opportunity; mistakes show that something is being done wrong. Some people have come to realize and accept their mistakes and they do not let it become negative baggage.

DR JOHN BARRETT

IDUSTRIAL AGE TO THE TECHNOLGY AGE

Chapter 3

WHAT IS INTELLIGENCE IN RELATION TO SELF-IMAGE?

What does intelligence have to do with the thinking process?

A great deal of our knowledge comes from the learning process the information that goes into our thinking and has a lot to do **with *who you are*** and ***what you are going to become and the successes*** in your life. The information is feed into the brain's limbic system which is perceived by the brain's circuits which make-up our emotions and thought process / rational thinking and choices / affects our decisions in the process. We are intelligent, but there is much more to know about the self-image of a person, we have discussed how our thinking process works we're not talking about your stature, but how we relate to who we are.

Definition of intelligence: Function: *noun*, Latin   {5}
  1a: (1) : the ability to learn or understand or to deal with new or
  trying situations
        : REASON; also the skilled use of reason
  (2) : the ability to apply knowledge to manipulate one's environment
  or think abstractly as measured by objective criteria (as tests)

Referenced from Merriam-Webster Collegiate.com

Merriam-Webster's Collegiate Dictionary Eleventh Edition / (date 1/30/04)

Here are some contemporary works on intelligence.
The different theories and organ of intelligence and what it means.
  1. Evolution states people came from a species over millions of
      years and evolved during the millions of years
  2. The state of the earth has been here for millions of years and
      man came into existence thousands of years later, the cave man
      theory has evolved from a primitive man.

3. Man came from intelligent design, but has it changed over millions of years which is a model which that most feel is realistic and is better than any of the above theories.

4. There are bases for God's creation of man, the Biblical account leaves two good theories of how the earth was created; the earth was recreated after the fall of Stan and his angles; another is the earth is a new creation with man as the head, both agree man was created by God.

5. The holistic approach of psychology deals with the emotions and feelings plus the spiritual aspects and makeup the whole person while others leave out the spiritual.

Charles Darwin, published his initial work, The ***Origin of the Species*** years later a second work, ***The Descent of Ma Today***,   [3]

"Darwin's ideas along with the views from his predecessors and some contemporaries formed a significant part of the framework for the "Theory of Evolution" they believed a man and women's intelligence came from a specie and that is their theory of where man came from. The theory essentially views man as a genetic accident a product of chance in time and space.

Which is a preposterous theory from my point of view there is a great deal of support in the evidence of evolution, yes man has psychical changes if we didn't everyone would say a baby there is evidence of the body cells changing every seven years. Their theory supports genetics, but there is no evidence of one species can change to another; it is another theory of many theories about creation. Our objective is to examine the theories that have to do with an intelligent being and how it influences a person. I base my studies and beliefs on the Bible accounts of creation and I know there is room for some of these theories of creation that will fit into the Bible; I deal with that in another series of books.

Evolution reduces man to a mere specie and man evolved from an animal and then from a specie, man's brain functions are completely different than the above theories which leaves us room to explore the intelligence of man. Since the history of man there has been a lot of studies and they have changed or been modified as to how man has the ability to think."

There are different theories on man's intelligence and where man came from:

There is a newer theory called **intelligent design** states that man came from an **intelligent creator** that contradicts Darwin's theory of creation, Darwin believed we came from a species, then an evolution of an animal to man that crossed over millions of years ago **"they created the pelt-down-man"** which has not been confirmed.

Secular Humanism is yet a newer version of the advancement of man and his intelligence is one of the most effective evidence of man's progress, but they dismiss the importance of God.

Darwin's theory of life starts there is no God, he states man as impersonal matter (chemicals) which came from a single cell organism that happened over millions of years this supports (the other theories that have to do with the evolution of man over time), how did we get to be reasonable and rational beings if that is true? I believe God made us intelligent beings able to process things and make decisions concerning our own well-being and to inhabit the earth. I look at what has been accomplished over the Centuries it had to come from God because the chemicals in a person's body can be bought at any pharmacy for a few dollars and we're 70% water. That is about the same relationship of the earth surface to water. He made man for the purpose of caring out His will we don't always understand His complete plain because He is God and the end is yet to come or is there no end.

This is the result of faulty reasoning.

Eat, drink and be merry for tomorrow we die, there is no here after and no end, this is what the humanist theories tell us, human wisdom gives us a self-centered attitude that can lead a person to become absorbed in self-satisfaction, greed, vanity, lust, and a lust for power. The human wisdom gives man the power of reasoning, but the theory of "eat, drink and be merry" and that is all there is to life leaves a hole to be filled.

General Intelligence

Despite some popular assertions, a factor for intelligence is called *g* intelligence, it can be measured by IQ tests some believe to some degree it predicts the amount of success in life. I am going to present other models that disprove this theory and look at other facts at the same time; I have drawn my conclusions from other studies that support those findings.

If we a scribe to that model of intelligence in terms of multiple layers, each layer built on top of the underlying layer, this would be their list:

1.   At the bottom level is *source* and *data structures.*

2.   The next layer is *sensory modalities* in humans, the archetypal examples of sensory modalities are sight, sound, touch, taste, smell; implemented by the visual cortex, auditory cortex, sensor motor cortex, and so on would probably have a different set of sensory-modalities. In biological terms the brain sensory modalities come the closest to being "hardwired"; they generally involve and clearly are defined stages of information-processing and feature extractions for people, sometimes with individual the neurons play a clear defined roles. Thus, sensory modalities are some of the best candidates for processes that can safely be direct coding by the programmers without rendering the system of a person fragile or very fragile. The visual cortex doesn't knows things its Hardwiring such as knowledge of why butterflies' system is so fragile, if such knowledge is considered "knowledge"; the hardwiring detection is something that the human brain seems to get away with.

3.   The next layer is the *concept* level. Concepts (also sometimes known as "symbols") are abstracted from our experiences; they describe some quality of common groups of experiences. Furthermore, this abstracted quality can then be *applied* to a mental image, altering it. For example, having abstracted the concept of 'redness', we can take a mental image of a non-red objects in the

brain (for example, grass) and imagine "red grass". Concepts are patterns within sensory modalities; concepts are *complex, flexible, reusable* patterns that have been abstracted and stored.

4.   The next layer is *thoughts,* built from structures of concepts. By applying a series of concepts to a single target, it becomes possible to build up complex mental images within the "brain space" which provides one or more sensory modalities. The archetypal example of a thought is a human "sentence" an arrangement of concepts, invoked by their symbolic tags, structured by the constraints of syntax, which constructs a complex mental image that can be used in reasoning.

5.   Finally, it is a sequence of thoughts that implement *deliberate intelligence* explaining and prediction,-planning-and-design.

    a.   What does the general intelligence do with its ability to use sequences of thoughts to carry out a connected chain of reasoning? What activities engage in thoughts?

6.   Creating and carrying out complex error-tolerant plans. Inventing and improving complex designs. Introducing a hypothesis based on a person's experience, this hypothesis comes from knowledge formed from theories about causation. Based on making predictions as to how a   person   will   react   to   the   expected   and-the-unexpected.

Intelligence, in the case of the human brain has a hundred trillion synapses and very complex neurons. What *causes* intelligence to develop in humans by knowledge and learning? Why do some believe intelligence is an evolutionary process? If that is the case it enables them to use it as a model, and manipulate their theory. Reality includes the external reality based on social reality, and the internal reality of their   own   minds. Our world has (internal and external factors) that exhibits a complex structure of the mind structure that might be called the "reductionist theory" or the "holistic theory", depending on whether you're looking down or looking up on the layers of the brain. Complex facts are composed of simple facts first; simple elements interact to form complex processes. Our world exhibits complex causal structure causes give rise to effects, which in turn cause further effects.

Emotional and logical Intelligence

There are two basic camps on the theory of intelligence those who believe in one unilinear construction of "general intelligence", and those who believe in much different intelligence that comes from the brain stretchers.

Most everyone is familiar with the basic theory of IQ and how it supposed to relate to one's ability to succeed in school and in a career. A relatively new and astounding study of intelligence identified in the 1990's has to do with ability of the brain to process both IQ and emotions at the same time. IQ as general rule in the past was the only potential standard form of intelligence, it was not known to work in relation to emotional and logic deductive reasoning. Emotions has a bearing on a person's behaviors, but more on the basic principles of behaviors and biological traits have just as much bearing on why and how a person thinks. Knowing one's Self-awareness is recognizing a person's feeling and emotions as it happens is the keystone in knowing how to use emotions in relation to how intelligence is used in making a decision. The ability to monitor what we are feeling moment to moment is crucial to the psychological insight and self-understanding.

There are 5 basic principles when it comes to inner personal intelligence, *by expanding these five abilities.*

1.*Knowing one's emotions.* Self-awareness is recognizing and coping with feeling *as they happen* it is the keystone of **inner personal intelligence**. The ability to monitor feelings from moment to moment is crucial to psychological insight and self-understanding. There is a problem when a person's has an inability to notice their true feelings that leaves them at the mercy of the problem. People with greater certainty about their feelings are better at piloting their lives, having a surer sense of how they really feel about their personal decisions from whom they marry to what job they take.

2. ***Managing emotions.*** The handling of one's feelings as they learn to appreciate their life, it is an ability that builds on **self-awareness**. I will examine the capacity to sooth oneself, to shake off rampant anxiety, gloom, or irritability; for instance the consequences of not being able to deal with failure, but now teaching people how to deal with their basic emotional tools and skills. People who are poor in this ability are constantly battling feelings of distress while those who excel in dealing with their feelings can bounce back far more quickly from life's setbacks and upsets.

3. ***Motivating oneself.*** The ability to manage motivations while setting goals, it is essential for paying attention, for self-motivation and mastery of your creative abilities. Emotional self-control delaying self-gratification and stifling impulsiveness underlies the accomplishments of every sort and being able to get into the "flow" which is a state of mind which enables outstanding performance in some or all walks of life. People who have this kind of determination tend to be more highly productive and effective in whatever they undertake.

4. ***Recognizing others.*** **Empathy** is the ability that builds on **self-awareness** is the fundamental to "people skills", as well as investigating in the roots of **empathy**, the social coast of being self-centered and this is the reason **empathy** kindles altruism. People who are empathic are more attuned to the subtle social signals that indicate what others need or want. This makes them better at callings such as the caring professions, teaching, sales, and management.

5. ***Handling relationships.*** The art of relationships is managing the emotions in others. Looks at social competence and incompetence and the specific skills involved. These abilities have to do with a person's popularity, leadership, and interpersonal effectiveness. People who excel in those do well at anything that relies on interacting smoothly with others; they are social stares.

Of course there are always exceptions and personal abilities in each person; some maybe adept at handling their anxiety, but relative inept at soothing someone else who is upset. The underling basis for personal levels of ability is no doubt based on a person's emotional well-being.

We see the inner-personal tools and skills are based on what a person feels is success for them and in learning how to deal with others. Lapse of inner-personal tools and skills can be redeemed to a great extent by responses governed by the mind and using good behavior habits that work with the right kind of effort, can be improved on with the right kind of help."

Copied

Multiple Intelligences Theory:
Education World Walden University   **Pages 1 – 6** [4]

A Theory for Everyone
"Howard Gardner's theory of multiple intelligences makes people think 'IQ,' is about being 'smart.' The theory is changing the way some teachers teach.
When Howard Gardners book, Frames of Mind: The Theory of Multiple Intelligences (Basic Books, 1983)

IMPLEMENTING GARDNER'S THEORY IN THE CLASSROOM

"When asked how educators should implement the theory of multiple intelligences, Gardner says, '(I's) are important when a teacher take the individual differences among kids very seriously. The bottom line is a deep interest in children and how their minds are different from one another, and in helping them use their minds well.'
An awareness of multiple-intelligence theory has stimulated teachers to find more ways of helping all students in their classes. Some schools do this by adapting curriculum. In 'Variations on a Theme: How Teachers Interpret MI Theory,' (*Educational Leadership*, September 1997), Linda Campbell describes five approaches to curriculum change:
Lesson design. Some schools focus on lesson design. This might involve team teaching ('teachers focusing on their own intelligence strengths'), using all or several of the intelligences in their lessons, or

asking student opinions about the best way to teach and learn certain topics.

Interdisciplinary units. Secondary schools often include interdisciplinary units.

Student projects. Students can learn to 'initiate and manage complex projects' when they are creating student projects.

Assessments. Assessments are devised which allow students to show what they have learned. Sometimes this takes the form of allowing each student to devise the way he or she will be assessed, while meeting the teacher's criteria for quality.

Apprenticeships. Apprenticeships can allow students to 'gain mastery of a valued skill gradually, with effort and discipline over time.' Gardner feels that apprenticeships '(…) should take up about one-third of a student's schooling experience.'

With an understanding of Gardner's theory of multiple intelligences, teachers, school administrators, and parents can better understand the learners in their midst. They can allow students to safely explore and learn in many ways, and they can help students direct their own learning. Adults can help students understand and appreciate their strengths, and identify real-world activities that will stimulate more learning."

Article by Anne Guignon Education World® Copyright © 1998
Education World
02/16/1998 Links Updated 11/11/2004
http://www.eduction-world.com/a_curr/curr054.shmtl   1/14/05

Cognition *leading to* Meta Cognition is Self-Awareness of one's Self-Image

One of the newest fields of studies on behavior is the **cognitive science of behavior** as it relates to (Person's self-image). Cognitive science is an interdisciplinary field that draws not only on psychology, but also on computer science, actual intelligence, logic, and the neurosciences.

Cognitive science is a new field that many are becoming interested in how it works, and I have research studies based in this field.

Cognitive science studies on behaviors, but in a different way than psychology. For most psychologists have base behavior on the objective cognitive sciences, behavior is a dependent variable; than cognition which is based on (environment and heritage / genetics). The cognitive science on cognitive behavior is only one part of this study. Cognitive behavior is where cognition is also evolved within a person's feelings, a good example of the difference between an evaluation of one's self and created cognition is how people reacts to a situation, an example is computers have the capacity for people to play chess. Chess is a game, but now computer programs can also play against a person. Once a year, the best programs play each other, and then, the winner plays a human grand master player. To date, people have always won; however, in the future computers will probably be advanced to the point winning. I believe as long as the Computer programs are able to develop programs by the human intellect the advantage will be built on those who learn how to develop technology. Humans display a completely different emotions, looking ahead a person will move about doing things while analyzing the current situation both computers and humans adjust to their behavior and are able to cope with the "cognitive" and cognition deals with the environmental stimuli presented.

Anything that thinks in any way could be a subject for a cognitive science. However, the behavior of a person will not be the point of this study; rather, the point of this study will be the mechanisms that lead to how a person behaves. That difference is an emphasis toward cognition and using behavior in the environment of a family. The clue that cognition differentiates between the cognitive science, it is strictly defined from psychological bases for the study of behaviors now we are able identify a person's behavior with their environment and how they perceive what the brain is responding. However, cognitive science is an inclusive result in its self without dealing with (self-worth) in terms of why a person does something many psychologists would consider themselves as cognitive behaviors theorists' without adopting the definition of cognitive science given above.

The way we're taught and how we think brings about a very definite mind-set regardless of the problem, but how aggressive behaviors will determine the outcome of a situation:

* When a person immediately jumps to conclusions,
* When and if a person becomes hostel toward another person,
* When a person doesn't try to think things through peacefully,
* When people think its okay, because this is just who I am.

The mind-set of aggression,

But, timely help can change those attitudes and stop or change a person's behavior toward some things:

- How does a person learn to control their antisocial behaviors, one is by studies, classes, group sessions, or counseling.

1. To see how many social clues could be interpreted as hostile, which were neutral or friendly

2. To look at others to get a sense of how others might think or feel

   a. about how they encounter addressing their anger

   b. classes, counseling on anger-control & management

   c. by interacting with others who get angry, such as in group sessions

   d. coming up with solutions for anger in your own life

3. To be able to control your temper when,

   a. people teased them

   b. is by monitoring their **feelings**

   c. by becoming aware of your own bodily sensations and vocal reactions

   d. such as facial expressions and muscles tensing

4. Take note of those **feeling** as **clues** will help you to stop and consider what is going to happen next.

5. How to deal with angry and being out-of-control, or is it just being too impulsive.

"Know yourself", speaks to this keystone of **inner personal intelligence**: **awareness** of one's own feelings as they occur. It might seem at first glance that feelings are obvious; a more thoughtful reflection may remind us that we may not have been aware of what we really felt or why at the time or do something without thinking a person may wake up to previously unknown feelings that alarms them.

Psychologist's use the term *Meta Cognition* to refer to an **awareness** of one's thought process, *Meta Mood* to mean **awareness of one's own emotions**.

Meta cognition" An Overview   **Pages 1 of 7** [5]
Meta Cognition Overview
© 1997 by Jennifer A. Livingston

"Meta cognition is one of the latest buzz words in psychology, but what exactly is Meta cognition? The length and abstract nature of the word makes it sound intimidating, yet its not as daunting a concept as it might seem. We engage in Meta Cognitive activities every day. Metacognition enables us to be successful learn, and has been associated with intelligence (e.g., Borkowski, Carr, & Pressley, 1987; Sternberg, 1984, 1986a, 1986b).

Meta cognition refers to higher order thinking which involves active control over the cognitive processes engaged in learning. Activities such as planning how to approach a given learning task, monitoring comprehension, and evaluating progress toward the completion of a task are meta cognitive in nature. Because Meta Cognition plays a critical role in successful learning, it is important to understand Meta Cognitive and development to determine how students can be taught to better apply their cognitive resources through meta cognitive control.

'Meta cognition' is often simply defined as 'thinking about thinking.' In actuality, defining Meta cognition is not that simple. Although the term has been part of the vocabulary of educational psychologists for the last couple of decades, and the concept for as long as humans have been able to reflect on their cognitive experiences, there is much debate over exactly what Meta Cognition is. One reason for this confusion is the fact that there are several terms currently used to describe the same basic phenomenon (e.g., self-regulation, executive control), or an aspect of that phenomenon (e.g., meta-memory), and these terms are often used interchangeably in the literature. While there are some distinctions between definitions (see Van Zile Tamsen, 1994, 1996 for a full discussion),

All emphasize the role of executive processes in the overseeing and regulation of cognitive processes.

Meta cognition consists of both Meta Cognitive knowledge and Meta Cognitive experiences or regulation. Meta cognitive knowledge refers to acquired knowledge about cognitive processes, knowledge that can be used to control cognitive processes. Flavell further divides meta cognitive knowledge into three categories: knowledge of person variables, task variables and strategy variables."

http://www.gse.buffalo.edu/fas/shuell/cep564/Metscog.html

1/14/050

Venture Capital Magazine   **Pages 1 - 2** [6]
Individualism methodology cognitivism

"Unpublished English version of '**Individualism methodology et cognitive**' In: R. Boudon, F. Chazel & A. Bouvier (eds.) *Cognition et sciences sociales*. Paris: Presse Universities de France, 1997. pp. 123-136)

"I would like to contrast two interpretations, a weak one and a strong one, of the notion of methodological individualism, and two interpretations, a weak one and a strong one, of the notion of cognitivism. This double contrast determines four ways in which one might choose to be at the same time a methodological individualist and a cognitivist in the social sciences. One way, where both positions are adopted with a weak interpretation, is of little interest. I argue there is another way, where both positions are adopted with a strong interpretation is incoherent. I will compare the two other possibilities. According to methodological individualism (whichever way you interpret the notion), social phenomena can be adequately explained by showing that they are the outcome of individual behaviors. Methodological individualism is standardly contrasted with holism, according to which social phenomena can be explained only by invoking the behavior or the properties of entities which are irreducibly supra-individual, such as culture or institutions."

(AI) ARTICLE INTELLIGENT
Virtual Christian Magazine: Artificial Intelligence: Improving on God's creation? Page 1 of 5

"(AI) ARTICLE NTELLIGENT - MACHINES will soon surpass the abilities of human beings, say enthusiasts of artificial intelligence. Such predictions are no longer espoused only by science-fiction aficionados. Some serious scientists are saying the same thing.

Why would anyone want to create an artificial entity more intelligent than man? The reasoning of some proponents of artificial intelligence (AI) is that, although mankind represents the pinnacle of intelligence on the planet, we have proven inept at handling many of our problems. Thus we need a new and better solution. 'We could turn to these superior intelligence's for advice and authority in all matters of concern--and the humanity-induced troubles of the world could at last be resolved' (Roger Penrose, *Shadows of the Mind,* 1994, p. 11).

Such thoughts set off alarm bells in the minds of people who fear such creations could take over society and enslave us or even decide they don't need us. This concept has provided the themes for several Hollywood action films, including the popular 1999 release *Matrix* and several *Terminator* movies.

AI developers hope 'heuristic' computers, equipped with vast databases and programmed to analyze and dissect problems, will be in extensive use around 2020. Heuristic computers might provide services normally supplied by a doctor or lawyer.
Designing such systems may prove more difficult than many envision. 'Ask a computer about a rusty car and it might blithely diagnose measles' (Michio Kaku, *Visions: How Science Will Revolutionize The 21st Century,* 1997, p. 62). Some scientists believe machines with even more humanlike traits will become commonplace. "It is reasonable to assume that by 2050 we may have robots that can interface intelligently with humans, machines with primitive emotions...and common sense"

(Kaku, p. 90). Some expect robots will have the capacity to actually love their masters.

Man is the only creature that puzzles over the reason for his existence. We are the only physical beings that demonstrably can ponder past, present and future. This ability did not evolve; God created it. He is the author of human consciousness and intelligence.

As for man developing a source of artificial intelligence that can supply answers to our insoluble problems, his new knowledge tends to produce even more problems in approximate proportion to the amount of new information he discovers. If we are wise, we will look to God for answers through His revelation, the Bible.

Man cannot find lasting solutions to his problems because they are at the core of spiritual aspects of a person (Isaiah 59). Unless and until humanity as a whole is ready to recognize the true source of its problems and seek God's solutions, we will continue to face the dilemmas and difficulties that have plagued mankind for thousands of years.

The Bible shows us human problems will not be resolved until Jesus Christ returns. 'Behold I lay in Zion a choice stone, a precious corner stone, and he who believes in Him shall not be disappointed' (1 Peter 2:6, New American Standard Bible)."

http://www.vcmagazune.org/vcm/artical.asp?volume=2&issue=7&artical =ia   1/14/05

HOW THE MIND AND INTELLECT INTERACTS WITH SELF-IMAGE

The mental and intellectual aspects of a person will it be more important within confines of a good healthy discourse, understanding, and attitude, will a good wholesome attitude bring about happiness within the confines as to who you want to be or is it something else, a person has to consider these different characteristics as they workout things. The mind is another important aspect in a person, but the heart of a person is a force, the soul is something different. Does the heart of a person have anything to do with the soul of course it does the soul is the inner core of a person.

There is another twist in a person's mind-set as people we need to be intellectual honest they can be miss lead by their conscience, which governs one aspect of self, self-well and your emotional involvement. A person's anxieties can run away with them and affects their mental aspects as well as the intellect, both are an under lying influence. It can get pretty confusing as you can see there are other ways to look at a situation and that is by not justifying the problem or that it exists. Does it boil down to what a person thinks of course not because there are other factors we just went through? A person has to look at what is best for them in light of what has gone right or wrong, yet the intellect of a person may have something to do with the outcome, but more likely it's their behaviors are the biggest factors not so much whether it's right and morally wrong. There are two concepts when something is wrong there is always a time of anxiety and doubt, did I make the right decision sometimes a person is not sure until they live through the experience.

An illustration is when you marry a person you really don't know them until you have been married for a while it is not always like you pictured them before the marriage. Sometimes it seems like they have become two different people. One time they think one way and another time they act differently under the same circumstance. A good illustration might be when you look at your spouse and look at the person you dated, "you may be saying who is that person I married?" Life does not always turn out like you planed like the number of children you planned and how many boys and girls you have.

What if there is a **cry for help** before and after the decision. The **cry from inside** is probably the most miss-understood feeling because it could be the quit before the storm and/or it becomes loud because of what a person is feeling and in that case there may or may not be any visible signs. The mind has to process things while it is dealing with what is right or wrong. You would think because we are intelligent we can reason things out, but if the person has bad memories of what has happened and don't understand why it is painful, another reason a person may not know what is "RIGHT or what's WRONG" because of past their experiences. Now think with me and follow my line of thought OK.

Emotional feelings are a domain of the mind and as surely as you know $4 + 4 = 8$, knowing how the mind works may be how you handle things. There are other ways of coming up with 8, $5+3 = 8$ different factors like two people with different ideas the ultimate outcome is a balanced approach like 4+4 = 8. The harder is to come with a solution to the problem, this could be 1+7 = 8 there is a greater need for balanced if the numbers don't match like even numbers or say they are odd members a person with lesser skills may have problems in communication. It may require a unique set of competencies or education to figure out a problem. How a person adepts and understands the situation, why one person thrives in life, while another person of equal intellect, has dead-ends.

A person needs an understanding how **emotional aptitude** is the primary influence in the *meta-ability theory*, what are the determining factors depends on how well a person is able to deal with their situation. The best way to determine how a person will do is how well they accomplish something their personal skill in coping with a situation, rather than their *raw courage, but rather their intellectual ability to think things through and some cases it takes both to work things out*.

Of course, there are many paths to success, and other aptitudes, which reward or destroy a person's self-image. One way is by increasing knowledge, social adjustments, and learning technical skills while others may go to college.

A person has to appreciate how their intellectual abilities are enhanced in this rough-and-tumble world we live in. In the day-to-day world our emotions plays a part in a person's **interpersonal relationships**. If you don't have the knowledge of how to deal with things and people, you are more likely to make poor choices and decisions.

1. Your Mind will cry out in confusion.
2. Your Soul will cry out in aguish.
3. Your Body will cry out in pain.

This is where understanding both intelligence and behavior comes into play, how a person deals with their **self-image,** and how self-well comes into play; both of these well dictate the way you think of yourself and others. There is a two-fold part in how a person deals with others, "You may say what you mean?" Because that is where we are going next, OK.

This is where **low self-image** comes into play as you focus on your problems. **Low self-worth** may cause a person to put things off because they look down on themselves. On the other hand, **self-image** can take on other characteristics. The war of the mind comes when we deal with our fleshly nature.

Sometimes a person's love takes on the form of admiration for a person or thing, but when it brings them down as a person, something is wrong. One of the symptoms is when a person has bouts of depression and low self-image can affect their relationships, work, etc.? Of course, love fits into this equation if there is no love and desire it makes for a bad relationship. If the relationship is based codependency the reason maybe because a person has become dependent on the other person, which enforces their low-self-image, it affects the way a person feels about themselves. If a person feels they can't live without someone or something, and they put up with their conflicts. The desire for something or somebody is not always easy to distinguish between their right and wrong motives. This kind of relationship can affect a person's good judgment and it can affect other relationships in their life.

When there is an improper balance in the relationship, or when a person feels alone and has a great deal of depression from time to time, it usually affects the way they feel in the relationship.

Is this relationship worth the ANGUISH and PAIN?

Look for these warning signs and consider to what degree your love has been violated in the relationship you need to conceder yourself first and make it a priority in any relationship. There needs to be a definite commitment to a relationship, marriage, or living together. The one big question before marriage is that the RIGHT person can you get along, do your temperaments match or do you disagree on important things that is a good question to ask each other if you are dating or getting ready to marry someone. Next have they violated your love, trust, and respect, if the answer is yes, they are not the right person or until it has been made right.

There are many forms of expression, love and empathy may enter into the equation. Another way a person expresses themselves in their emotions and their attitude toward another person or when a person expresses their feelings and opinions about things. When a person's doesn't agree and their emotions are too highly charged and that becomes an outward expression of their feelings for others. They can become violent emotions and even get out of control to the point of anger and rage sometimes do you really want to put up with those feelings. It can be an expression of the stress in the situation. There can be an expression of love and joy by creating and building empathy and trust with others which takes on the **expression** of (love and caring).

I want to take it a step farther if possible and relate to your emotional needs for **self-expression** as a person. You have to deal with the need to express your love and that takes on many forms. There are other expressions concerning your personality they may come in the form of some kind of art, crafts, writing or creating something, and there is creativeness from within.

Another way is how a person identifies with their love and passion for something or someone. If there is a conflict in a relationship and that causes a person to loss their joy and happiness. If you are dependent on a person and they may rob you of that joy and happiness. This is one way of knowing when something is wrong, when they don't give back to you the joy and happiness you disserve, and you are not able to enjoy the feeling of two being one. This will leave a void and emptiness; another is the need for self-fulfillment. If these two things don't balance, and you are not in control of your life; you are not going to have that joy and happiness. If you do not have one or both you are incomplete.

The passion for some kind of creativeness can also be a **stress-relief** for you and add that other dimension in your life that will enable you to cope. How do you feel about what we have been talking about in this aspect of your life?

This is where you need that something or someone that will allow you an escape from time to time and increase your joy and happiness. Be careful this can become an obsession in your life and cause an imbalance in your relationship or relationships. There is tendency over do things or under react.

If there are personal problems in a marriage and other relationships one of the problems is immorality and infidelity. I will discuss these subjects and talk openly about divorce in our (book on "SOS New Beginnings") also I will discuss some of my personal experiences concerning my divorces in my biography "Facing the real me, Run John Run, the real cry for help and the real hurt and pain."

There are many avenues of escape in this real world there are ways to deal with any situation. The problem can be finding the right answers for you, which do not add another stress in your life, there is a stress level in anything you do, but we need to be wise enough to know the difference between good or bad stress. There was a time when everything I tried seam to add more stress, I felt I was in a valley of despair over a situation.

I liked the kind of stress that added pressure to my life I like being in business, making money, and being successful. My pride in relation to the wants, needs and desires lead me into other adventures and you may want to read about them in my family biography "Facing the Real Me."

Does the human spirit and the will of a (man or women) have anything to do with us being intelligent beings of course it does it helps us in knowing the best or worst in a conflict or crisis, and does the dowel facets of our being show up in the right or wrong, should I, or I should not.

The psychology of a (man or women) is not complete in the nature and make-up without understanding the third part of our (character), but the very nature of creation is in God who created us, a God who lets us make choices. We are twofold beings, it shows up in our thinking idealistically there is a (right and wrong, sometimes there are gray areas) the gray is where we often have problems deciding how much is right and how far can we go before it becomes wrong. The functional side may seem to have everything to do with our intellectual side. A person is probably going to say is it right or wrong before they do anything, this brings out the make-up of a person's (character) and how it affects a person's self-image, they are two different aspects of a person's being. Our emotions are transacted into feelings which include our actions or reactions to any given situation or relationship. God gave us a heart, in this way we are able to feel and communicate with each other on a personal and spiritual bases; our heart and mind lets us know what is right and what a person should do, what happens a person doesn't always do the right thing?

Therefore, a person needs help in making the right choices/decisions. There are defiantly conflicts in relationships especially when it comes to the will of two people. You can hardly get two people with the same values and morals let alone two people with same viewpoint. Of course, there are two viewpoints from the (male and female) point of view because of their emotional levels are not the same. In addition, there is just the plain truth of I will or I want something; how does the will relate to spiritual applications, how a person's deals with what God wants and expects.

Will pretty well defines it specifically as "believing you have both a **will** and **determination** to accomplish your goals whatever they maybe".

Most people think of themselves as being able to handle their own will or some feel they can get out of a jam, the problem is finding ways to solve your problems, while others do not have the energy, ability, or means in solving problems, and some have problems in reaching their goals based on their well-power.

I believe these traits and abilities will help bring about success:
   * Motivating themselves
   * Feeling resourceful enough to find ways to accomplish their objectives
   * Reassuring themselves when in a tight spot they can do things and it will get better
   * Being flexible enough to find different ways to get to your goals or to switch goals are among other possibilities
   * Having the sense to break-down formidable tasks into
   smaller parts; can make them more manageable tasks.
   * Being self–assured and interested in the tasks being done
   * Knowing what is expected and living up to expectations
   * Knowing how to believe in one's self
   * Knowing when to rein in the impulses that cause misbehaviors
   * Knowing how to wait and being patient with others
   * Knowing how to follow instructions, and carry them out
   * Knowing how to get help and knowing when to let things go
   * Knowing how to express your needs while getting along with others.

I think the basic difference is how much a person relies on their physical abilities, but more important is the emotional make-up of their mind. Another is be aware of set (patterns, routines, and of course medications/natural foods, supplements, & addictions) be careful when using one or all of these as solutions in dealing with a situation or problem. On the other hand, some of these are good you may rely more on the psychological aspects to solve problems, or the combination of both physiology and psychology ideally having a proper balance of the two is vital.

That is why this part of our study will make sense as we look at a person's needs according to their wants, it is very important for a person to know how to fix or mend the broken pieces, and put things in perspective.

I hope I haven't lost you at this point stick around it will be worth your time and energy. The human-spirit and will is another aspect of your life that will have an effect on what happens and what you accomplish. Again, this deals with the very heart of the person your well to do something will add to how well you accomplish things. The well to survive and live is one of the strongest instincts and assets a person will have in solving problems it will show up when a person faces a crisis or situation.

The fact is your **spirit** and **well** will never quit or give up unless it is limited by the person's own **determination**. This is where the conflict of **two wells** can come together. What happens when both people think they are "RIGHT"! Can both people be "RIGHT" and equally "RIGHT"? This is a situation everyone has faced many times in your relationships the key is being willing to compromise and still feel good about the decision. We have to dig down deep inside if a person is going to set aside their prejudices, self-well and their personal desires to take on a situation.

Then your defensive mechanism kicks into gear because someone has challenged you before. All of these motives come into play when we think of a person's self-well, and the well of others. Both parties are equally responsible and could be that one is not necessarily Right and should be equally guilty in some way, but when there is a point of disagreement some tend to become an adolescent, selfish rather than mature adults. It still leaves the question unanswered if they cannot come up with a solution, but we do have some idea of the magnitude and gravity of these situations and the problems people are dealing with.

At this point, a person can feel wounded or emotional crippled; the human spirit can give up if they are not careful. There are a couple of things that can happen, when the **spirit** and **well** is suppress by another person and they impose their **well** on another person the obvious question is when a person becomes stubborn and subdued by another person over a long period of time there can be a great deal of damage when this happens. The prolonged stigma can cripple a person mentally and sometimes take on physically ailments. That is when a person may need help in overcoming personal issues.

The conscience and the subconscious feelings and beliefs are involved in any situation or problem because that is how the human mind responds, but a person can overrule the **human spirit** and **well to overcome**. As we have studied person has to have the knowledge and then the desire to make the right decisions, even if it is not what they may have wanted personally. If you can't make the decision or know what is best you may need advice or personal counseling.

Again, you may need to understand and know a little more about the **human spirit** and **well**. They are the driving forces in overcoming in any given situation and can be the equalizing force in some situations. A person has to deal with every part of their life and in every situation, but even more than that, a good illustration is how it affects a life-threatening situation or health problem. The human **spirit** and **well** can surprise a person at times Doctors and Psychologists cannot understand or predict what the **human body, mind** and **the human spirit** and **well** can do I like to add that to the power of Prayer. We have a powerful force and we need to activate those powers at times, I believe it can take on the form of a miracle. There are many types of miracles and we don't always see them as that.

Then you need to respect yourself and your body, and your **mental well-being**. There are mental and physical changes as a person gets older and then a person has to deal with the different situations and problems that go along with those changes another way of saying it be kind to yourself, but don't feel sorry for yourself. The critical point in a situation or problem is when you feel helpless and when you feel there is no help or hope. When you are at the bottom of the well, so to speak, don't despair look for the answer it could be hidden somewhere in the back of your mind waiting for you to call it back the heart of the matter is another aspect of your inner being.

Some have a tendency to feel dejected and let down while others wonder why did this happen to them? Sometimes the help comes when a person goes through the situation and the circumstances bring the answer or it may come from other sources. Wait is probably the hardest thing a person has to do we get impatient waiting for the right answers while life goes on ticking. We need to stop and evaluate the situations and problems before going on this is where we need love, support, guidance and encouragement.

It may come from the most unlikely sources. A person can even feel or want a change of direction in their life, and it may or may not be the answer. "A person may be going through a crisis at the time". If we can only get you to take on the present challenge before it builds into full-blown crisis.

The answer is there if you could only see it before it gets worse in the mean time you need to make good decisions and keep trying to find the answers. In searching for an answer you may feel helpless or don't know what else you can do. I believe in having faith in yourself will be tied to the limits of your human endurance in a crisis. The problem maybe that you cannot see the real problem and you may not want to accept the answer. You can get confused about this time, it is always much more difficult when you are going through a crisis or problem, as you look it, it is always the darkest before you see the light there is always hope.

You may not be able to see the light at the other end as you look through the tunnel there is an end because others have gone through the same thing. At this point, it can look bad, as you feel engulfed by despair, your journey must continue because there is always hope to lean on. Another thing look for an obvious solution, someone else may be able to shade some light at that point. There are short cuts and they may not be the answer, remember to stay calm don't panic, or get overwhelmed at any point and time.

In my case, I was able to find myself and harness the powers in me and that help me. It takes a great deal of care and understanding on both sides of the human spirit. The human side and spiritual side, the two don't always agree at any given time. I have been dealing with the human side, the human spirit became a part of my healing process, I know life gets fustigating at times I am going to show you how I dealt with this human aspect and my makeup. There are many different avenues and channels that go through your life and life system, this can leave a lasting impression to deal with.

We want you to look at your positive or negative nature, your **spirit** and **well** has a bearing you may have a tendency to feel down this can become a dominating force it is a very strong factor in your determination.

The **human spirit** and **well** can do some funny things at times. This is a great force, but knowing how to use those powers of the mind, I am of the opinion that a person can do great things when they put their mind to it. It is a matter of which power you want to rule and to what degree a person needs to understand their **will power** at the same time.

* The Human-Well has motivations
* The Human-Well has awesome powers.
* The Human-Well is a driving force.
* The Human-Well is also fragile.

A person has multiple powers and influences depending on their background, as we look at a person's character, their ego is a major factor in their self-image it can be fragile if the ego is broken then the well is broken. The well to do something hinges on the balance of the ego self-image is especially in regard to the human mechanisms, transference of guilt is one, reality is another the testing of the human well. Let me try to explain by looking at the difference between LOVE-HATE, GOOD-BAD they relate to opposite ends of the spectrum in our emotions. Now let's look at the HIGH'S and LOW'S that are involved in the human spirit in a way they are like the North and South Pole they are relevant to each other, but they are at opposite ends of the world each person can have extreme feelings and they are at the mercy of those esteem feelings. This is a critical point is when they become too high or too low. Let me illustrate by saying there are various degrees of emotions such as love and then it becomes to the point hating someone.

There is a sense of unworthiness when bad thoughts prevail, your joy is gone and gloom is crowding the mind, a sense of dread and alienation, and above all a feeling everything is wrong, and a stifling to anxiety sets in.

Then there are the emotional marks:
* Confusion
* Failure
* Mental focus is gone
* Lapse of memories

In any stage in life the mind may become "dominated by doubts and fears," and "a sense of loss in the process and a person may be engulfed by toxic feelings.

This can be the physical effects:
* Sleeplessness, feeling of listlessness, and becoming a zombie,
* A kind for numbness, but more particularly having odd feelings.
* They want to be alone, feeling fragile restlessness,
* Then loss of pleasure.
* Finally the vanishing of hope "the loss of hope and horror", then despair is like the physical pain in the body that has over taken you, when suicide seems to be a solution.

Are you there?

The point is how much stress can a person take before they bend or break. When there is too much stress and too much bending over time when these reactions have been taking place for too long a person can only take so much before the breaking point something has to give. Sometimes it only takes a push or shove because of all the things that have happened in the past.

I worked as a maintenance foreman in a power plant we had to measure the amount of wear on a part and the stress point on a part; we used a mic to measure the 1,000's of an inch. If there was too much wear, we would have to replace it with a new part. Our lives take on some of the same principles the wear and tear on our lives can get to be too much at times. Can you replace the damage in your life (no); you can change things in your life to the point of having a better life? (YES) Stay with me and see how we do this!

When there is too much stress! We know there is breaking point every person has a different breaking point this can be a very dangerous time. When you have drastic reactions taking place it may not be a life treating situation, but if it is or it is a very serious illness or problem. When people can't seem to do anything and don't see the need for help, at that point we do have people who think about suicide or killing someone else because they have hurt them. At some point a person may feel out-of-control ready to hit the panic button and what does that mean.

The Panic Button.

That means you are stressing out or almost out-of-control, or maybe you are just having a bad day, or needing some loving care and understanding. The president of the United Sates has a "The Hot Line". We call ours "The Panic Button" that is when you need to contact us or a support partner.

Let the stress out and talk to someone or find away to cope. I have been so angry and even out-of-control a few times. My hope is that we can help you get back on track and add some new demonstrations in helping your image.

(Our Self-Help Books) brings out different studies and information, we want to help the person accomplish things they never considered before and we want you to find new activities. We are going to continue to deal with emotions, pride, and love as we go on. We want to help you define *who you are* and *what is best for you when things get tough.* Our self-help studies has a major emphasis on the person, next is your need to understand more about your self-image and living with your circumstances and relationships.

The advice *you* get is not always the best. Because *you're* family, friends, are not counselors, but they should be a part of *your* support team. There are books a person can read and some are not always helpful. *You* may say if that is the case what should I do now, and that is a good reason for wanting the right kind of counseling. I know, I have been there, and when I listened to others and society influenced some of my decisions I made and again I made my own mistakes.

WHAT IS WISDOM? THINKING THING THROUGH & WISE DECISIONS

Chapter 4

CRITICAL THINKING & WISDOM

The value of wisdom

This is not the END when things go wrong it may be the BEGINNING of WISDOM in knowing one's self-image, and when a person knows how to apply wisdom to their personal life. Remember to look for other kinds of help in other sections of our studies and services.

It may be hard to believe there is a lot more that has to do with your self-image and that is in the way a person looks at themselves, but more importantly is how you take on the challenges of the circumstances in your life and relationships. Next how are things affecting your value and value means self-worth? I know that there is an interaction with everything that happens, but on the other hand, the outside influences can affect your self-image and how you to deal with your motives.

Another thing this chapter is another conception of one's self how do you're motives affect what you do how are these influences affecting your motivation. A person can get emotionally up set and that has a bearing on their decisions which is based on how they feel. How about self-motivation or dealing with things you can't control? That is why you need to understand what Meta Cognition really means one's own THINKING.

There is another thing to consider when a person wants to get even for what has happened; the problem with getting even it becomes a never-ending cycle of who got who last.

This is where we deal with the person and then their role which means self-assurance and self-assurance helps you at the same time. Your needs may vary in how (you) meet those needs how a person incorporates the thinking process along with what they want to accomplish.

What you think of yourself will determine whether you succeed. You may think of yourself as the "king on the mountain", but one of the guidelines is the amount of determination a person has. You may not know all of your inner strengths and weaknesses and how to deal with them.

Pride

Sometimes it is a matter of the right kind of pride, with others it can lead to a low-self-image which is one in the same as you deal with how you feel about yourself, and that may very well affect how you think of others when you compare others to yourself. This is a good time to talk about pride if a person has a positive attitude how does pride fit into a person's attitude as they deal with a situation or relationship. A person's pride is a very strong influence. I have a pride in the way I look, therefore, there has to be a balance in the area pride and how a person sees themselves. Regardless whether they are (male or female), we can't base everything on how things look, each person has to deal with their personal traits and how they see themselves.

We are going to look at three real problems and how pride works. A person may not want to face the real truth because of their pride and a false pride also affects the way they see themselves. There is another problem with pride, it is summed up in the way a person processes the real truth about themselves. That is when they feel bad about themselves and they don't do anything to help themselves.

Secondly let's look at a person's mannerisms and conduct towards others in the way they feel really boils down to what they think of themselves and how they control their feelings for others. It effects their interaction with others and some believe their never wrong and it is always the other person's fault.

Third pride affects their relationships if a person has too much pride they are unable to take criticism it is crucial because this will determine what others think of them. Another is how a person interacts with the outside pressures and influences, and how well they govern their principles and morals.

I think if this part of your life has problems and even worse when you think you are better than someone else it is okay to feel good about yourself, but not at the expense of others. When pride is puffed up a person needs help in understanding how it is affecting others in your relationships. There are multiple problems when things get in the way of them saying I'm sorry. This may seem like a minor problem, but when it becomes a major obstacle in a relationship and when a person has a problem for giving others; it will show up in how it affects their relationship with others.

I have individualized our self-help studies as much as possible to meet a person's different needs. Regardless who they whether they are (young or old). My hope is that you will be able to understand the person you think you are and how affects your reacts in a situation and look at how it influences others. Whatever a person says or does can hurt someone be careful again! That is of the most importance because people need each other.

Success is a part of that joy of course just because you failed and have problems does not mean you can't find happiness, because you may have had a bad relationship does not mean the next one will be bad, whatever you've done in the past does not mean everything will turn out wrong. This could be the stepping-stone it takes to turn your life around I found this to be very true in my life I had to learn how to give yourself.

The thing to look for at this point can you find your way? The right kind of help is the next question. "RIGHT" I want you to separate the two, forgiveness is the beginning in helping making things right and do this whenever possible.

Then you need to try and express how you feel toward others without hurting them, next what needs to be done, and see how someone else identifies with how you feel and it is important to let them know what you are going through. See how others are dealing with the same situations and circumstances, and how they are coping with their situations and circumstances. It is ok to look at why others have failed and how they learned from their mistakes. They can be an encouragement and then see what you can do different ask them if they would have done something differently, knowing what they know now.

A person may think it is the other person's fault because you can't get along when in reality it lies at your own door step. It is easy to blame someone else; I want you to look at your own problems first and find ways to solve your problems that may help more than anything.

This is where a neutral party can be of help if you are going to help someone you will need to be honest with them, but not when it will hurt them or cause an augment. This is where another person's pride stands in their way and pride can stand in the way of them being honest with themselves, or their lack of self-worth. Until they face the truth about themselves nothing is going to happen the hurt is still there and will stay there until they decide to do something about who they are. They need to be careful if they are unable to get past what is or has happened. A person has to deal their faults and short comings as well as the other person's short comings and faults.

When Abuse is involved

When things get out of control it lead abuse? How to deal with abuse in relationships is one the toughest things because people don't see what they do as abuse that is why it is hard to define and deal with. There is always some miner abuse and they feel they need to get over their bad feelings and attitude, but if the other person feels or sees it as abuse, it is usually shows up in how they are over compensating for the other person's bad behavior in some way. The paramount question is how bad is the abuse a person has to put up with, and what can be done about it does either one or both want to deal with it.

How does a person deal with the impact of abuse, but on the other hand how does it affect the person, this is a very important question? How does a person react if there is abuse and what affect is it going to have on a person's life and that is very important too?

One is the abused person and the one that causes the abuse, is it affecting both of them. Sometimes both of them are very helpless individuals because one of them has become a codependent. This does not take anything away from each person's responsibility for themselves I think the key is how each looks at the abuse and how seriously is it affecting each other. The problem comes when they cannot be honest about the abuse, and can each person deal with it objectively. If not the answer always comes down to doing what is right and the answer should be good for both persons in a positive way. They will probably need help in reaching the right decision and how to deal with the abuse.

There are so many kinds of ABUSES, Physical-Mental-Sexual and Domestic Violence I have dealt with these over the years. I find there are three main categories one is the degrees of abuse of course, two is how it is affecting them. The third comes when they are unable to deal with the abuse; the judge and jury is out on how to deal with abuse because each person has to decide if something needs to be done. I find it is hard to help a person when they don't know what needs to be done especially when they have lived with abuse as a child. They feel they deserve the abuse they may need help in understanding when it started in their relationship and what caused the abuse. How much they will allow before they blow-up over things and most of the time they don't know how much their life is being affected by the abuse. Why haven't they done something about it before it got out of control, and they would like for it to end, but they need to be willing to do something?

If the abuse is there in their adolescent years it carries over into their future relationships. The person who has been abused over the years are not able to define how bad the abuse has become because they feel they dissever the abuse, abuse becomes a part of their life.

When the assaults take place the person is glad when it's over, they usually live in consent fear of the next assault; the problem is the next one maybe too late. They walk on eggshells, because any little thing can trigger a drug addicted or alcoholic person to fly into a rage and attic them. I find this to be very true in most of these cases abuse and addictions is the bottom line and how it affects their life and relationships.

The addicted person doesn't even know who they are when they are under the influence of alcohol and drugs or why they do things. There is a real danger at this point when a person wants to dominate and control the other person and in that case they become a victim of the abuser, in many of these cases they don't know how to deal with it! In many of these cases, they lose their identity as a person, low-self-worth and depression sets in. They feel inadequate, helpless, and unsure within themselves they become a codependent with that addicted person, the abuse becomes a way of life, and they can't move without the other person's approval. They never deal with the other person's anger and disapproval of them and they live with violent out bursts, they are trapped when this happens. They need to stop it before the next attic takes place does this sound familiar to you, do you feel trapped in some way! There are shelters for those who have been abused, check places in your local area.

This is classified as a traumatic experience and they have gotten to where they can't think for themselves and can't make their own decisions, they can't stand up for their rights, they feel they have no rights as a person. They are beaten they feel trapped, and they feel they can't get out because they feel helpless and the worst thing they don't want to get out, they feel lost because that is all they know! My hope is that I can encourage them to do something to help themselves.

I am asking you to look at your relationships and see if there is any abuse in your life! You need to be able to distinguish between yourself and the abuse involved. You are your own judge this can happen to either (male or female).

Children and young people are victims of abuse too and they don't have many ways to deal with adults who cause the abuse. The parent needs to find for themselves if no other reason for their children. There are other relationships, which have some of the same trade marks in their relationships I think of it as "A living Hell on earth". If a person's inadequacies, insecurities are the result of abuse it will affect their ability love and be loved, the need for love adds to the situation of course.

Your childhood influences affects every relationship especially if they have been abused, does this fit you or your relationship. The church, society and family usually set the guidelines for dealing with abuse, what can you do if you are caught in this kind of situation?

Sure, we can do something about abuse if the person is willing to work with a counselor or support group, or get help through the court system. What are the consequences if they don't and is it worth the effort to get help? We have tried to look at the whole picture and see if they can see the damage and do they want to do something about it. Do you need help, but, the most important thing is for the person to realize they need to change things and go on. It can be done, there are all kinds of help, the abused person is the key and there are all kinds of keys to unlock those prison doors in a person's life.

To sum it up they are Social-Problems: but more than that it becomes personal when a person depends on Alcohol-Marijuana-Drugs-Pills relating to addictions. These are some the common social disorders in our society this can also relates to smoking it could fit into this category all of these are considered abuses in some way. What about the other person that has to live with their addictions, in some cases both have addictions to deal with, every person suffers. It affects their family, even the children, wives-fiancé, mother-dad, and the whole family. These addictions can lead to mental problems and illnesses!

These addictions can and do destroy the brain cells that creates a chemical in balance. When it gets so bad they can't cope, it has gone too far at this point, they have become dependent on the addiction and it has taken over. They can break the chains of any addiction if they get help the earlier the better chance for defeating the addiction, there are all kinds of support help and support groups out there to help them. But, they usually don't take advantage of the help and if they don't I'm not sure anyone can do it on their own. I have heard of some who have stopped on their own, most of them say with God's help and they didn't have any more problems, anything that works will help them at that point. I have studies on Christian and faith based self-help study guides.

You have to find your identity as a codependent the help comes when they find interdependence from those addictions I hope our self-help studies can be of help. There are many ways to deal with these problems, there are several programs one is the twelve step programs, and alcohol anonymous, AAA choose which direction you are going to take and stick with it. There are studies, books and all kinds of information that offer support information, group sessions and ours is based on cognitive identity and behavior modification "SOS LIFE ENHANCEMENT". At Support outreach Services www.sosselfhelpbooks.info, we can help a person find a support partner, or you can become a care-partner or become a mentor or coach if you would like to be a part of our service. It is not enough to say you need help unless you seek help counseling and professional help I have an on line counseling service and if you do need our self-help study guide SOS NEW BEGINNINGS. My question is how can I help, our motto is let us *help you help yourself*. When these programs work and these studies build on a person's self-image and after going through these programs their lives are changed and then they can help others in our services. I know of people whose lives and marriages are changed and others who remarry and become leaders in their church.

GENETIC INFLUENCES

Look at the reflections in your life

Your attitude is a reflection of yourself it is so much like looking into a mirror it is the reflection of one's self, if you look deep enough within yourself you may be able to see yourself. When a person looks at their reflections, there can be a problem. The first things to look for are your PRIMARY INFLUENCES because you won't see them by looking in a mirror and how they are affecting your life. To sum up what I'm talking about or to understand what we are saying examine YOUR MOTIVATION. This is a real reflection of what is or as happened in your life. A person tends to see what they want to see and not what caused the problem; what has happened will reflect on how you go about dealing with the problem. All of these will determine what you are going to do and say and how it is affecting your personal well-being. There is another way to look at it, a cancer can take over and the same is true with what is happening.

Now you are going to see a good example taking place in a person's life it is very important to determine *who you are* and *what you are made of.*

I was DETERMINED not to make the same mistakes over again, but I did. I thought I was doing the right things by trying different methods, and they helped, but I ended up with same results. WHY? Something had to happen fine the things that have worked and get rid of the things that didn't work at that point I didn't know what to change to make things better! I found I was the same person, after I made the CHANGES. I found I was able to deal with the things I couldn't change! I began to look at the old patterns, now I began to see my faults as patterns that could be changed, now I look for the good things I could change and see the bad in different way, I'm not as critical of myself and others.

Now I look at how things were affecting and controlling me. How are you holding up under health problems and there was a break through by breaking the chains that were holding me captive.

When everyday things become a burden, you have to deal with them and when things don't get resolved, you can harbor bad feeling toward someone and that can eat at a person and destroy their love and understanding in a situation or relationship. If you cannot forgive a person for something that has happened in the past, when something reminds you of the past things they have done or someone else may have done something that influences your present life in the wrong way. When people and things remind you of the hurt its time to do something about it.

One of the biggest setbacks may not be the worst thing that could have happened, it becomes from the dread of what could happen. In the long run it could destroy you if you don't do anything; the worst thing is when you don't know how bad things have become. The evidence is when it destroys your joy, robs you of your happiness and brings out the negative thoughts and feelings. You don't have any fun because you have been robbed of your joy, how can all this happen; it is a serious offence against yourself it is like heaping coals of fire upon yourself.

Now I try and remember the good things as quickly as possible and know that I am not their judge, and "I don't live there any more". You are going to need all of the love, support and guidance possible. This is a major step in the healing process. That is why our support group programs are available, and there are other organizations out there.

There is another factor that we have not explored at all and that is how your motives figures into all of this. You need the motivation to stop those bad feelings that are relevant in any situation or relationship, divorce, breaking-up, or separation as a result there are different influences, and you may want to weigh all of the evidence before making any decision.

Divorce, separation and failed relationships are one the most devastating circumstances to deal with outside of death almost 50% of marriages end up divorce. There are so many multiple families and blended marriages in today's society. I do not know of anything that can leave person, family, and children so mentally crippled or leave anyone with any worse feelings to deal with. The utter sense of failure and rejection is so common in these situations. The whole family has to deal with the hurt feelings, and some even feel they are at fault they feel the pain and guilt associated with these problems.

This all starts with a wonderful marriage the cheer joy and happiness people are so full of expectations when they marry they are usually a highly emotional feelings. At one time they thought this was the person they would spend the rest of their live with how could they have been so mistaken about this person.

They could be caught up a warfare of who's right and who's wrong and in most cases each person thinks they are RIGHT and has a point of view each one has their own prospective of what has happened or who is RIGHT and who is WRONG. This is a classic example of each person looking at it from their own prospective; it becomes a point of trying to persuade their spouse they are right, children and family think they are RIGHT consequently people take sides. In this case, they have destroyed their emotional stability! In some cases, the parents are so bitter they do not realize what they are doing to themselves and the children.

All I can say at this point what a mess I have been there and gone through this I know what it's like to go through the war zone of a bad relationship and divorce!

The children are the ones who suffer and pay the biggest price because they are hurt. They take it just as personally as the parent's and even take sides, because children look it from a child's point of view. When a child deals with a divorce or a separation, they can be just as prejudice and selfish as the adults. Their human element is going to show up too. They can use both sides to get what they want and get even their security is jeopardized when they don't have a peaceful home; they are thorn between two people they love. The stable atmosphere they need is gone and now they have to adjust to the fighting and most of the time it is over them.

This will affect them for the rest of their life. It will likely affect their relationships as young people and adults. It is a little like the abuse we just discussed it will leave a mark on their life, such as being insecure they will have all kinds of feelings to deal with.

Mental, Emotional, Thought process = safety factors

I want to expand on Abraham Maslow has 5 basic needs.

1. Physical 2. Safety 3. Belonging 4. Esteem 5. Self-actualization

He uses the term Hierarchy. (Prioritize your needs)

1. Physical needs = food /place to live /survival

Most people work on meeting these basic needs.

2. Safety = protection and feeling safe.

3. Belonging needs = a. relates to self-worth b. physical needs - a place to live people / friends – join a group, organizations, and be socially involved with others.

Relationships – is called attachment: Family/friends – people you love

= relationships take on many different forms and identities.

= romance is a strong physical attraction & emotional feelings.

= belonging is a basic need, it starts as far back as kindergarten, in the teen years they look at romance and the physical attractions, they may be able to deal with their emotional feelings because someone has hurt them.

In the core of understanding *interpersonal intelligence* includes the "capacities to discern and respond appropriately to a situation, temptations, and personal desires". In the *interpersonal intelligence* the key is the acknowledgement of a problem; being able to "access to one's own **feelings** and the ability to discriminate between bad feelings from good feelings in a way that does not cause someone else to be hurt or cause them to misbehave.

That transformational act of aggressive behavior could be transmitted into an innocent act, an implausible mistaken repressive passive aggression it captures the whole the bad behavior. People who habitually over react with emotional-out-bursts usually don't change their bad behavior, what needs to be done in that case. The subconscious mental avoidance is a larger pattern in their behavior, a pattern of tuning out their emotional upsets as an inability to control their true emotions; it is a cousin of alexithymics behavior. Perhaps their current thinking is bound up in the way they think of themselves as being proficient in regulating their emotions, when in reality they are not. They become adept at not being aware of their negative feelings. Rather than calling them oppressor behaviors which are a more appropriate term for self-unawareness.

What triggers an **emotional upset** with a harsh tone and incompetent behaviors need to be modified their different responses are noted as aggression and also show up passive aggression in many cases they want to get even and in extreme cases leads to abuse.

These thoughts trip the ***neural alarm system*** leaving no room for **emotional alarms**. This generally leaves the person with alternative distress signals and follows a pattern that could border on a pessimistic a false view of their own thought process.

To some degree genetics plays a role in a person's thinking and behavior patterns they may result in fear phobias and may very well come from biological **genetic tendencies**, I am not necessarily limiting genetics to specific **traits** because their environment and how a person is raised has a lot more to do with a person behavior the leading indicators to these behaviors can be changed by cognitive behaviors reinforcement.

The range of **emotional temperament**, which adds a different concept in dealing with your personality, which is relevant to a person's background and your basic disposition, is tempered by your **feelings**. (The balances of Right/Wrong) could be governed by a person's temperament which can be best defined in the terms of **mood** that most typifies a person's **emotional make-up**. The big question is can a person change their **biological** and **emotional demeanor**, of course by relearning, reeducating, and reinforcement and changing their behavior patterns; does that change the biological make of a person, no?

Does our chemistry change? Yes, does our emotional make-up change of (course not) or probably no! That would mean a complete makeover, but the amount of adrenaline released in the body does change the chemistry in an emotional situation. Can we change our personality? (Maybe/Yes & maybe/No) or more than like probably No! Why not Yes? Only if we manage our intelligence and put learned lessons into practice.

Beyond *temperament,* the readiness to evoke a given **emotion** that makes people melancholy, timid, or cheery. Beyond the **emotional dispositions** are the outright *disorders* of **emotion** such as depression or unremitting anxiety, in these cases someone feels ***trapped in a toxic state of mind***.

Psychological changes develop as children mature, yet by the mid-late teens temperamental preferences stay more or less fixed. The theory becomes useful on a practical basis because as temperamental preference becomes fixed, we can then make reliable assessments of a person's personality, learned habits, and communication skills, to name a few areas.

When you understand, the basics covered in this section; "On Temperament and Personality Typing" it will help if you understand your own type.

* Attempts to see things as they are in reality focuses on the "here-and-now."
* Compelled to pay attention to your surroundings.
* Focus on what is actually happening to you.
* Lean toward reality, and you may be able to minimize the importance of intangible   feelings, or the spiritual side of things.

Feeling
* Attempts to see things and look at the possibilities.
* Take action use your ability to focus on all situations.
* Focus on your dreams, in vision what could happen, improve the possibilities.
* Lean toward inspiration and seeing your dreams come true minimize the importance of measuring the results in light of what is happening.

Thinking
* Attempts to see things by using logic or principles.
* Compelled to look for the truth as you perceive it.
* Focus on understanding the facts or principles needed in helping a situation.
* Tend to organize, sum up, or categorize the "data" as you perceive it.
* Lean toward the measurable or objective solutions minimize bad behaviors and feelings.

Extraverts
* Attempt to understand people and things and act wisely.
* Analyze and organize your thinking try to instigate your feelings with others.
* Focus on enjoying things.
* Attempt to act according to your internal perceptions or judgments.

* Analyze or organize your thinking try to make sense from their standpoint.

* Focus on the situation as it relates to your past experiences and knowledge of one's self.

It takes emotional feelings and energy when it comes to changing your viewpoint, the introvert person will become drained if they have encounters that are too hard to deal with or there is too much controversy. A person maybe described as an introvert, the example of a monk they are taught they should not to talk, but meditate, pray, or they may be mistaken for an extraverted person because of their title. Of course, people vary in their need to change their thought process. This concept within a performance is called "the power rating of the mind," or a particular preference to one's self or job.

The two ways are not mutually exclusive they may feel they have no choice, but to turn outward at times and have concerns for themselves with the everyday tasks of living, while others look inward to ponder and dream. Such excursions can even be stimulating and satisfying, but neither type can be in both worlds at once, and each will usually show a strong preference for one over the other. In those types, they lose their vitality and the significance for life, the center of their world and may seem relatively foreign, uninteresting, and unimportant.

Does intuition always shut off observation of life? I think not. People can multi-task in their perceptive abilities. Of course, there's a point when a person is able to perceive things as they are, whether they can sense intuitive-perceiving, or a combination or both. There is a time to make a decision or take action.

Everyone has thoughts and feelings, but some pay more attention to their thoughts rather than to their feelings while others pay more attention to their feelings than to their thoughts. Those who pay attention to their thoughts are said to govern themselves with their head, their concepts and precepts converts their feelings into action. In contrast, those who pay more attention to their feelings are said to follow their heart, which means they are based on emotions or desires. If we make a distinction between the pragmatic term some people are more "tough-minded" and others more "tender-hearted" each type has a distinction between those who can be called "tough-minded" and those who can be called "friendly."

There is some criticism exchanged between these types the tough-minded are often accused of being "inhuman," "heartless," "strong-minded," "remote," "having ice in their veins," and of living "without human kindness." In the same way, the friendly is chided for being "too soft-hearted," "too emotional," "bleeding-hearts," "fuzzy-thinkers," and for "wearing their heart on their sleeve."

Such people can be vehement in marriage and other family relationships, when two people of different orientation conflict over an important decision. A wife for example, might want her husband to open up emotionally and "let his feelings show," while he might wish for her "to be logical for once." A father might want his son to be stronger or "use his head" for a change, while the son might wish his father could "lighten up" and be more understanding of what he really is and what he can do.

Another polarizing stereotype is known as the friendly type who have deeper emotions than the tough-minded one type is seen as sensitive and warmhearted, and the other is seen as insensitive and cold-hearted. However, the truth is that both react emotionally with similar frequency and intensity, the difference being a matter of their emotional display in a situation. The friendly tend to make their emotions known and wishes are quite visible, while others see themselves as capable of deep feelings. To be sure, when they show their feelings others cannot help being affected, their own emotions even aroused by their display of emotions. The tough-minded in contrast are embarrassed by an exhibition of intense feeling, and will hide their feelings rather than be seen as losing self-control. Because of this, they are often described as "cold" and "indifferent," when in fact they are feeling something quite strongly, but they don't display it as emotion they work hard to contain themselves.

When we get past these stereotypes, there are two observations usually found they can complement each other quite well, but if you have two people with the same serotype whether in business or in marriage, with the tough-minded partner providing a source of clarity and toughness, and the friendly partners provide a source of compassion and personal consideration.

I find it helpful to think of these two as one who has a preference solely based on decision-making it has little to do with whether a person has feelings of course they do while thinkers have feelings. While it is true that emotions are generally more emotional than thinkers, I think this is based on one's observations on the facts rather than on their outward emotions the generalization seems to hold true in either case.

The tough-minded take on a job and finishes it before they play or rest, they tend to look upon deadlines as mere challenges, others are like people who turn off or ignore the alarm to catch an extra forty winks, almost as if the deadline were used more as a signal to start than to complete a project. Some are more insistent on working to the purpose of taking on a task they are directly instrumental in finishing the task, they may balk at doing it, but they get it done, or others wonder why they need to do it or leave it to someone else.

This difference extends to the physical environment as well they like their desk at work to be tidy, and their house picked up dishes done, bed made, car washed, and so on. Not that they always manage all of these chores, but they are unhappy when their personal space is a mess, and straightening things up is often near the top of their list in contrast they have a much greater tolerance for disorder in their physical environment. They seem absorbed in whatever they are doing or thinking at the moment, and are somewhat oblivious to the details. They are more occupied by their personal space, office, house, garage, car are often cluttered with a variety of objects they have not picked up, used, and then dropped when they have finished with them.

These two styles are brought out in Oscar and Felix "The Odd Couple" each get on the other's nerves. Schedulers can become impatient with probers for what seems to them passiveness and playfulness, and can be described as "indecisive" and "dragging their feet," "aimless" and "lazy," as "uncooperative," and "laid back." On the other hand, people can become impatient with schedules and pursue other things, and described as being "in too big a hurry" and "rude," "personal driven" or "wearing blinders," as "uptight," "stressed-out." Others are described as "slave-drivers," as "arbitrary," "rigid and inflexible," and even as "neat-freaks."

* The ultimate **emotional triumph** is over fear itself.

* There is a wide range of possibilities even in the genetic constraints in achievers

* When genetics are observed, the gene patterns are determine by some behaviors,

1. Nor does your environment mean a person will turn out good or bad,

2. Nor does a person's behaviors make them an over or under achiever,

3. Nor does the learning process teach a person how to learn any more than their genetics will determine their temperament.

4. The passion of expressions are **emotional capacities** and are very influential if given the right guidance

5. The relearning is vital to your changing and improving of your temperament and behavior.

* It is amazing how much can be accomplished when a person **matures**.
* Learning good behaviors is another way of dealing with the mental well-being of a person.
* Normal and abnormal define good and poor mental health & well-being.
   1. abnormal self-defeating behaviors, habits, treats, and patterns
   2. abnormal level of competency
   3. abnormal relationships is a bad indicator
   4. abnormal rejection, insecurities, and introvertedness.
* Symptoms Characteristics of good Mental Health.
   1. normal people with good mental health have balanced their behaviors
   2. normalcy is to be able to adjust without going over the edge of reality
   3. normalcy is meting needs and reaching goals
   4. normalcy is a liking in ones-self and having some independency and self-assurance.
   Now let's look at the warning signs of bad mental health and well-being.
* Anxiety
   1. Anxiety brings about a feeling of uneasiness.
   2. Anxiety brings about fear.
   3. Anxiety brings about a sense of insecurity.

4. Anxiety brings about apprehension that something bad is going to happen.
5. Anxiety brings about unpleasant thoughts and escapism.
6. Anxiety may lead to using drugs and alcoholism.

* Defense mechanisms
    1. defensive mechanisms are used in hiding anxiety
    2. defensive mechanisms are used to protect one's self
    3. defensive mechanisms are used to defend one's position and feelings
    4. defensive mechanisms are used to prevent hurts and miss-giving's about one's self.

* Repressive mechanisms
    1. refusing to think of something bad
    2. refusing to deal with something that upsets you.

* Denial mechanisms
    1. conscious refusal to take a treat seriously
    2. consciously forgetting something bad
    3. consciously denying guilt for wrong doing.

    * Projection mechanisms
    1. accusing someone else for your bad attitude and bad feelings
    2. projecting your anger on someone else for your miss-giving's
    3. transfer of guilt to someone else.

* Displacement mechanisms
    1. emotional rejection and shifting the real anger to someone else or thing
    2. this is usually a normal reaction to hurt and anger
    3. miner announces maybe ignored or forgotten in a short time.

* Dysfunctional Relationships
    1. one of the biggest is low self-worth and confidence.
    2. they are usually filled with conflicts
    3. they are not self full-filling
    4. for the most part, they are not functional
    5. poor communicators and poor communication
    6. there is a like trust, respect, and confidence in each other
    7. usually a withdrawal and shutting others out when this process takes place

8. usually two people living their separate lives
9. usually the <I> syndrome
10. demands on the emotional and physical aspects of a person
11. expecting someone else to make you happy
12. last, expecting love for love when it is not there.

* Phobias
   1. irrational fear of something you cannot see
   2. irrational sense of close places
   3. irrational apprehension like hearing something that is not there
   4. irrational emotional reactions to normal situations or problems
   5. irrational can be led by health issues
   6. irrational mental anxiety to hurt and pain.

Now we are going change our focus to another aspect of the personal exchange of inward feelings to the outward expressions of one's self-esteem.

The challenge comes in methods of changing human behaviors. There will be the challenges to do right, and accomplish things there is also a conflict of what to do. The way to do this is by being able to relate to *your* personal life experiences, relationships.

There have been advances in mental-health, and personal-well-being, there have been greater advances in self-help books: over $750 billion a year is spent on self-help books. This has revolutionized the way to deal with the mental and the physical well-being. There is a need for such information in today's society, because there is more stress, anxiety, depression, and phobias.

I had to learn the hard way; I don't want *you* to do that. When I made a mistake, did I ever hear about what I had done wrong? It seemed like I always made the wrong decision in who I married! I have learned to live with my past, and not judge myself in the way others see me. But, I began to understand that I'm only human. I learned why I made the mistakes in those relationships, and my quest is not to make the same one over again.

SELF-ESTEEM
IS AN
EVALUATION OF
YOUR SELF

Chapter 5

BUILDING SELF-ESTEEM

Introduction to Self-Esteem Assessment II

WHY DO PEOPLE FAIL?

No person plans to fail they fail because they fail to plan!

People do fail for any number of reasons, but does it correlate with their self-esteem or what are some of the reasons a person fails. They may get tired of facing the same old situations and problems, and what is happening to them, it's what a person does or doesn't do that causes a failure.

You are probably thinking does self-esteem have anything to do with a person who knows they are losing the battle. When they feel "what's the use", or "I am going to live with my situation and they believe that is the only solution." Again, that reminds me of when I was a child, when I got tired of playing a game I would find something else to do, and people play games with their life and life is not a game.

Some will say to you quote "everything is going to be alright if you do the best you can", and your problems will be solved or get better. "Why worry about it, how many times have I heard this from a person?" You can try all sorts of things to solve the problems, but what if they have not worked before. This is the most dangerous time in a person's life there are two times when a person is most likely to fail "when things are going good and when a person is down and feels bad." This is when most people are saying my life is fine or I'm dealing with my problems don't worry about me things will work out.

They are kind of like a fighter saying "I'm OK" and he is about to be knock out. As I look back on my life, it was a mess for a long time and it has been a fight dealing with my health problems.

I felt like a failure and maybe I was, I was not satisfied with me as a person; I felt I was in a rout. Now let's take a look and see what a person can do, let's take it a step farther and see what is keeping you from reaching your goals. In this chapter I will remind you your goal is to find out *why they failed*? If a person doesn't have knowledge of why something went wrong, I believe a person needs a good foundation for making better decisions, it doesn't make any difference how you are doing things and why things may get worse. If you are making the same mistakes in your decisions look for a better way.

Self-Improvement and Self-Esteem

Again, everything in your life starts with you applying self-improvement techniques what does that mean when it comes to assessments that lead to improving your life? Your thinking is the foundation in every decision you make, self-esteem either builds character or destroys confidence, the actions you take are what influences what you do or become. If your life is not the way you want it to be; then who can change it, only you can change it don't let others dominate your thinking or put you on the defense. Yes you can get help from other people, but only if you accept the right kind of techniques.

It is often difficult for a person to accept the fact that they are responsible for the conditions in their life, you will find that is not always true as we have dealt with self-image, but before we deal with self-worth you have built your self-esteem, but for now I will expand on what self-esteem means to a person.

Full Definition of *ESTEEM* {6}
transitive verb
archaic : APPRAISE
  a : to view as : CONSIDER <*esteem* it a privilege>
  b : THINK, BELIEVE
  : to set a high value on : regard highly and prize accordingly <an *esteemed* guest>

Examples of *ESTEEM*
1. <I had *esteemed* the whole affair to be a colossal waste of time.>
2. <although the works of the Impressionist painters are *esteemed* today, they met with scorn when they were introduced>

Origin of *ESTEEM*
Middle English *estemen* to estimate, from Anglo-French *estimer,* from Latin *aestimare*
First Known Use: 15th century

Related to *ESTEEM*
Related Words
BELIEVE, DEEM, FEEL, SENSE, THINK; CONCEIVE, FANCY, IMAGINE
  Learner's definition of SELF–ESTEEM
  : a feeling of having respect for yourself and your abilities
  ow/high *self-esteem*
  programs to raise/build *self-esteem* among children

What is a Narcissistic Personality?

There is a lot of good formation on self-esteem, first let's look and define what narcissism means and what is a narcissistic personality? A narcissist is not just one who likes themselves, but someone who is absorbed in their own actives, seeks attention, or values their dreams and goals above others. They can be charming, charismatic and they tend to play mind games that serve their purpose.

Sarcasms comes in the form of making light of something or somebody else is not "pretty in part 97 any langue"; they are not just someone who wants power, but needs others to treat them as if they are beautiful or brilliant. If this were the case, a lot of people would have these traits and would be labeled as narcissistic, and they are sadly mistaken if a person feels that way about themselves.

According to several top psychological theorists of the 20th century, who have made a distinction between a healthy attitudes, versus an unhealthy power over others, for example? The desire for power over others makes them feel good, unless it is a "neurotic power over others." It is not a healthy core for individuals to be driven by the desire for success that brings out the best and in some it brings about the worst that means their motivates were selfish in nature and want to be successful at any cost.

Nothing is more natural than to want to influence others in a good way, to move a person to want to cooperate, value and be loving and caring toward someone else. We often forget this, especially when a couple is dealing with their relationships, when we throw around the fact we are "controlling" someone else.

If you're human, regardless of your gender, economic status or age, from the moment you were born, a child cries out to see who cares and understands what they want. The parent wants to see their child happy and wipe away the tears. The purpose in life is to influence others to move them by "assisting others" rather than have the attitude to get what you want in some form or another throughout your life is being selfish.

(Conceivably, the most powerful drive has to do with our thoughts and feelings, in some cases it is not at all about your love for others, but how you feel toward others and how you treat them that counts. In some cases it is increasingly more important how mature a person is and sad to say some put their feeling first or wanting to be wiser than someone else. Your love for someone should matter, and brings meaning to your life in around about way.)

In short, the word narcissist is too casually used and in many cases it is misplaced. It is a healthy love for others that builds a person and values one's self and builds self-esteem; and it is healthy to have wants, to want others to want you to be happy, to feel your own sense of value, to want attention or to passionately seek to realize your dreams, but not at the expense of others.

On the other hand, the extreme expression of these traits in negative terms may mean a person has a personality disorder. However, this speaks to a subconscious inner self a wounded ego, or a super-fragile self-esteem is lowered. The opposite in a person who has compulsion to be powerful, attention to details, which can be thought of as the side effects of *three key identifying (and interlocking) traits*, as follows: a lack of empathy for others, connected to a compulsive need to prove their own superior status (which would be impossible if they fail to empathize with others, right?). If this is coupled with taking pleasure in hurting or treating those who they consider inferior or weak. To the point of scorn or disdain such as (a competition of sorts, to win at all costs with displays of superiority, making others feel like losers, etc.).

Without the presence of the three *interlocking* traits or of lack of empathy, compulsive need to prove superiority and seeking pleasure in (hurting) treating others with scorn or disdain.

Whereas, every healthy person has an inner emotional-drive to feel important and gain the admiration from others, the narcissist's has a compulsive need for attention and admiration based on an unrealistic expectations of self so they can feel superior and get others to buy into this illusion of their self-esteem. It is this belief that keeps them dependent on others to prop them up, bolster their ego, and makes them vulnerable to any criticism, and keeps their "self-esteem" fragile at the same time they are dependent others to bust their ego whether they like it or not.

It makes sense that they perceive any request for change as a threat or "criticism" their mission is to find others who recognize their top-dog status. And, according to their belief system, a person of lowly status needs to be reminded they need others to bust their self-esteem.

Speaking of unhealthy power, a person who seeks to control another person by getting them to surrender their focus on their own wants, values and dreams to instead solely promote the their happiness. They may not feel ashamed or guilt within themselves or for others; because they can't give in without feeling venerable they don't necessarily want to hurt others feelings, but it does. However, if they feel wronged and they become critical, but in reality they really want approval from others they have the "need" to be happy (regardless of what others "want" it may be harmful to them and their relationships, or other's it may be making a large purchase when in their in debt, etc. to make them feel good.) This is what psychologist Alfred Adler referred to "neurotic power" or using punitive tactics to subvert another's will.

These people have a lack empathy for others, they relish and admire their own ability to get out of trouble and dismiss others feelings about themselves; and they view this as a strength, proof of their superior over others. Thus they are experts at getting out of making any changes that would truly make another person feel happy, they view others as a failure, they think of others as "losers" and they don't "give in" to others.

The similarities between a narcissistic personality and social disorder comes in the form of a social personality disorder.

These social disorders show up in sex addicts and other addicts have the same symptoms, but they should not have an air-of-superiority over others. They are masked by a deep-seated loathing of others, lack of connection to genuine self-esteem, which would require them to see others as they see themselves. Many of their wounds are self-inflicted by their own unrealistic expectations of one's self, the need to look down on others in order to feel worthwhile. They are mostly interested in getting their ego satisfied (sensory) needs met, and thus can only relate to their superficial feelings for others and it show up their relationships. Others are not "important" only to the extent that they can make them look and feel good, watch out if this fits your personality. They are experts at scrutinizing others, to cut them down to size with their judgmental attitude, strong opinions, in order to enforce their will and agenda.

Narcissistic Personal Disorders, Symptoms of Disorders
Pages 1 – 4   [7]

"Narcissism is a term used to describe a focus on the self and self-admiration that is taken to an extreme. The word "narcissism" comes from a Greek myth in which a handsome young man named Narcissus sees his reflection in a pool of water and falls in love with time image.

Narcissistic personality disorder is one of a group of conditions called "Cluster B" or "dramatic" personality disorders. People with these disorders have intense, unstable emotions and a distorted self-image. Narcissistic personality disorder is further characterized by an abnormal love of self, an exaggerated sense of superiority and importance, and a preoccupation with success and power. However, these attitudes and behaviors do not reflect true self-confidence. Instead, the attitudes conceal a deep sense of insecurity and a fragile self-esteem. People with narcissistic personality disorders also often have a complete lack of empathy for others.

What Are the Symptoms of Narcissistic Personality Disorder?

- Are self-centered and boastful
- Seek constant attention and admiration
- Consider themselves better than others
- Exaggerate their talents and achievements
- Believe that they are entitled to special treatment
- Are easily hurt but may not show it

Preoccupation with fantasies that focus on unlimited success, power, intelligence, beauty, or love

- Belief that he or she is "special" and unique, and can only be understood by other special people
- Expectation that others will automatically go along with what he or she wants
- Inability to recognize or identify with the feelings, needs, and viewpoints of others
- Envy of others or a belief that others are envious of him or her
- Hypersensitivity to insults (real or imagined), criticism, or defeat, possibly reacting with rage, shame and humiliation
- Arrogant behavior and/or attitude

What Causes Narcissistic Personality Disorder?

The exact cause of narcissistic personality disorder is not known. However, many **mental health** professionals believe it results from a combination of factors that may include biological vulnerabilities, social interactions with early caregivers, and psychological factors that involve temperament and the ability to manage stresses. Some researchers believe that a narcissistic personality disorder may be more likely to develop when children experience **parenting** styles that are excessively pampering the child, or when parents have a need for their children to be talented or special in order to maintain their own self-esteem. On the other end of the spectrum, narcissistic personality disorder might develop as the result of neglect or abuse and trauma inflicted by parents or other authority figures during childhood. The disorder usually is evident by adolescence or early adulthood when personality traits have become consolidated."

http://www.medicinenet.com/narcissistic_personality_disorder/I.htm
8/15/2014

Let me give you another good example of what I'm talking about, I had an assonate in Florida who was a theorist we would meet once a month and discuss our case load. One of our clients seemed to have some narcissistic tendencies and were talking about how to deal with this person. My assonate said he was a narcissistic person at one time and didn't know it, I thought sense I was a theorist I knew everything when I would talk with my wife about things she didn't like it she felt things were going wrong in our marriage. I didn't realize my attitude was causing problems her problems in our marriage and my wife wanted a divorce, I couldn't believe my wife felt that way, after all I knew all the classic signs of divorce in others.

She felt he was looking down on her and he was a know it all kind of person especially with her she was supposed to look up to him because he was a man, a therapist, and she felt he did this with everybody he knew and dealt with. There are two kind of narcissistic people in most cases these people are very controlling which we have just profiled. In this case he did not allow her to have any ideas or thoughts on any problems because she didn't have a degree, you get the idea. He said I wanted to know how she felt and how she feels matters to me, he said now we have a great marriage I listen real close when she has something to say because I love her. Now I listen to what my clients have to say because it is important them, I may not agree with them, I want them to know I care. The most important things as a person or psychologist is to listen and give the other person a chance to express their feelings.

The Thought process, Mental Health, & Well-being

I am dealing with self-esteem in relation to mental stability and it is not an exact science, but that is what we're trying to deal with in this part of our study.

When I talk about self-esteem for the most part I'm talking about people with ego problems, and not mental disorders. This is where people usually need help in today's society people don't seem to able to control their personal wants, needs, and drives, their actions cause avoidance behavior as I call them (withdrawing from someone who has hurt them in the past).

The development of the connections in the brain that have to do with **self-analysis** and **the improvement comes from being able to adjust your behavior**. It starts with the first manifestations known as a phenomenon, which is a routine that has been established by a person's previous ecological framing of behaviors or traits. There are close family genetic ties to a situation in relation as to how strong these ties become a part of the behavior. Now a person's esteem depends on how far back we can trace their ego. This is one of the reasons a person actions and the way they do things is known as framing their ego from their parents and grandparents. Pasted behaviors and ego even go as far back as three generations, for instance if one or both parents has ego problems the child grows up with ego issues, they may not know why they are dealing with an ego in their life.

The next thing which is just as strong, addictions are also passed from generation to generation the scientific explanation is passed on through the blood; the brain also processes every action relating to how it is perceived. The biology characteristics can go back generations even if the present parents don't do drugs, some alcohol studies for some unknown reasons don't know why it is so strong in the second and third generation. I know of parents who were very good Christian parents and yet two of their children were on drug and the third did not go into addictions, from a logical deduction we would think all three would have gone into drugs there is a good explanation on their grandmothers side she did not use drugs and alcohol. I will not go any farther on the subject of addictions and alcohol, but I do have an in-depth study on addictions in my book on "Preparing for New Beginnings".

These factors call attention to the surface of the **brain, right underneath cortex**, there exits an area containing several nuclei of gray matter (neurons), which determine a sense it is ok, it forms an entire structure later named the "**limbic system**".

In our studies, **this is known as the rational brain** it is a highly complex network of neural cells capable of producing language, thus enabling a person to exercise skillful intellectual tasks such as reading, writing, and performing mathematical calculations. The neopallium is the great generator of ideas, and/or "the mother of inventions and the father of objective thought".

This is because there is disruptiveness in the selective neurons while some actions are oblivious like ego responds to what is happening in the brain and it can't deal with something it does not already know; while others are more favorable and are allowed to occur because it is a present experience.

"I believe that within certain limits the affective participation of certain areas the brain reinforces the cognitive behavior components to respond giving more flavor to the day-to-day experiences and facilitating and adapting to other behaviors causing a person to compensate."

Nevertheless, when things go above these limits of human understanding the mind and emotions hamper reasoning and when low levels happens these behaviors become infective or passive, unless they are at a normal level, in this case it improves the quality of life.

Life is about the journey and trying to understand one's self and the traits you pick-up can become habits they are a part of the journey, but learning the meaning of *how* and the *why's* in relation to the challenges in any given situation. Certainly, the degree of emotions and feelings largely has to do with a person's reaction to actions taking place. What else transpires during any given situation can boil down in terms of the "cause and effect" of course this is very important, probably the most over looked factor in relationships are the problems involved in the relationship and certainly the outcome of any situation is important too.

A person's journey begins in part by new discoveries about one's self and the architecture relating to a person's ego and feelings.

Here are some explanations as to some of the most baffling moments in live, when your feelings are overwhelmed and your rationality is set aside for a brief span in time. Understanding the interplay of the brain structures may in some cases give us some insight as to how fare a person is involved in their own well-being, there is a lot to be said about passion and wanting to get things done, but when the ego takes place in a **situation** it works in two ways. Much can be learned from **a person's ego** it can undermine their best intentions and can subdue their **well to want to do something** and at the time revealing destructive tendencies and those **emotional drives** that can be good in a situation, fear can keep you from doing something wrong. I like this example of fear it keeps a person from running out in front of a Mac Truck.

Your **Ego** can cause you to rise or fall in a given situation. I do believe the brain is governed by how bad a person wants to do something, but rather the knowledge of one's self has grown especially in the last fifty years. I have given you some insight into the brains functions, here is some insight and knowledge of it's working, so that you can understand how the mind works with a person's mindset.

HOW THE BRAIN WORKS FUNCTIONS INTER ACTS WITH THE HEART

ASSESSMENTS I, II, III, IV

Chapter 6

EMOTIONS & FEELINGS

Does the brain control your Self-Esteem?

The brain has a memory, but it is one of the ways to help a person, the way to do this is by keeping a record / journaling the events in your daily life, we keep track of birth days and other memorial events in a person's life by using the same logic writing about those personal feelings by showing how they interact a situation.

The Break Down of the Brain:
1. Emotions and Feelings:
2. Moods, Mood-swings, and Depression:
3. Temperament and Personality:
4. Character and Morals:

   Our journey began in "Part One Self-Image" of this book; there are new discoveries about the **brain's architecture,** but the esteem relate to more than that **determination** relating to **self-worth**. Now what is ticking, or clicking on the inside that relates to self-esteem?

More often, there is a symbolic threat to self-esteem or a person's dignity:
1. Being threatened unjustly or rudely,
2. Being insulted or demeaned,
3. Being frustrated in pursuing a goal.

   These perceptions act as a triggering device the **limbic surge** that has a dual effect in the brain now we are taking about esteem issues. Part of that surge is a release of *catecholamine's*, which generate a quick, episodic rush of energy for few moments to fight or flight depending on how the **emotional brain** sizes up the oppositions.

Meanwhile, another **amygdala-drive** ripped through the **adrenal-neocortical branches of the nervous system**, creates a general a background of action or readiness, which lasts longer than the *catecholamine energy surge*. This is generalized by **shot of adrenalin** and **cortical excitement** to get things done and can last for few hours and even days, keeping the emotional brain in readiness and becoming a foundation on which subsequent reactions can build esteem, which is reflected in excitement or a climax in a situation. In general, the higher *catecholamine energy surge*, a person is much more prone to the excitement if they have not already experienced or provoked it into energy.

Energy of any sort creates adrenalin **neocortical arousal**, lowering the threshold for what provoked the energy.

Empathy for others helps build **self-awareness** for others; the more open we are with our emotions, the more skills we should have in being able to get along with others.

For instance, the transition to middle school and junior high marks a child's devolvement, and is in itself a formidable **emotional challenge** there are abnormal changes during this time. Putting all other problems aside, as they enter high school virtually all have a dip in **self-confidence** and a jump in **self-consciousness**; their self-esteem is affected the notions of them-selves are rocky and in emotional turmoil taking place. One of the greatest blows is in "**social self-esteem**, a teenager or a person's confidence may be shaken as they try to make new tasks and keep old friends. It is at this juncture a young person may need some help in their ability to build on their self-esteem and usually their confidence builds self-esteem. A person needs to find a way to navigate and deal with social changes, and to nurture in their **self-confidence** at the same time.

There is something different about dealing with personal adjustments, they may become more **emotional** as they are dealing with new peer pressures, there are more academic demands, and the temptations to smoke and use drugs because of peer pressures. If they have not mastered their **emotional abilities**, or at least for the short term, this may correlate or cause some turmoil and pressures they have not faced before.

RESULTS:
* They are more sensitive to others' and their own feelings
* They may have problems understanding the consequences of their behavior
* They have increased inability to "size up" interpersonal situations and plan appropriate actions
* They have lower **self-esteem.**
* They are more social in their activities.
* They are more likely to seek other outlets for pleasure not realizing the consequences.
* They are less antisocial, **self-destructive**, and impulsive behaviors, even when followed up in school or adult life they need to improve learning skills.

There others who are better at **self-development**, social awareness, and social decisions-making in school and throughout their adult life.

Here are some other explanations as to some of the most baffling moments in our life when we **feel overwhelmed** and our rationality is set aside. Understanding the interplay of **ego** and how the **brain structures** give us some insights into how and why we act the way we do in a given situation. In some cases, our **ego** will give us some clues into amount of ego, and the amount of achievement involved, our passions, but for beyond that there can be joy in fulfillment in any **situation**. There is much that can be learned from our **ego** and maybe we can understand a person's determination our best intentions to the undermining why we do certain things. We can be subdued by our **ego** or **controlled** our ego, while revealing destructive tendencies, such as our **selfishness, self-will,** and **emotional impulses** in a situation, or when there is joy and happiness in the working **mind-set** and **making things happen.**

Yet, in order for these functions to occur in a good way, they must have passion, emotion, and desire to make it happen expecting a positive results. The deep limbic system adds to what happens, it could be either a positive and negative reaction.

The physical make-up of the Brain.

Definition of brain: *noun*   {7}
    1 a: the portion of the vertebrate central nervous systems enclosed in the skull and
continuous with the spinal cord through the foramen magnum that is composed of neurons and supporting and nutritive structures (as glia) and that integrates sensory information from inside and outside the body in controlling autonomic functions (as the heartbeat and respiration), in controlling and directing correlated motor responses, and in the process of learning – compare forebrain, hindbrain, and midbrain.

      2 a: (1) intellect, mind <has a clever brain>
              (2) intellectual endowment: intelligence – often used in   the plural
        b: (1) a very intelligent or intellectual person
              (2) the chief planner of an organization or enterprise – plural
      3 a: something that performs the function of a brain;
      especially

Definition of midbrain: *noun*   {8}
:   the middle of the three primary divisions of the developing vertebrate brain or the corresponding part of the adult brain between the forebrain and hindbrain that include the tectum, tegmentum, and substantia nigra – called also *mesencephalon*.

Definition of hindbrain: *noun*   {9}
    1:   the posterior of the three primary divisions of the developing vertebrate brain or the corresponding part of the adult brain that includes the cerebellum, the medulla oblongata, and in mammals the pons and that controls autonomic functions and equilibrium called
- *rhombecephalon*.

    2:   the posterior of the brain of an invertebrate.

Definition of forebrain: *noun*   {10}
    :   the posterior of the three primary divisions of the developing vertebrate brain or the *corresponding* part of the adult brain that includes especially the cerebral hemispheres, the thalamus, and the

hypothalamus/*hyopocampus* and that especially in higher vertebrates main control center for sensory and associative information processing, visual function, and voluntary motor functions called the *prosencephalon*.

Definition of left-brain: *noun*   {11}
:   the left cerebral hemisphere of the human brain especially when viewed in terms of its predominant thought process (as in analytical and logical thinking) left-brained *adjective*

Definition of Right-brain: *noun*   {12}
:   the right cerebral hemisphere of the human brain especially when viewed in terms of its predominate thought process (as creative and intuitive thinking) Right-brained *adjective*

Brain Functions in relation to the Limbic System as it (Controls Mood, Ego, Temperament / Attitude)

Function
1) The Ego sets the tone of the mind
2) Filters external events through internal stats (emotional coloring)
3) Tags events as internally important
4) Stores high charged emotions
5) Modulates motivation
6) Controls appetite and sleep cycles
7) Promotes bonding

Problems
1) Moodiness, irritability, clinical depression
2) Increased negative thinking
3) Perceive events in a negative way
4) Decreased motivation
5) Food, negative motions
6) Appetite and sleep problems
7) Decreased or increased sexual responsiveness

The deep limbic system lies near the center of the brain it is power-packed with functions all of which are critical for human ego system.

There are literally thousands of functions that happens without a person being aware of them happening as it has to do with self-esteem. We are discussing all parts of the brain as it works on how you react and how it affects you as a person. All of these functions in the brain suggest the need for proper balance of our **ego** and **feeling** about ourselves when something goes wrong it affects our ego it could recruit the rest of the brain to action as a person reacts, but now is the big question, in some cases a person has an emergency and that causes irrational reaction then what?

When the ego interrupts a reaction and triggers a response during those crucial moments before the **thinking brain** has a chance to override the emotion at the time or has had a chance evaluate and grasp fully what is happening. Let alone decide what to do, a person could be strictly working on the raw courage in most cases reacting to a bad situation or circumstance.

This part of the brain is involved in setting a person's **emotional tone** and **personal esteem**. When the **deep limbic system** is active, there is generally a hopeful state of mind, having a positive reaction or when the opposite takes place, it shows up low self-esteem. Yet, we have noticed again and again when this area is overactive it correlates with **depression** and **negativity**. It seems when the **deep limbic is inflamed**, painful **emotional shading** results. Due to this **emotional shading,** the **deep limbic system** provides the filter through which you interpret the events of the day. It tag's or colors the events in the emotional state of mind When you are sad (with an **over action the deep limbic system**) it is likely to be interpreted by the neutral events through a negative lens.

For example, if you have a neutral or positive conversation with someone whose deep limbic structure is over reacting in creating "a negative mind-set" (he or she) is likely to interpret the conversation in negative ways.

When this part of the brain is "cool" or it functions are interacting, a neutral passive interpretation of the events are more likely to occur. **Emotional tagging** of events is given to certain events in our lives it drives us to action or causes avoidance of a situation (withdrawing from someone who has hurt you in the past).

Here is a good example; PMS is another classic example of **emotional shading** of the **deep limbic system** when it becomes inflamed or overly active there is a drop in the hormones. Most women color these cycles in a negative sense, then in a few days after her cycle starts, she is back to bring positive and loving again.

In what ways does the brain have control over Self-Esteem?"
THE TEMPORAL LOBE & LIMBIC SYSTEMS   Pages 1-9   [8]

John R. Hesselink, MD, FACR
"The limbic lobe is a complex set of three C-shaped structures containing both gray and white matter. It lies deep within the brain and includes portions of all the lobes of the cerebral hemispheres. A myriad of fiber tracts connect the limbic lobe with numerous deep nuclei and the olfactory apparatus to form the limbic system. Phylogenetically, the limbic system is one of the more primitive parts of the brain. It has a central role in memory, learning, emotion, neuroendocrine function, and autonomic activities. Clinical conditions involving the limbic system include epilepsy, congenital syndromes, dementias, and various psychiatric disorders.

ANATOMY
Limbic System
The outer arc of the limbic system (also called the limbic gyrus) includes the subcallosal area, the cingulate gyrus, the isthmus of the cingulate gyrus, and the parahippocampal gyrus, including the uncus and subiculum. The subcallosal area includes a cluster of small septal nuclei that lie immediately anterior to the paraterminal gyrus and anterior commissure. The septal nuclei receive input from multiple midbrain nuclei, the substantia nigra, the CA1 region of the cornu ammonis, the subiculum, amygdala, lateral hypothalamus, cingulate gyrus, and mamillary bodies. Efferent fibers project to the entire hippocampal formation, the habenula, hypothalamus, thalamus, amygdala, mamillary bodies and the cerebral cortex.
Cavazos JE, Wang CJ, Sitoh YY, et al: Anatomy and pathology of the septal region. Neuroimag Clin NorthAm 1997; 7:67-78.
The middle arc (also referred to as Broca's intralimbic gyrus) consists of the paraterminal gyrus, the indusium griseum, and the

hippocampus. The paraterminal gyrus is wedged between the septal nuclei and the anterior commissure. Posterior to the anterior commissure is the hypothalamus. The indusium griseum, extending from the paraterminal gyrus, consists of gray matter and white matter tracts named the medial and lateral longitudinal stria. The indusium griseum is closely applied to the superior surface of the corpus callosum. Posteriorly, it courses around the splenium and inferiorly merges with the tail of the hippocampus.

The mamillary bodies, fornix, alveus and fimbria form the inner arc. The alveus and fimbria are the major efferent fibers tracts of the hippocampus. Posteriorly, the fimbria form the crura of the fornix that continue upward deep to the splenium of the corpus callosum. As the two crura converge, a thin triangular sheet of fibers passes to the opposite side to form the commissure of the fornix. The crura merge as the body of the fornix, which continues forward along the inferior edge of the septum pellucidum and roof of the third ventricle. At the foramen of Monroe, the fornix divides into two columns which course inferiorly. Just superior to the anterior commissure, the columns divide into pre- and postcommissural tracts. The precommissural fibers connect to the septal nuclei and anterior hypothalamic nuclei. The postcommissural fibers continue inferiorly to end in the mamillary bodies.

Sitoh YY, Tien RD: The limbic system: An overview of the anatomy and its development. Neuroimag ClinNorth Am 1997; 7:1-10.

The hippocampus is a part of the middle arc of the limbic sys tem. It is located in the medial temporal lobe inferior to the choroidal fissure and temporal horn. In the sagittal plane the hippocampus is a club-shaped structure divided into three parts: head, body, and tail. The more anterior head is marked by digita tions and is also called the pes hippocampus. The body is more cylindrical in shape, and the tail tapers posteriorly.

The gray matter of the hippo campus is an extension of the subiculum of the parahippo- campal gyrus. In coronal plane the hippocampus and parahippocampal gyrus form an S-shaped configuration. The hippocampus itself consists of two interlocking C-shaped structures: the cornu ammonis and the dentate gyrus.

Histologically, the hippocampus is further divided into four sections: CA1 to CA4.

Mark LP, Daniels DL, Naidich TP, et al: The hippocampus. AJNR 1993; 14:709-712.

The amygdala is positioned directly anterior to the pes hippocampus and above the tip of the temporal horn. The alveus and fimbria, white matter tracts along the superior surface of the hippocampus, continue posteriorly as the fornix and serve as the major efferent pathways to the rest of the brain.

Hui F, Cavazos JE, Tien RD: Hippocampus: normal magnetic resonance imaging anatomy with volumetricstudies. Neuroimag Clin North Am 1997; 7:11-30.

ETIOLOGY of EPILESY

Birth Ischemia

Hirpocampal

Tumors

Vassular – Hraumatic

Others Symptoms

Infectio, Intract

Migrational Disorders

Tubrous scterosis &nCortical Dplasia

The hippocampus, fornix, and mamillary bodies have an integral role in memory and learning. Much of what we know about temporal lobe function comes from patients with temporal lobectomies for tumors or intractable seizures. Impaired verbal memory is associated with left anterior temporal lobectomies, whereas right temporal lobectomy may result in visual/spatial memory disturbances. The degree of impairment is directly related to the age of the patient. Young children have considerable plasticity, allowing for other areas of the brain to take over the function of the resected portion. The decrease in memory function after temporal lobectomy is directly related to the amount of medial temporal lobe resected and the level of memory function prior to surgery (the more you have, the more you stand to lose), and it is inversely related to the degree of hippocampal sclerosis of the resected lobe.

Gabriel EM, Haglund MM: Neuropsychiatric complications after temporal lobe limbic system surgery. Neuroimag Clin North Am 1997; 7:155-164.

(…)

With high resolution imaging, loss of the normal internal architecture of the hippocampus can be identified.

Bernal B, Altman N: Evidence-based medicine: neuroimaging of seizures. Neuroimaging Clinics N Am.13:211-24, 2003.

MR imaging is reported to be 80-90% sensitive for detecting hippocampal sclerosis.
Quantitative volume measurements from thin-section 3D MR sequences can increase the sensitivity.

Sheth RD: Epilepsy surgery. Presurgical evaluation. Neurol Clin 20:1195-1215, 2002.

Associated findings include atrophy of the parahippocampal gyrus, decreased volume of the adjacent white matter, and temporal horn dilatation. Since the fornix is the primary efferent pathway from the hippocampus, severe damage to the hippocampal neurons can result in atrophy of the ipsilateral fornix.

Baldwin GN, Tsuruda JS, Maravilla KR, et al: The fornix in patients with seizures caused by unilateralhippocampal sclerosis. AJNR 162:1185-89, 1994.

Gadolinium enhancement is not helpful for the diagnosis of hippocampal sclerosis.

(…)

The common signal characteristics of gliomas include high signal intensity on T2-weighted images and low signal on T1-weighted images. Gliomas infiltrate along white matter fiber tracts and have poorly defined margins. The higher grade gliomas, particularly glioblastomas, appear heterogeneous due to central necrosis with cellular debris, fluid, and hemorrhage. Peritumoral edema and mass effect are common. Most exhibit irregular ring-enhancement. The lower grade astrocytomas tend to be more homogeneous without central necrosis. Large cystic components may be present. The cysts have smooth walls, and the fluid is of uniform signal, to distinguish them from necrosis. Enhancement is variable, depending on the integrity of the blood-brain barrier.

Metastatic disease needs to be considered when multiple lesions are present. Occasionally, lym-phoma will present in the medial temporal lobe.

It is not uncommon to find an incidental arachnoid cyst in the choroidal fissure. They are generally small and of no clinical significance. Also, an epidermoid tumor in the adjacent basal cisterns may extend into the choroid fissure.

Vascular Lesions

Most cavernous angiomas are asymptomatic, but they may be a source of temporal lobe seizures. They invariably contain hemosiderin from chronic hemorrhage and are distinctly hypointense on T2-weighted MR images. Lesion margins are "fuzzy" due to the magnetic susceptibility effect of the hemosiderin. Calcification is often present. Mild enhancement can be obscured by the hemosiderin.

Horowitz M, Kondziolka D: Multiple familial cavernous malformations evaluated over three generations withMR. AJNR 16:1353-1355, 1995.

One-half of patients with arteriovenous malformations present with seizures. CT features of an AV malformation on plain scan include a high- absorption irregular mass with large feeding arteries and draining veins, focal areas of calcification and no surrounding edema or mass effect. The contrast scan shows serpiginous enhancement with prominent arteries and veins. Due to the rapidly flowing blood from these lesions, a flow void is observed on MR scan. As a result, the characteristic feeding arteries and draining veins can be imaged without any injection of contrast material.

Infection

Any CNS inflammatory condition can involve the temporal lobe. Herpes simplex is one organism that has an affinity for the medial temporal lobes. Herpes simplex is the commonest and gravest form of acute encephalitis with a 30-70% fatality rate and an equally high morbidity rate. It is almost always caused by Type 1 virus except in neonates where Type 2 predominates. Symptoms may reflect the propensity to involve the inferomedial frontal and temporal lobes - hallucinations, seizures, personality changes and aphasia. Early involvement of the limbic system and temporal lobes is characteristic of herpes simplex encephalitis. The cortical abnormalities are first noted as ill-defined areas of high signal on T2-weighted scans, usually beginning unilaterally but progressing to become bilateral. Edema, mass effect and gyral enhancement may also be present.

Tien RD, Felsberg GJ, Osumi AK. Herpesvirus infections of the CNS: MR findings. AJR 161:167, 1993.

(…)

Trauma

The anterior temporal lobe is susceptible to traumatic injury. Deceleration forces compress the cortex against the protruding edge of the sphenoid wing. Brain contusion results in encephalomalacia and gliosis that can lead to posttraumatic epilepsy. Intracranial mass effect can result in major shifting of brain structures that can damage the temporal lobe. With downward pressure, the uncus of the temporal lobe is displaced medially and inferiorly through the tentorial incisura. The combination of compression against the sharp edge of the tentorium and compromise of the blood supply to the medial temporal lobe can result in significant damage.

(...)

Developmental Lesions

Epilepsy is commonly associated with developmental anomalies, particularly disorders of neuronal migration and cortical organization. This long list of disorders includes lissencephaly, pachygyria, polymicrogyria, cortical dysplasia, schizencephaly, gray matter heterotopia, microcephaly, and megalencephaly. All are characterized by a disordered cortical architecture, abnormal deformed neurons, and apparent loss of inhibitory neurons.

Barkovich AJ. Morphologic characteristics of subcortical heterotopia: MR imaging study AJNR 21:290-95,2000.

Two neurocutaneous syndromes are associated with epilepsy in 80% of cases. The classic features of tuberous sclerosis include autosomal dominant inheritance and the clinical triad of seizures, adenoma sebaceum, and mental retardation. Multiple nodules or tubers are distributed throughout the cerebral cortex and subependymal regions. Histologically, the subpial regions of the involved cortex disclose gliosis and proliferating astrocytes that are large and bizarre with abundant processes. (…)

DISEASES RELATED TO THE LIMBIC SYSTEM

Developmental abnormalities

The limbic system is directly involved by congenital abnormalities of ventral induction, namely holoprosencephaly, and septo-optic dysplasia. Clinically, alobar holoprosencephaly displays microcephaly, hypotelorism, and cyclopia. The brain is grossly malformed with a monoventricle, fused thalami, and absent interhemispheric fissure, falx, septum pellucidum, and corpus callosum. All 3 arcs of the limbic system are affected, and the septal nuclei and hypothalamus are often hypoplastic. Semilobar and lobar holoprosencephaly have lesser degrees of abnormality.

epto-optic dysplasia is caused by failure of the optic vesicle and commissural plate. The septum pellucidum is absent and the optic nerves and chiasm are hypoplastic. Hypoplasia of the hypothalamus, pituitary gland, and septal nuclei are other features.

Limbic encephalitis

Limbic encephalitis is a paraneoplastic syndrome that has been reported with carcinoma of the lung, breast, and some other primaries. The mechanism of disease is not known but it manifests as an encephalitis that primarily involves the hippocampus, amygdala, cingulate gyrus, insula, and orbital-frontal cortex. Afflicted patients develop subacute onset of memory loss, dementia, involuntary movements, and ataxia.

Shaw CM, Alvord EC: Neuropathology of the limbic system. Neuroimag Clin North Am 1997; 7:101-142.

ALZEIMER'S

Severe momery Defect
Path Senile Plaque
Neurofibrillary Sengles

Hypomctabolism CBF Temporal Lobes
Cholineryic nurons
Subcullosal nuclie

Dementia

Degenerative changes in the limbic system likely have a role in the genesis of neurodegenerative diseases, particularly Pick's disease and Alzheimer's disease. The frontal and temporal lobes are predominantly affected by Pick's disease. Marked atrophy is also found in the limbic system, most notably the dentate gyrus and hippocampus.

Alzheimer's disease is a chronic progressive dementia of unknown origin. Early on, patients develop memory impairment which eventually progresses to global intellectual dysfunction. Brain atrophy is more diffuse in Alzheimer's disease. Senile plaques and neurofibrillary tangles are dispersed throughout the cerebral cortex and basal ganglia, but the hippocampus and amygdala are often severely involved. Secondary atrophy of the fornix can be seen in chronic cases. Hippocampal atrophy may be a prominent feature on imaging studies, but the finding is nonspecific and the diagnosis of Alzheimer's disease requires clinical correlation. Volumetric measurements of the amygdala and hippocampus as a unit may be helpful for distinguishing patients with early Alzheimer's disease.

Lehericy S, Baulac M, Chiras J, et al: Amygdalohippocampal MR volume measurements in the early stages ofAlzheimer's disease. AJNR 1994; 15:929-937.

Links to the limbic system are suspected for several psychiatric disorders, but the structural alterations are subtle and generally require volumetric analysis for detection. The most studied diseases are schizophrenia and bipolar (affective) disorder. The limbic system has also been implicated in psychopathic and amnestic disorders, but no specific imaging criteria have been developed.

Anxiety disorders include stress disorders, phobias, and panic attacks. The amygdala attaches emotional significance to sensory input. Functional MR studies have revealed over activity of the amygdala during facial recognition tasks. Also, neuroscientists have identified a fear circuitry, whereby the amygdala modulates neural circuitry in orbital, ventral and prefrontal cortex, the anterior cingulate and the entorhinal cortex. Another theory is that anxiety disorders result from failure of the anterior cingulate and hippocampus to modulate the activity of the amygdala.

Brown GG, Jernigan T, Cato MA: Functional MRI in Neuropsychiatric Disorders. *in* Edelman, Hesselink,Zlatkin & Crues, eds., Clinical Magnetic Resonance Imaging, 3rd edition, Saunders-Elsevier, Philadelphia, 2006, pp 1806-39.

Multiple studies of patients with **schizophrenia** have shown ventricular enlargement and reduced limbic volumes.

Byrum CE, Thompson JE, Heinz ER, et al: Limbic circuits and neuropsychiatric disorders: Functionalanatomy and neuroimaging findings. Neuroimag Clin North Am 7:79-99, 1997.

Bipolar or affective disorder features severe depression alternating with episodes of hyperactivity. Patients have defective regulation of emotions, and they have difficulty with judgment and behavioral decisions. The most popular theory is that a deficiency of serotonin is the primary cause of the disorder. Serotonin is normally produced in the raphe nucleus in the midbrain and upper pons and is distributed to the rest of the brain. Ventriculomegaly is observed in affective disorders, but the finding is nonspecific. Reductions in volume of the frontal lobes, basal ganglia, amygdala, and hippocampus have also been reported. Functional studies have revealed decreased activity in the prefrontal cortex and anterior cingulate gyrus.

Psychopathic disorders are characterized by aggressive and impulsive behavior. Patients are thought to have deficits in informational and emotional processing. A likely root cause is malfunction of neural circuits in the prefrontal temporal-limbic."

REFERENCES
http://sinwarp.uesd.edu/NeuroWeb/Text/br-800epi.htm   5/15/2014

SELF-ESTEEM & AS IT RELATES TO YOUR- IMPORTANCE

Chapter 7

WHAT IS TICKING, or CLICKING?

Low-Self-Esteem

We are going to be looking at some of the negative responses and how a person may respond. The **short term memories**, along with the deep temporal lobes has also been recorded and stores them as highly charged **emotional memories**, both positive and negative. If a person has been traumatized by a dramatic event, such as being in an accident or watching their house burn down, if you have been abused by someone, the emotional component of the memory is stored in **the deep limbic system of the brain**. On the other hand, if you have won the lottery, graduated magna cum laud, or watched the birth of your child, those emotional memories are stored as well. The total experience of our **emotional memories** is responsible in part for the emotional tone of our mind. These emotional memories are intimately involved in the **emotional tagging** that occurs.

The **deep limbic system** also affects our motivation and drive it helps get you going and getting things done as you to go throughout the day. When over activity happens in this area it is associated with lowered motivation and drive, which is often seen in depression or low-self-esteem. The deep limbic system controls the sleep and appetite cycles of the body both of these components are often a problem within **abnormalities** in the way a person sees themselves known as personal esteem.

The **deep limbic structures** are also intimately involved with bonding and social connectedness which has everything to do with our self-esteem. This system affects the bonding mechanism that enables you to connect with other people and your ability to do this successfully in turn influences your social activity. When we are bonded to people in a positive way, we feel better about ourselves. This capacity to bond then plays a significant role the tone and quality of our relationship or relationships.

As mentioned above due to the larger deep limbic system, women are more in touch with their feelings than men, but there are advantages and disadvantages to each gender. Each person has an increased ability to bond and connect with others (which is why women are the primary caretakers for children – there is no society on earth where men are primary care takers for children). Having a larger limbic system leaves a female somewhat more susceptible to depression, especially at times of significant hormonal changes such as the onset of puberty, before menses, after the birth of a child, and at menopause.

This "hard-wired response", happens immediately upon activation, such as seeing or experiencing an **emotional** or **physical threat.** In this response the heart beats faster, breathing rate increases, and blood pressure increases, the hands and feet become cooler because it shuts the blood from the pupils, they dilate (you see better). This "deep limbic" translation of emotion is powerful and immediate. It happens with more covert emotional threats. This part of the brain is intimately connected with the **prefrontal cortex** and seems to act as a switching station between the runaway emotions in **(the deep limbic system)** and the **rational thought process** aids in problem solving **both** have to do with the **prefrontal cortex.** When the **prefrontal cortex** is cooled down, more activation is possible, current research on depression indicates there is an increased activity in the **deep limbic system** and activity can shut down in the **prefrontal cortex,** especially on the left side.

The entire structures were later named the "**limbic system**" the neopallium called the rational brain, a highly complex network of neural cells capable of producing language, the neopallium is the great generator of ideas, and/or "the mother of inventions and the father of abstractive thought" in terms of the **thinking brain.**

The **neocortex** is the seat of thought; it contains the centers that put together and comprehends what senses are perceived at the time. It adds to feelings as to what we think and allows us to have feelings about ideas, art, symbols, imaginings, and love. Due to the neocortex gives way for strategizing, long-term planning, and other mental abilities.

This new additional thought process allows the **limbic brain** to act on emotions and feelings of love, pleasure, and sexual desire. Also, with the addition of the **neocortex** and its connections to the **limbic system** allows for mother child bonding, that is the basis for the family unit and long-term commitments to relationships. Species have no neocortex, the neocortex allows for subtlety and complexity of emotions such as having feelings about feelings. Thus, showing a greater range in our reactions and in our emotions this is a very complex system, it is more essential for the flexibility. This is very evident in our feelings, emotions, reactions, and in our social environment and that has a direct correction to self-esteem. The **limbic system** and **neocortex** gives the emotions to the event and immense power to influence the functioning of the rest of the brain centers including the thought process.

One is the **hippocampus** and **memory** a long with the **amygdala** reflects FEAR, **to** understand exactly how the **hippocampus** is involved in memory. The term is the working memory, (long-term memory) enables a person to look back on what they said or did**.** Working memory is like the RAM in your computer it is crucial for performing some common operations in your brain structure. It is able to recycle as soon as a person turns to something else; it does not become a permanent memory.

The **second type** is what we commonly associate with **"long-term memory** or **declarative memory**. It composes the facts, figures, and names you have learned and it becomes conscious memory. It is like the hard drive in a computer although no one knows exactly where this enormous database is stored, it is clear that the **hippocampus** is necessary to file new memories as they occur.

I know I sound like a broken record when it comes dealing with emotions and feelings they do play a big role in dealing with your self-esteem, there is much more to be learned in our quest to know more about what makes you and me click and tick. We have just scratched the surface in regards to our self-esteem, but when it comes to gloom, doom, and despair in a person's life.

Some emotional reactions and emotional memories can be formed without any conscious cognitive behavior changes or with any predicative behavior like our ego. The **amygdala** can house memories and responses, interacts without quite realizing why we have done something, because the shortcut comes from the **thalamus** to the **amygdala** and completely bypasses the **neocortex**.

Other research has shown that in the first few milliseconds of perceiving something are not only unconsciously comprehended by what we think and at the same time what it means. We decide whether we like something or not; the "**cognition awareness conscious**", presents our awareness with just the identity of what we see and that gives us ways to do things. Our **emotions** seem to have a **mind** of its own, which can hold views quite independently of our rational mind.

The **third type** is procedural memory is the most durable form of memory. These actions can become habits, or skills that are learned by simple repetition. Examples are playing tennis, playing an instrument, solving a puzzle, etc. The **hippocampus** is not involved in procedural memory, but it is likely that the **cerebellum** plays a role in some instances.

Out-of-Date Neural Alarms

One drawback of such neural alarms happens when there is an urgent message, sometimes it does not send a message relevant to the emotional memories the **amygdala** scans the experience, comparing what has happened in the past up to now. The response may be the mild shutting down and the person doesn't want to deal with it, the situation may bring back old memories similar to some kind of dangerous situation in the past. The trouble comes when it is a highly charged **emotional memory** that triggered a crisis response or something equally as bad. The emotions of a situation can and do set off alarms going through the brain are stored in the critical narrative as far as memories are discerned, and the **neocortex** helps a person deal with **rational thoughts**.

The **amygdala** and **hippocampus** work hand and hand; each stores and retrieves information independently. The early childhood can be triggered by wordless emotions when an infant feels things before they can talk or communicate, in other words it only takes a reminder of those emotional memories to trigger something later in life it can be an emotional response to a present or past situation or event.

At this point we're going to use an illustration of **amygdala** in action when I heard a noise around three in the morning I thought a piece of the ceiling might have fallen, there was a big crash in the corner of our bedroom I jumped up thinking something had fallen. I got out of bed realizing I was safe, but what had happened; my wife had cleaned out the closet the day before and left the books in the corner.

I was half-asleep when I leaped from bed it might have saved me from injury if the ceiling had really fallen. Before the **neocortex** has time to fully register what has actual happened. The emergency route from the eyes or ear to the **thalamus** was an interaction action with the **amygdala** was crucial in my actions "you may not need to know that something is dangerous to react, but you can react to the potential danger."

The direct route has vast advantages for the **amygdala** to confirm what happens. The test was performed on rats they begin a response to a perception in as little as twelve-milliseconds, twelve-thousandths of a second. The route from the **thalamus** to the **neocortex** to the **amygdala** takes about twice as long.

Some emotional feelings are based on prior feelings and thoughts, which set off the thought process. This is called "**precognitive emotions**", a reaction based on neural bits and pieces of sensory information that have not been fully sorted out and intergraded and may not be recognizable in a bad situation. It's a very rare form of sensory information, something like a neural response, there use to be a TV show called "*name that tone*", a snap judgment of the melody is based on a few notes, a whole perception is grasped on very little information. If in the case of the **amygdala** sensors, sensory patterns are of importance and emerges when a person jumps to a conclusion. Triggering their reactions before they are in a full confirmation of the information or any confirmation is reached that is called "jumping to a conclusion."

Small wonder we have little insight into our more explosive emotions, especially when they still have a grip in our memory. The **amygdala** can and does act and react before the **cortex** knows what is going on because such raw emotion is triggered prior to what was thought.

Therefore, the **hippocampus** is critical in laying down the **declarative memory**, but is not necessary for the two other types of memory,

1) procedural memory,

2) memory storage.

When there is damage to the **hippocampus** it only affects the formation of new **declarative memories**.

Ordinarily the **prefrontal area** governs our emotional reactions from the start. The largest sensory information comes from the **thalamus**, remember it does not go into the **amygdale** until later, it has to go through the **neocortex** first it has many centers as it tries to make sense of what is being perceived; that information is coordinated by the **prefrontal lobs** the seat of planning and organizing actions toward a goal, including emotional ones. In the **neocortex** there is a cascading series of circuits that registers and analyzes information, it comprehends the thought before it axially happens, the **prefrontal lobes** orchestrates a reaction. If in the process an emotional response it is called for, the **prefrontal lobes** sends it to the **amygdale**, which works hand-in- hand with the **prefrontal lobes** and other circuits in the brain's functions all thoughts go through the brain at some point or almost at the same time.

This progress allows for discernment in an emotional response and is significant when there are emotional emergencies. When an emotion is triggered within moments the **prefrontal lobes** performs what amounts to a risk/benefit ratio a myriad of possible reactions, before a person decides which action seems best.

The **neocortex** is slower because of the circuits it has to go through before there is a response so that the person can respond late after thinking about what happened now the thought or action becomes more judicious and while it considers what is actually happening at the time there is a sense of what is happening rather than the actual thought was which precedes your feeling of what happened.

Emotional hijacking presumably involves two dynamics, **triggering** of the **amygdala** and failure to activate the **neocortex** that usually keeps **emotional responses** in balance and that is what a person wants. If the **rational mind** is swamped by the **emotion,** the **prefrontal cortex** acts as an efficient manager weighing the **emotions** before acting or by dampening the signals for activation which is sent out by the **amygdala** and the other **limbic centers**. It is like a parent asking a child (to wait) for what they want.

This is known as the "off switch" for getting emotions under control it seems to come from the **left prefrontal lobe**. One of the tasks of the **left frontal lobe** is to act as a neural thermostat regulating unpleasant emotions. The **right prefrontal lobes** have to do with negative feelings, which is known as the "the right brain / left brain" which is a common term now we know how people think the process works while the **left lobes** keep those raw emotions in check. Probably by, inhibiting the **right lobe** to act on those feelings before things go through the **left prefrontal cortex**, which are prone to catastrophic worries and fears the "right brain / left brain" they are consent factors because people have patterns of behaviors.

The connections between the **amygdala (**and related to **limbic structures)** and the **neocortex** is the hub of battles or cooperative treaties struck between what a person thinks and the heart is relevant to their thoughts and feelings. This circuitry explains why each emotion is so crucial to an affective thought, both in making wise decisions and in simply allowing us to think clearly, I hope this helps you understand the thought process.

The emotion is another factor it has power to disrupt the thinking process. Neuroscientists use the term "**working memory**", for the capacity of attention that holds the facts essential for completing a given task or problem, whether it be the ideal fluctuations of what has just happened. One illustration that might fit while a person is looking for a house and also looking at another house, the comparison allows reasoning while taking the task of which house might be best.

The **prefrontal cortex** is the brain region responsible for **working memory** this starts developing in the early teens. If the circuits from the **limbic brain** to the **prefrontal lobes** signals a **strong emotion**, this could indicate anxiety, anger or they can create neural sabotaging, the ability of the **prefrontal lobe** maintains the **working memory**. That happens when a person is emotionally upset, they "just can't think straight", and why continual emotional distress can create problems in a person's intellectual abilities, crippling their capacity to learn, that is why some use IQ as indicator, but it is not a true indicator of success or failure.

These deficits are more subtle not always shown up in IQ testing and it shows up more in neuropsychological testing which measures the emotional level as well a child's continual aggressive or passive impulsive behaviors. For example, boys who have above-average IQ scores, the question is why do others do poorly in school may have to do with a learning disability rather than a behavior identified with ADHD, via the neuropsychological tests something has affected the **prefrontal cortex** from functioning like it is supposed to. Here are some reasons, they maybe too impulsive, anxious, and often disruptive in class, this shows up when they have trouble at school and home it suggests a faulty performance of the **prefrontal cortex** over riding their **limbic** urges. Despite their intellectual potential those children who have problems with academic failures are more likely to become alcoholics and criminals, because they are not able to control their emotions. The emotional brain is out of balance from those cortical areas tested by IQ tests, they don't want to do anything at school and are unable to control their anger, it comes down to them being unable to control their emotions. What if their circuits in the brain are short circuited throughout their childhood and into their adult life they have a behavior pattern.

Contrary to what is considered a normal reaction it does matter if a person has a process of thinking things through, then their **feelings** and **thoughts** are facilitated by disrupting the **rational mind** from coming up with a rational action, it enables the destructive emotions to take over or disabling the thought process and come up with a good response. Likewise, the **thinking brain** plays an **executive** role in your **emotions** except in those moments when **emotional surges** are out of control and a person lets the emotional brain run rampant.

DEALING WITH DEPRESSION

Gloom, Doom, Despair, and Depression

There is a correlation between gloom, doom, and despair; they are cousins to depression all of these are setup by the mood a person is in, which reflects in their state of mind, how they feel at the time. Mood also sets the tone for the way a person is going to meet and handle life's ups and downs.

Definition of mood: *noun*   {13}
    1 a: a conscious state of mind or predominant emotion
      : feeling
      : the expression of mood especially in art or literature

2 a: a fit of anger : rage
3 a: a prevailing attitude : disposition
  b: a receptive state of mind predisposing to action
  c: a distinctive atmosphere or context
   : the form of a syllogism as determined by the
        quantity and quality of its constituent propositions
:   distraction of form or a particular set of inflectional forms of a
verb to express whether the action or state it denote is conceived as
fact or in some other manner (as command, possibility, or wish)

Definition of depression: *noun*   {14}
  1 a: the distance of a celestial abject below the horizon
  b: the size of an angle of depression
  2: an act depressing or a state of being
  a: a pressing down : lowering
  b: (1) a state of being sad : dejection
(2) a psychoneurotic or psychotic disorder marked especially by
sadness, inactivity, difficulty in thinking and concentration, a
significant increase or decrease in appetite and sleeping, feeling of
dejection and hopelessness, and sometimes suicidal tendencies
  c: (1) a reduction in activity, amount, quality, or force
(2) a lowering of vitality or functional activity

Definition of bipolar: *noun*   {15}
   : any of several disorders of mood characterized usually by
   alternating episodes of depression and mania—called also *manic*
   depression, manic - depressive illness
Referenced from http://www.merriam-webstercollegiate.com/
Merriam-Webster's Collegiate Dictionary Eleventh Edition / (date
4/19/04)

***Bipolar Disorder: Manic Depression, Symptoms*:**
- Severe changes in mood-either extremely irritable or overly silly and
  elated
- Overly-inflated **self-esteem**; grandiosity
- Increased energy
- Decreased need for sleep-able to go with very little or no sleep for
  days
- Increased talking-talks too much, too fast; changes topics too
  quickly; cannot be interrupted
- Disregard of risk-excessive involvement in risky behaviors or
  activities.

People with depression may have a hard time coping with everyday activities and responsibilities. While others may have difficulty in controlling alcoholism or an addiction, both kinds of people may suffer from low **self-esteem**. Signs of depression are often include sadness that won't go away:

- Hopelessness, boredom; unexplained irritability or crying, loss of interest in usual activities;
- Changes in eating or sleeping habits;
- Alcohol or substance abuse,
- threats or troubles in their home life;
- outbursts of shouting, complaining; reckless behavior;
- headaches and pains that don't get better with treatment;
- thoughts about death or suicide.

Daniel Goleman

"In another rendering by Gardner, noted that the core of *interpersonal intelligence* includes the 'capacities to discern and respond appropriately to a person's **moods**, temperaments, motivations, and desires'. In *interpersonal intelligence* is the key to knowledge of one's self, he included' having the access to one's own **feelings** and the ability to discriminate among themselves, and draw upon their own discernment to guide their behavior'."

Other types of mood disorder include:

Chronic Low Grade Depression (known as Dysthymia or Dysthymic Disorder).

Dysthymia greatly affects the quality of life of the person experiencing it. There is a sense of gloom, a lack of pleasure in life, **low self-esteem** and little confidence. For a person to be diagnosed as having chronic low-grade depression (Dysthymia), these symptoms alter a person's mood if it is present for at least one year if dysthymia can start during the teenage years, it may be expressed as irritability.

Chronic Low Grade Depression is equally common in boys and in girls and increases with age, this condition is likely to lead to social avoidance and low self-confidence, which will affect their social activities, vocation, and personal development of a person. Moreover, there is an increased risk of a Major Depressive Episodes and possibly suicide attempts.

Manic Depression or a Bipolar Disorder.

This illness is marked by extreme mood swings these changes are more intense than the changes of mood, which are not a part of normal life. Usually there is a "high" (manic) phase alternating with a "low" (depressed) phase, with a period of normal mood level at times. There are wide variations; however, depression affects a person and their families.

Postnatal Depression

Depression occurring after the birth of a baby is normal. Risk factors, such as poor personal support, relationship difficulties, and stressful life events indicate that mother's may be vulnerable to postnatal depression.

Seasonal Affective Disorder - SAD

Some depression coincides with the onset of seasonal changes.

Substance Induced Mood Disorder

Alcohol and other drug misuse can change the body's chemistry, causing depressive symptoms in additions, incidents of depression.

Precise data relating to the prevalence of depression in the community are unavailable because it often goes unreported. However, even the conservative figures indicate that depression is a major health problem. There are about as many people with depression as there are people with asthma. (What is Depression?)

Psychologist's use the term *Meta cognition* to refer to an **awareness** of one's thought process; *Meta mood* means **awareness** of one's own **emotions**."

MOOD DISORDERS

What causes mood disorders?

Researchers believe most serious mental illnesses are caused by complex imbalances in the brain's functions, the body's chemicals, and the addictive substances. They also believe environmental factors can play a part in triggering an emotional behavior which comes from related mental illness.

Like other diseases, mental illnesses can be treated; the good news is that most people who deal with mental illness, even serious disorders can lead productive lives with proper treatment. Mood disorders are one form of the more common mental disorders.

One of the most common mood disorders are kin to depression and bipolar Mood Disorders, National Mental Health Information Center, also known as "manic-depressive illness."

They are known as gloom, doom, and despair, **mood** often leads to depression there is a tendency to feel dejected and let down, again **mood** definitely dictates a person's frame of mind, but we're are sure bad circumstances can lead to a bad **mood,** neither if the person is in a bad mood causes doubts and fears.

We need to let the air out of the situation by using a pressure-relief tactics of some kind to relieve all kinds of feelings, discouragement, or depression as we examine our self-esteem; we need to understand our **moods,** especially if they are negative.

The University of Washington
People with low self-esteem are less likely to break a negative moods
Page 1 of 2 [9]

UW HOME >UMIN > News and Events
FOR IMMEDIATE RELEASE
FROM: Joel Schwarz
206-543-2580
joels (UW. Washington.edu
DATE: Aug. 5, 2002
    "People with low self-esteem are less motivated to break a negative mood
People with low self-esteem are less motivated than people with high self-esteem to improve a **negative mood**, even when they are offered an activity that will change their frame of mind, a team of American and Canadian psychologists has found.

The finding is contrary to the common belief that all people are motivated to **evaluate negative moods**, according to Jonathon Brown, a University of Washington psychologist and co-author of the study. 'Many people with low self-esteem believe sadness is part of life and that you shouldn't try to get rid of it, while people with high self-esteem believe in doing something to feel better if they have a negative experience or get in a **bad mood**,' said Brown.

The researchers conducted five studies involving nearly 900 people. In the key experiment, the researchers created a **sad mood** by having subjects listen to music and found that people with low self-esteem were significantly less likely than people with high self-esteem to select a comedy video from among six tapes to **break their mood**.

A group first read descriptions of the six videos —which included stand-up comedy routines, a discussion of global warming and the story of a polio-crippled runner who dreams of becoming an Olympian but fails — and rated how happy or sad each would make them feel if they watched it. Most people, regardless of their self-esteem, said the comedy video would make them the happiest.

Then 116 people, half of whom had been tested to have high-esteem and half to have low self-esteem, were exposed to music that induced happy or **sad moods**. Some of the subjects heard a jazz version of Bach's Brandenburg Concerto No. 3 to put them in a **positive mood**. The others were put into a **negative mood** by listening to Prokofiev's 'Russia Under the Mongolian Yoke' played at half speed, a piece of music described by Brown as 'slow, sad, laborious and boring.' Each recording lasted about 10 minutes.

Afterward, all subjects were given the descriptions of the six videos and asked to rate how they thought each would make them feel, ranging on a scale from very sad to very happy. Finally, they were asked to select one to watch.

The subjects, regardless of their level of self-esteem, agreed that the comedy video was the one that would put them in the **happiest mood**. However, among the people exposed to the negative music there was a sharp difference in the videos they actually picked to watch. Just 47 percent of low-self-esteem people picked the comedy video while 75 percent of high self-esteem subjects selected it.

People with low self-esteem are less motivated to break a negative mood Page 2 of 2

A different pattern emerged among people who heard the happy or positive music. More people with low self-esteem *(75* percent) than those with high self-esteem (54 percent) chose the comedy video.

Brown said it appears that a combination of resignation and sadness leads to less motivation among people with low self-esteem to rise above their **mood**, and make an effort to change it.

'People with low self-esteem feel resignation because they question whether anything will help and say 'I'm not good at **breaking or changing a mood**,' he said. 'They also believe sadness is not something you get rid of and that you learn and grow from sadness. They feel it is **not appropriate to try to change a mood**. These are not people who would necessarily go to the movies or shopping to feel better.'

There are things that people with low self-esteem can do to snap a **negative mood**, according to Brown.
'If you have low self-esteem, you should actively try to rise above the sadness and learn that you will feel heifer if you do not passively accept sadness. You can get better if you remind yourself to do something. You may have to kick yourself to a movie because it will require a conscious effort rather than something that comes automatically,' he said.

The other four studies reinforced the idea that low self-esteem people are less motivated to change a **negative mood**. The initial study asked students to record in a diary a positive or negative experience that happened to them in the next 7 to 10 days and what they did afterwards. Among those who listed a negative experience, only 55 percent of people had a low self-esteem of themselves and expressed a goal to improve their **mood** compared to 77 percent of those with high self-esteem. The second study found that people with low self-esteem are equally knowledgeable as those with high self-esteem about strategies to **repair negative moods**.

The final two studies asked people about their experiences when they were in a negative mood. Those with high self-esteem were more likely to express the need to do something to change the mood, and less likely to recall instances when they didn't find a way improve their mood. Those with low self-esteem, however, were more likely to say such moods are acceptable, and that they couldn't change a mood even if they tried. They also were more likely to say that negative moods sapped their energy.

Self-esteem is generally defined in terms of feelings of affection one has for oneself. In a normal population, high **self-esteem** is characterized by a general fondness for oneself, **Low self-esteem** is marked by mildly positive, ambivalent or slightly negative feelings.

Co-authors of the paper published in a recent issue of the Journal of Personality and Social Psychology are Joanne Wood, a psychology professor at Canada's University of Waterloo, Sara Heimpel, a graduate student at Waterloo, and Margaret Marshall, a doctoral student at Washington."

The research was funded by the Social Science and Humanities Research Council of Canada. For more information, contact Brown at (206) *543-0679* orjdb@u.Washington.edu
http://www.washington.edu/newsroom/news/2002archive/08-02archive/k080502.html   6/19/2004

The Moody News Newsletter for Depression, Mania and Other Mental Disorders
Mood Disorders — Test Your Knowledge   Page 1 of 6 – 15 [10]

"Here are the facts behind some basic conceptions and misconceptions about **mood disorders**, and the people coping with them.

The **mood disorders**, major depression and bipolar disorder depression are rare diseases, and affect very few people.

FALSE. Although the statistics seem to vary by whichever source, or one thing we do know is that **mood disorders** are extremely common, researchers say that at least 50% of all visits to physicians are depression related (examples include: "stress", high blood pressure, fatigue, and bowel problems, chronic undefined illnesses, fibromyalgia, etc.).

Among the facts and figures available: at least I in 5 people will suffer a major depressive episode over the course of a lifetime, usually before the of age of 40; more than 2.3 million people in the U.S. have bipolar disorders, million have a depressive disorder. The Center for Mental Health Se Rockville, MD estimates that 5.4% of all Americans have a serious, ongoing with mental illness.

The Moody News Newsletter for Depression, Mania and Other Mental Lisoraers - nome (…)

Other reports state that 23% of Americans aged 18 and older have had diagnosable mental disorder in any given year, while 9-13% of children ages 9-17 have a 'serious emotional disturbance with substantial future impairment'. These numbers are absolutely chilling, but luckily it is apparent that a large number of children and adolescents do recover from the diagnosed or diagnosable mental illness.

Women experience depression twice as often as men, which the Arr. Psychological Association (APA) says is directly related to women's subordinate roles in American society, and to the higher incidence of violence, poverty and sexual abuse in women's lives.

Mood disorders made up 27.6% of psychiatric office visits in 1980—most common presenting illness.

The number of psychiatric hospital beds (for all brain disorders) in the United States exceeds the number of hospital beds for all other medial illnesses — and **mood disorders** make up a large percentage of psychiatric beds; of the more than 1,000,000 total hospital admissions in the United States during 1998, nearly 270,000 (or 26%) were psychiatric admissions.

Workplace studies show that 17% of all female employees and 9% male employees have a **mood disorder; mood disorders** cost American businesses $43.7 billion in lost productivity each year. (The total cost of mental health services in the U.S. in 1990 was $148 billion, which in both direct costs — treatment and rehabilitation — of $69 billion, in indirect costs — lost productivity at home, school, and/or work — estimates at $79 billion.

The Moody News Newsletter for Depression, Mania and Other Mental Disorders - Home Page 2 of 6

Mood disorders are caused by poor parent role-modeling and result of the breakdown of the American family because of the Industrial Revolution.

***Primarily* FALSE.** Most experts finally agree, based on pretty extended research, that **mood disorders** are biochemical in origin with both genetic and environmental triggers and exacerbators.

What this means is that the three (biochemistry, genetics & environment play off one another: someone with the 'right' biochemistry and genetics background is probably more likely to develop a **mood disorder** under certain environmental circumstances, than another person might.

The biological piece is the result of an imbalance in brain chemicals neurotransmitters, which control electrical transmission between nerves sort of like being "wired" wrong. Medications help to restore proper brain functions.

We also know that the greater the depression "load" in the family (noted close relatives with a **mood disorder**, or other related, disorder), the chances of a child developing a depressive disorder.

The Moody News Newsletter for Depression, Mania and Other Mental Disorders – Home Page 3 of 6

Studies have found that 40% of children with a depressed parent deep major, long-standing impairments, particularly mood disorders. The kids who lose a parent to death or divorce before the age of 14 will develop major depression.

So what chance would the statisticians give someone like me to escape **mood disorder** of some type: not only do I come from a family with a depression load, but my mom died when I was ten. Pretty grim, huh' not surprising I developed bipolar disorder — and we didn't even know the odds were stacked against me in the wrong way!

Are **depressive disorders** caused by poor parent role-modeling? No. But, we can develop depressive personality traits and habitually ineffective ways of responding to our environment, as a learned research what we live with when we are young, makes it even harder for us to cope with as adults, and without **depressive episodes**.

It's for this reason that counseling is recommended: to teach people healthier ways of responding to and interacting with their social environments. Note that I said counseling, not psychotherapy — it's personal conviction that counseling is helpful, but psychotherapy for disorder is a waste of time. However, psychotherapy can be helpful in dealing with other issues, and may be the best way of handling a person's disorders and other deep-seated problems.

There's also evidence that a greater percentage of the U.S. population copes with a diagnosable **mood disorder** than there were one hundred years ago. That's not just in sheer numbers, but also as a percentage total population.

The Moody News Newsletter for Depression, Mania and Other Mental-Disorders-Home

Depression and manic depression "run" in families, very definitely TRUE.

Bipolar Genetics: If there is no family history of **mood disorders**, the chance of someone developing one of these illnesses is 1.2%. If a brother or sister has bipolar disorder, the risk is 12%. If one parent has a manic disorder, the risk is 27%, and if both parents have a **mood disorder,**' is 74%. If an identical twin develops a depressive disorder, the risk increases to 74-80%.

Major Depression Genetics: If there is no family history, the chance of someone developing a **depressive disorder** is about 5%. The risk increases to 15% if a brother or sister has a **mood disorder**. If one parent has a depressive disorder, the risk is also 15% (I was unable to find the static's both parents having depression, but it's surely quiet high). If an incidental family member has a mood disorder, the risk is 59%.

Mood disorders affect mainly mates.

FALSE. Bipolar disorder affects men and women equally, but major depression affects twice as many women as men.

If people would just take their medications, they'd be cured.

FALSE. There is no cure for depression, bipolar disorder or any of total related illnesses, any more than there is a cure for diabetes. **Mood episodes** are lifelong illnesses that affect most of us every day of our lives, the reoccurrences of full-blown episodes is a real problem.

More than half of the people affected by depression will have some functional disability that persists throughout their lives. As a rule, the more episodes a person has, the more likely he or she is to have future episodes.

The earlier we can get in to help someone with a **mood disorder** (or practically any other major illness), the greater the chance of success. Research shows the success rate for treatment of a first episode of depression is 65-70%, and 80% for bipolar disorder.

Mood disorders have the highest rates of completed suicides, than those with psychiatric disorder. **Mood disorders** are very dangerous illnesses, and we should never take them for granted. I know someone who seemed to have it all together after years of struggling with her illness— she had a job, was well-respected and loved by her co-workers, and, we thought she hadn't had a serious episode of either mania or depression for quite some time. A year and a half ago, she made an extremely well planned suicide attempt with devastating results... and those who were close to her didn't have a clue what she was going through. (It was only by accident they found her, just barely in time — and the overdose she took caused a stroke and permanent physical disability; she'll be in rehab for the rest of her life.)

I can't say it strongly enough: mood disorders are extremely dangerous, life-long, and life-threatening illnesses. We always feel be on the alert for new episodes; in ourselves, or in those we love.

Clinical depression affects mainly younger people, not the elderly.

FALSE. Depression is not a normal part of aging, but 58% of older adults think it is; late-life depression affects some 6 million American adults women; but only *10%* get treatment. Older adults are considered the most at risk for suicide.

The Moody News Newsletter for Depression, Mania and Other Mental Disorders - Home ... Page *5* of 6

Rates of depression in nursing homes are up to 25%. Clinical depression can be triggered by other chronic illness such as diabetes, stroke, health disease, Alzheimer's, Parkinson's, and arthritis. In men, the rate of depression peaks at age 55-70, and the highest rates of suicide in a category occur in white males over the age of 69.

Bipolar disorder often begins in the late teens or early twenties, but it strikes at any were from age; 1 in 4 children with Attention Deficit (Hyperactivity) Disorder (ADD or ADHD) will develop bipolar disorder.

'**This too shall pass**' is good advice for a depressed person.

FALSE. Sure, depression is typically episodic (meaning there are depressions and periods without the more overt symptoms) and it targets about 40% of those having a first episode will be depression free for the rest of their lives.

But this means that 60% of those affected will have repeat episodes of which will recur within 2 years. In these recurrent depressive disorders the average number of episodes of depression in a lifetime is about the same as people with bipolar disorder, about 11. The episode may pass, but it likely to return, and once it does, it may be more frequent, 1 harder than the last, and be even more difficult to manage. Suicide is always a common statistic, most suicides occur in the early years of the depression, the toll of poor concentration and organizational skills, memory lapses, and constant fatigue while trying to maintain a job, a home, and social responsibilities is enormous.

Major depression is easy to diagnose because the person is obviously sad.

FALSE. There are many different ways that depression can manifest itself biologically (with aches and pains, chronic conditions and/or stress-related-illnesses) emotionally (unhappiness, self-doubt, defeatism, hypertension to criticism, etc.); intellectually (belief that one is a failure, incompetence unloved or rejected by others); and behaviorally (indecisiveness, procrastination, avoidance of change, disinterest in or abandonment formerly enjoyed activities, crying, slowing down of mental and physical activities).

Bipolar disorder can be even more difficult to diagnose; like depression there is no definitive laboratory test, blood test or x-ray that can diagnoses to confirm bipolar disorder. According to The Greater Cincinnati Bipolar Support Group 'persons diagnosed with bipolar disorder have seen, average, 3+ doctors and spent 8 —*10* years in agony before getting an accurate diagnosis and then beginning treatment." Like depression, bipolar disorder can manifest itself biologically, emotionally, intellectually and behaviorally.'

The Moody News Newsletter for Depression, Mania and Other Mental Disorders - Home Page 6 of 6"

Some References, Resources & Bibliography:

"Atypicals for Bipolar Disorder: Efficacy & Side Effects", Gary S Sachs, M.E, Asst Professor of Psychiatry, Harvard University; Director, Bipolar Research Program, Massachusetts General Hospital. From a talk given at the 12th Annual U.S. Psychiatric & Mental Health Congress, Atlanta GA, Nov 1999

"Bipolar Disorder—You Are Not Alone!", Greater Cincinnati Bipolar Support Group.

Center for Mental Health Services. 1998. "Survey of Mental Health Organizations and General Mental Health Services". Rockville MD. Center Mental Health Services (CMHS).

"Finding Peace of Mind—Medication Strategies for Depression", National Depressive & Manic-Depression Association, 1999.

Friedman, R M, et al. 1996. "Prevalence of Serious Emotional Disturbance Children and Adolescents". In Mental Health, United States, 1996. Edited by R W Manderscheid and M J Henderson. Rockviile MD, Center for Mental Health Services.

Kessler, R.C., et al, 1998. "A Methodology for Estimating the 12-Month Prevalence of Serious Mental Illness." In Mental Health, United States, 1999, Edited by R W Manderscheid and M J Henderson. Rockville MD, Center for Mental Health Services.

Mental Health: A Report of the Surgeon General. Rockville, MD. US Dept of HHS, SAMHSA, SMHS, NIMH, National Institutes of Health, 1999.

Murray, CJL and AD Lopez, eds. 1996. "Summary: The Global Burden of Disease." Cambridge, MA, Harvard School of Public Health on behalf of the World Health Organization and the World Bank, Harvard University Press.

NAMI Advocate, Spring 2001.

National Mental Health Advisory Council. 1993. "Health Care Reform for Americans with Severe Mental Illnesses." American Journal of Psychiatry 1 (10): 1450-1452.

Regier, D A, et a!. 1993. The De Facto Mental and Addictive Disorders Service System. "Epidemiologic Catchment Area Prospective One Year

Prevalence Rates of Disorders & Services", Archives of General Psychiatry 50 (2): 85-94.

Rice, OP and LS Miller. 1996. "The Economic Burden of Schizophrenia". In the Handbook of Mental Health Economics and Health Policy: Schizophren Vol. 1, edited by M. Moscarelli, A Rupp, and N Sartorious. John Wiley & Son New York.

US News & World Report, Marcy 26, 01, Science and Ideas: Criminal Justice Vol. 130 No. 12, p 50: "Psychosis and Punishment" by Marianne Szegedy Maszak

MOOD DISORDERS

Mood

"Dysthymic Disorder

- On the majority of days for 2 years or more, the patient reports **depressed mood** or appears depressed to others for most of the day.
- When depressed, the patient has 2 or more of:
- o Appetite decreased or increased
- o Sleep decreased or increased
- o Fatigue or low energy
- o Poor self-image
- o Reduced concentration or indecisiveness
- o Feels hopeless
- During this 2 year period, the above symptoms are never absent longer than 2 consecutive months.
- During the first 2 years of this syndrome, the patient has not had a Major Depressive Episode.
- The patient has had no Manic, Hypomanic or Mixed Episodes.
- The patient has never fulfilled criteria for Cyclothymic Disorder.
- The disorder does not exist solely in the context of a chrome psychosis (such as Schizophrenia or Delusional Disorder).
- The symptoms are not directly caused by a general medical condition or the use of
- Substances, including prescription medications.

- The symptoms are caused clinical important distress or impair work, social or personal functioning. **Specify whether:**

Early onset, if it begins by age 20 late onset, if it begins at age 21 or later the only specifier that can apply is With Atypical Features.

Mood
Coding Notes
In children, the **abnormal mood** may be one of irritability and the time required is only one year.

A Major Depressive Episode may precede Dysthymia if it has remitted for a full two months before Dysthymia begins. Also, Dysthymia may begin first, if it lasts at least two years before the major depression begins. In this case, the two diagnoses may be made together. After the first two years, Major Depressive Episodes may also be diagnosed with Dysthymic Disorder, if the symptoms are met for both.

Cyclothymic Disorder

- For at least 2 years, the patient has had many periods of hypomanic symptoms and many **periods of low mood** that don't fulfill criteria for Major Depressive Disorder.
- The longest the patient has been free of **mood swings** during this period is 2 months.
- During the first 2 years **of** this disorder, the patient has not fulfilled criteria for Manic, Mixed, or Major Depressive Episode. Schizoaffective disorder doesn't explain the disorder better, and it isn't superimposed on Schizophrenia, Schizophrenifonn Disorder, Delusional Disorder or Psychotic Disorder Not Otherwise Specified.
- The symptoms are not directly caused by a general medical condition or the use of substances, including prescription medications.
- These symptoms cause clinically important distress or impair work, social or personal functioning.

Coding Notes
In children and adolescents, the time required is only one year.

After the required 2 years (1 for children), a Manic, Mixed or Major Depressive Episode may be superimposed on the Cyclothymia. Then, a Bipolar I or II diagnosis may be made concomitant with Cyclothymic Disorder.

http://www.themoodynews.com   6/19/20

Mood Disorder Due to a General Medical Condition
- The patient's clinical presentation is **dominated by a mood disorder** that persists and is characterized by either or both *of:*
  o **Depressed mood** or markedly decreased interest or pleasure in nearly all activities, or
  o **Mood** that is elevated, expansive or irritable.
- History, physical exam or laboratory findings suggest a general medical condition that seems likely to have directly caused these symptoms.
- No other mental disorder (such as Adjustment Disorder secondary to having a medical disorder) better accounts for these symptoms.
- The symptoms don't occur solely during a delirium.
- These symptoms cause clinically important distress or impair work, social or personal functioning.

Specify whether:

With **Manic Features. Mood** is mainly elevated or irritable.

With Depressive Features. Mood **is mainly depressed, but criteria for Major Depressive Episode are not fulfilled.**

With Major Depressive-Like Episode. All criteria (other than the general medical condition exclusion) are fulfilled.

With Mixed Features. Manic and depressive symptoms are present in about equal parts

Coding Notes

Depression associated with the general medical condition of Alzheimer's or vascular **dementia** is designated as part of the Axis I code for the dementia (see pages 27 and 32). Depression that occurs with other dementias must be coded separately on Axis I.

On Axis III, also code the specific general medical condition that has caused the mood disorder. The name of the specific general medical condition also goes into the **Axis I diagnosis.**

Substance-Induced Mood Disorder
- The patient's clinical presentation is dominated by a mood disorder that persists and is characterized by either or both
o **Depressed mood** or markedly decreased interest or pleasure in nearly all activities, or
o **Mood** that is elevated, expansive or irritable.
- History, physical exam or laboratory data substantiate that either - these symptoms have developed within a month of Substance Intoxication or Withdrawal, or -Medication use has caused the symptoms.
- The symptoms cause clinically important distress or impair work, social or personal functioning.
- This disorder does not occur solely during a delirium.
- A nonsubstance-induced mood disorder does not better explain the symptoms. * Code according to the specific substance involved:

6/19/2004 Mood
Page 12 of 15
291.8 Alcohol
292.84 Amphetamine [or Amphetamine-Like Substance]; Cocaine; Hallucinogen; Inhalant; Opioid;
Phencyclidine [or Phencyclidine-Like Substance]; Sedative, Hypnotic or Anxiolytic; Other [or Unknown] Substance

Specify the type:
With Depressive Features. **Mood** is mainly depressed
With Manic Features. **Mood** is mainly elevated or irritable
With Mixed Features. Manic and depressive symptoms are present in about equal parts
When criteria are met for substance-specific intoxication or withdrawal, specify whether:
With Onset During Intoxication
With Onset During Withdrawal
Coding Notes

Use this diagnosis instead of Substance Intoxication or Substance Withdrawal only

1.   when the symptoms exceed those you would expect from a syndrome of intoxication or withdrawal

2.   when they are serious enough by themselves to require clinical care.

Although the diagnosis of Substance-Induced **Mood Disorder** has no time or symptom requirements, there must be no **non-substance mood disorder** that better explains the symptoms. Look for these indications of a **non-substance mood disorder**:

a)   Previous episodes of Bipolar or Recurrent Depressive Disorder

b)   Previous manias

c)   Symptoms that are much worse than you would expect for the amount and duration of the substance abuse

d)   Mood disorder symptoms precede onset of substance abuse

e)   Mood disorder symptoms continue long (at least a month) after substance abuse or withdrawal stops

f)   Strong family history of mood disorder Mood

Page 13 of 15

Mood Disorders caused by most medications taken in therapeutic doses would be coded as, for example:

Axis I 292.11 Reserpine-Induced Mood Disorder, With Depressive Features, With Onset During Intoxication

Axis III E942.6 Reserpine

311 Depressive Disorder Not Othe rwise Specified

296.80 Bipolar Disorder Not Otherwise Specified

296.90 Mood Disorder Not Otherwise Specified

Specifiers that Describe the Most Recent Episode With Atypical Features

For the most recent 2 weeks or more of a Major Depressive Episode or predominating during the most recent 2 years of Dysthymic Disorder:

- The patient experiences **mood reactivity**, with improved **mood** when something good happens or seems about to happen (e.g., presence of friends).
- At least 2 of the following:
o Material increase in appetite or weight
o Excessive sleeping
o Arms or legs feel heavy, leaden
- Work or interpersonal relations are impaired by sensitivity to rejection that is long-standing and not limited to periods of depression.
- During the same episode, the patient does not qualify for With Melancholic Features or With Catatonic Features.

With Catatonic Features
- Two or more of the following dominate the clinical picture:
o Immobility (catalepsy or waxy flexibility) or stupor
o Apparently purposeless hyperactivity not influenced by external stimuli
o Mutism or extreme negativism
o Prominent posturing, stereotypies, mannerisms, or grimacing
o Echolalia (repeating words or phrases someone else has just said) or echopraxia (mimicking another's gestures)

Mood
With Seasonal Pattern
Mood
With Seasonal Pattern
- Major Depressive Episodes regularly begins at a particular season of the year.
- Complete recovery or change of polarity also occurs regularly during a particular season.

- These seasonal changes have occurred in each of the previous two years, during which no other nonseasonal Major Depressive Episodes have occurred.
- Over the patient's lifetime, seasonal Major Depressive Episodes materially outnumber nonseasonal=episodes.

Coding Note
Disregard examples where there has been a clear seasonal cause, such as being unemployed **every** summer."
http://www.geocities.comlmorrison94/mood.htm   6/19/2004

Mood disorders do not have be a way of life and **Mood swings** can become a problem if they are excessive in nature. If any **mood develops** and **presets** over a long period of time you're probably facing some **depression.** There is usually a pattern, all you have to do is find the pattern and break the pattern, set new ways to deal with a **mood disorder**.

Modern psychology
1.   Common enemies of a person.
a.   Pride/ego
b.   Pride, beauty can be a snare,
c.   How to deal with pride.
d.   Humility: **A look at the personal influences inside and out?**
e.   The answer to pride is a humble spirit.
2.   Controlling Lust & Addictions
a.   Love, the need to love and to be loved is a driving force and is characterized by your need for love.
b.   Take a love test!
c.   Appearance and Reality,
d.   What is Knowledge?
3.   Love of Money
a.   Dealing with a budget.
b.   Now let's look at some Scriptural truths about money and the results.
4.   Is how to avoid the pit-falls in life.

a. God is willing to forgive all things.

It usually takes a crisis to shake a person up and get their attention.

That has given me a different prospective on how I see the breaking point or in a crisis as I look back at things it damaged my self-perception it took several crises to get me to change things. When I help people, I want them to start with some common sense goals I call them common sense guidelines that gives them away to make sound judgments and the best directions to follow.

The emotional pull is there of course, but using sound principles and your values are the beginning of wisdom, don't let your emotions take over and rule you. I found that good principles and values helped me to understand why I behaved a certain way. If it doesn't fit into these common sense guidelines I know it's likely to turn out wrong for me.

Common sense rules:
A. Don't go overboard, (use good judgment, don't OVER REACT)
B. Don't get in a hurry, WAIT. (take your time and THEN SOME!)
C. Don't give up to soon. (look for the RIGHT ANSWERS)
D. Don't ever say I won't, (be willing to accept the RIGHT ANSWER)
E. Don't get discouraged, (in will doing, accept the CIRCUMSTANCE)
F. Don't for get to acknowledge, (our responsibility, in THE SITUATION)
G. Don't forget the wisdom, (in understanding both sides of THE SITUATION)
H. Don't forget the wisdom, (in discernment, of RIGHT & WRONG)
I. Don't forget the wisdom, (in knowing, when to STOP & LISTEN) # 6 Wait.

I do believe in changing a person's behaviors when they don't work, here is a good point, "we are never as tall as when we are at the lowest points in our life." It's not so much when things are going good, but when things are going bad that "makes or breaks a person."

At my age, I have finally gotten some peace and control of the storms, but this was not always true in my life. I found good decisions made me feel better it seemed like a series of bad decisions for a long time. I had gotten off track; it seemed to be a roller coaster ride because of the ups and downs, when the roller coaster gets off track they have to fix it the same is true in a person. I thought nothing would ever going to change, I thought I deserved bad things, I felt hurt. I think it will help if I give you an idea of what happened.

When I keep losing the same battles over and over, that made me feel I felt I deserved all of the bad things that had happened I am not going to tell you if you go to church "everything is going to be alright", "I am going to say pray about it" and see if there are any changes needed. Do more for God and He will bless you of course, but if you don't apply good sound principal and good judgment, prayer won't help either, you have brought about what has happened, "the law of sowing and reaping if you sow a "whorl wind you will a whorl wind" "the chickens will come home to roost" if we plan well, will we be successful in everything you do, NO, if you put your mind to the task or situation will that solve the problem, NO. I am talking about hard work and determination will changing things. If you don't have those basic qualities of perseverance, you are not going to be successful and solve the problems in your life.

At this point in my life, I realized things had gone wrong, the problem I was not OK with what happened, but I do feel better about myself, now you need to deal with your problems it is more important how you deal with things and in away that makes sense if you feel good about yourself. Then how you live with a bad situation, because you want something doesn't make it right, and it may not be good for you in the long run. I think these are some good principles to fellow when things go wrong.

I had to deal with my self-esteem at this point and what was happening to me during this time. There is a chain reaction when things go wrong I started to get better and other things will come together if you want to do something about them, OK. This can be a time of trying different things and trying to find out what you can do. Don't worry if takes time and effort, but don't give up to soon that is one of our common sense rules.

You have to decide what direction your life is going as it relates to your present circumstances.

How do you go about using sound principles if you don't know what will help you feel good about yourself. There is more to it, you have to make good choices, but they have to be applied in the right way. This can be a little bit confusing because you have been trying things and they have not worked, you need to keep on trying. Let me say failure is not always bad, but it can influence your self-esteem, now you know what work doesn't try other things until you find out what does work.

I hope you can see by now, if you are not getting to the root of the problems and deal with them, you maybe just deceiving yourself. You can hide them, but it's like the cat's litter box, the smile is still there, you have to clean the litter box from time to time. A person needs to look there life from time to time, you can do the same thing in their life. If a person is just covering up their problems and feelings, they are still there. How do you find a better way to deal with solving your problems?

The answers are there, but if you don't know how to find the answers they are not going to get better. How in the world do you expect to change your life for the better, learn how to discern the primary problems from the secondary problem areas?

The thing that really helped me learning how to cope with my problems coping may be the best and only answer and don't blame it on something else, some problems never go away. This was not an easy for me to accept because of my pride there are so many different variables and influences that cannot be controlled. I tried to find good solutions, but I learned to accept things rather than saying I don't like what has happened or feel like I don't deserve what happened. I dealt with the things I could change. There are many ways of handling what happens, I think I had tried most of the alternatives at one time or the other. I set goals and stuck with the things I knew in my heart to be right for me, that is when things changed, and I got control of my feelings and thinking this is when things turned around in my life.

I have talked about myself now I want to talk about my goals, I think it helps others to know how someone else has dealt with their feelings, but the most important thing is how my studies help me. You may choose other methods of help in your life and that is OK. I have a fresh new approach as you can see I have a different concept in how I have dealt with my problems and maybe my studies can help you decide what is best for you.

We should never "judge a book by its cover", in other words we should not "judge another person until we have walked a mile in their footsteps." A person needs to learn when they judge someone they are putting a stumbling block in their own life. I have dealt with my problems some for the good and others not so good, I think that is one of the bad things I thought they should have been punished for what they did wrong. I found good things came out of all my problems, I certainly have no right to judge another person. What is done is done is done, I use to think God should punish them because I felt I was punished; now I pray for them because God loves them and He loves me too.

There are other contributing factors a person has to deal with how do you fit into the equitation of what is happening in your life. Some would say this is the providence of God and others may say this was just bad luck. When you make a decision in your life, what methods did you use? Do you flip a coin or say whatever will be, will be. Again you can look at it from the human side did you use a logical course of action or used intuition as a point of view. I'm not so concerned how you deal with things, but rather are you dealing with your problems and how are you going to deal with your problems and set goals think it over before making a decision.

Please consider both aspects of a situation before you make your decision. I have prayed for things and they didn't happen or change things, rather than asking how did I fail in dealing with the situation. I did what I could and that has helped me to understand not everything has a successful conclusion. The good thing that happened out of all my failings I am still working on fitting the pieces of the puzzle together and that is exciting. I think we need to look at both sides of the coin if a person is going to be honest with themselves.

When you make a decision or a promise in your heart and mind to do something do you follow through or fail at every turn. A person has to work on solving problems as we use some illustrations from chapter 2.

Let's use a term all of us can understand "The honey noon stage" we know that is for a few weeks, months, to some it may last for years. What a person thinks has a lot to do with how a person goes about solving a problem usually within a few weeks things are right back where they stated. The decision part of any change may be the hardest step you take. When it is an up-hill battle a person begins to see things that are not working out.

The thing I have tried to emphasize there are several reasons why things go wrong and things don't get solved. There are idealisms within a person's thinking "don't worry about it until you have to" we think of ourselves as failures. The driving force should be weather you've done the right thing, next in line did you solve the problem? Some have the drive and motivation to get things done, but we cannot let that be the dominate factor in your life. Even if a person has successes, there is always the fear things will go wrong or failing to live up your expectations I know that seems like a paradox success does not guarantee happiness. Then on the other hand, we have the person that is a failure as for as societies standards and if it doesn't bother them, to them everything they do is a failure or can we change things.

A person has to deal with *their* **ideals** in a **situation,** and also in *their* mind-set. Say for instance love is supposed to make a person happy, that is the **ideal**. The ideal person is supposed to come along and make them happy for the rest of their life. That is an **ideal situation** of course. That is a storybook setting and ending, and it doesn't happen because people are not perfect. When a couple has children come into *their* life that adds to a couple's **ideal** of wanting **children** in their marriage. **Realistically** there is the sharing in a relationship, and I am using the term "who is the one going to wear the pants in the family?" Don't ask me who that should be because I know it is different in each marriage. In some marriages it's the man, and some cases I see the women being the dominant person. To me marriage is like this, "It is like a bed of roses". It can be beautiful, but you have to watch out for the thorns. The **ideal** should not be classified as perfect, but being **realistic,** the **real** truth in a **situation** or relationship is working together, and not pulling each other apart. I hope we can agree!

In theory an **ideal** is a hypothetical hypothesis set in principle for being a good person.

-    Esteem needs = is the value and worth *you* place on *your*self.

    (1) Self-actualization – achieving one's goals and possibilities.

    (2) Self-concept – **ideals** and **idealisms** they have about one's self,

This could relate to **ideals**:

- Conception – poor/low self-esteem.
- Self-concept – how *you* see yourself and how it influences *yourself* worth and esteem.
- Self-actualization needs = achieving possibilities,

This can bring about joy and happiness, another way to help a person is by describing *their* **feelings** about themselves and others, and another way to feel good by doing volunteer work. (Illustration)

    (1) The Spartans trained their young boys/men to believe in physical strength as an ally defending themselves and in war."

    (2) The Greeks believed in development of both body and mind. The arts, culture, sciences, and the intellectual.

    (3) Most societies/cultures follow the Athenians traditions similar to their culture.

Idealism

Here is another factor a person has to deal with **their idealism's** of one's self and others. The ever present the ability to fight against self and self-will, a person has to deal with the ever present *who am I?* There is another problem when a person lets *you* down, and a person ends up having to live with the **situation** and relationship whether it's **good** or **bad**. Why not try to make things better.

The psychology behind in **idealism** is not complete because in the nature of man, their **make-up** is about the **character** of a person. Their past creates a mixture of behaviors, but to be more specific a person's nature does not necessarily fit the criteria of what some people think. Some believe God is the final authority in a situation, others believe what a person wants is their right to choose in the situation, but never the less a person is faced with choices. If a person could be right more than half the time some play the "Stock Market" and become rich, some do become rich and never play the "Stock market" I hope *you* make the right choices.

There is a two-fold approach to rational thinking, **idealistically** (right always wins, and wrong always loses), but what about the third area, the gray area where people often have problems deciding how much is right and how far can they go before it becomes wrong. This is the functional side and **makeup of a person's character,** and how they deal with the different aspects to *their* being.

The help process continues when dealing with a person's demands and high self-awareness is essential in meeting the person's needs. You need to work out problems and keep in mind their needs for accomplishing set goals and living a better life along the way. Be sure the goals are achievable and they have the right prospective concerning the situation. It takes critical planning to meet those goals. Goals should be realistic and attainable so they can reach their goals and be successful in controlling their behaviors. In the course of helping a person they should see realistic goals if they are going to achieve a successful outcome in their situation. It may mean changing strategies and interventions techniques along the way if they don't succeed at first. It is important to clear up the demands or stresses that caused the situation in the first place.

ADDICTIONS&
IMPOWERMENT
RECOVERY FROM
MENTAL ILLNESS

Chapter 8

MENTAL DISORDERS & SELF-ACTUALIZATION

Actually, there are three basic areas in the brain which go through three primary responses for self-actualizations relating to one's self. It is there that the acts of aggression starts and being able to recognize those bad behaviors as they are developed during a child's growth stages it is also true as adults look at things. It is there the instinctive reactions and emotions occur and develop; called reflex actions, the commands which allow some involuntary actions to take control. They may seem to be uncontrollable acts at times, but the person for some reason can't control certain behaviors. I have given you some reasons why people do things without thinking. Now I am going explain some of these technical terms and help you understand why people do things. I have discussed human reasons why people act the way they do, but there is more to this study.

When people are going through a change in their life it can affect their ideal of one's self. We want to show you some of the diagnoses by professionals and what they think as they deal with addictions, and physical ailments. They may indicate why alcoholism and addictions maybe classified as mental illness, but there are many other studies showing the need for support services and programs that help as well or even better, we recognize and deal with them as cognitive behavior solutions and others treat those disorders, as diseases.

With professional help, many of these people can be helped with the right kind of treatment. Here are some ways where people do respond well to counseling and group sessions and live a normal productive life; I have seen hundreds of lives changed during my professional career. Others live with these disorders and some need professional help and others use medications. Some people don't respond to either of these treatments and continue to deal with these problems in their own way; as a result they continue to deal with the same problems for the rest of their life.

In spite of all this evidence, most people in this country still believe that when a person has been labeled with mental disorders they can recover. Even most rehabilitation professionals believe that mental illness is a condition. We believe that fear is a large factor in perpetuating the myth of no recovery. Those persons who are temporarily labeled normal are afraid that they too could enter the realms of mental problems. They are more comfortable thinking that those who have displayed severe emotional distress are qualitatively different, that somehow we have a genetically-based brain disorders that they don't have. This myth could not be continued if people who are labeled with mental illness can life a productive life, and no longer need medications in some case. In fact, if we are to better understand the recovery process we need to see that anyone can have mental issues. We need to see the connection between recovery and healing process. (See the expanded areas of our empowerment over mental disorders.)

* Bipolar Disorders
1.   a wide shift in feelings
2.   extreme mood swings
3.   can't tell the differences between fancies and realities
4.   overly depressed
5.   need professional help and/or medication

* Hallucinations disorders
1.   seeing a situation or things that did not happen
2.   making up a fabrication of the truth

* Delusion disorders
1.   might think or believe they are someone else
2.   a combination of twisted ideas and beliefs
3.   out of touch with reality
4.   living in dream world
5.   odd, peculiar in nature
6.   this behavior can be frightening and dangerous

* Reality disorders
1.   a very serious mental balance
2.   a twisted and false ideas and values
3.   usually very negative thinking

4. I'm right, everyone else is wrong
5. Serial killers and mentally disarranged

Three kinds eating disorders

* Anorexia
1. Description
   a. emotional problems
   b. weight loss
2. Characteristics
   a. affects more females than males
   b. extreme dieting
   c. no food or little food
   d. compulsive exercising
   e. frequent dieting and weight loss
   f. intense fear of becoming fat
   g. treatable with medication and psychotherapy when found early
3. Consequences
   a. low malnutrition rate
   b. menstruation stops
   c. low metabolism
   d. heart problems
   e. even death

* Bulimia disorders
1. Description
   a. emotional problems
   b. eating large p
   c. ortions in a short time
   2. severe dieting Characteristics
   a. inability to stop eating
      b. detect vomiting or use of laxatives
      c. extreme concentration on appearance
      d. feeling of being out of control and depression
   e. treatable with medication and psychotherapy
3. Consequences
   a. enlarged stomach

    b.   poor teeth

    c.   behavioral problems

    d.   psychological problems

    e.   over medication and drug use

* Compulsive overeating

1. Description

    a. emotional problems

    b. no purging

2. Characteristics

3. Consequences

    a. obesity / extreme body fat

    b. heart disease

    c. diabetes

    d. some kinds of skin cancer

    e. reduced life span

Just as the mind works with the mental, emotional works thought the mental process, we need to take care of our body. It is just as important maintain a good healthy mind.

First is getting to know more about this wonderful creation.

1. Body System

a. the body has more than 200 bonds.

b. provides our body structure.

c. protects the organs.

d. stores important minerals.

e. produces certain blood cells.

2. Nervous System and Sense Organs

a. The body system is the body's communication network.

b. There are two parts to the nervous system

The central nervous system is made up of the back brain which is connected to the spinal cord.

Now let's look at any situation and see what could have caused the alarms to go off, when you look at something that looks good, but you know in your heart if it's bad or wrong.

Some people use excuses, "Be Careful in CAPITAL Letters." If the bad looks good at the time it is probably wrong, there is usually some excitement and fun in the wrong thing for a while, a person may be in more trouble if it seems innocent at the time. Be careful this is when a person tends to let their guard down.

We need to understand when something is wrong in our everyday situations people can get into a routine and the excitement takes over. I think this should sound familiar when this happens people have gotten into routine, which can lead to boredom and burn-out.

These are some of the cross over benefits from the other aspects in your life. There can be a multitude of different factors and complexities to deal with and in any given situation. In addition, this makes your life is complicated a personal wants and needs take over people tend to make excuses because things are not going their way. Let's see if we can't make your life more interesting and fun at the same time.

The idea is to get a good balance in all aspects of your life. The next thing a person needs to deal with is their Self-Expression. This is going to be a challenge when it comes to balancing your self-esteem against your self-will, a person's pride should not stand in the way of expressing yourself, look for ways that helps you grow.

There is something within that keeps a person going and allows them to find a way to rebound mentally if their spirit is not broken, and their well is not broken, that is where some people fail. I think if a person rebuilds physically they are also building some mental toughness by this I mean it can give a person a mental edge at times having this part of your life under control, but not a prerequisite. A person has to deal with their self-esteem and understand *who they are*, there is that delicate balance from our self-image to dealing with our self-esteem I want emphasis that does not mean how much money you have.

Of course, thinking too much of one's self is a false narrative we want a person to consider their pride a person should not be boastful at the same time. The "Bible says "pride comes before a fall", consider your self-esteem as you look at yourself I ask this question are you too hard on yourself, a person can get down and feel bad about themselves, "RIGHT". I know that it is going to be difficult to do in respect to self-esteem because a person should feel good about themselves, we should want to better ourselves, one way is to feel good about yourself and someone else may see you as bragging or boasting about your accomplishments. Value and balance is usually measured in self-worth not by wealth or success. There has to be a better way to value a person's life; I hope I can shed some light on that kind of value, which is placed on a person's self-worth in chapters 9 - 14. The materialistic side of a person and the soul of a (man or women) are two different aspects of *who you are* and what you want out of life.

What (he or she) has done make either makes or breaks their character and what a person is made of will establish their value and esteem? The person is what counts because (he or she) is the only one who can set themselves free or give a person peace of mind. There is a saying "if momma is not happy no one else will be happy." Now we need to know how the body soul and mind correlate with each other in regards to self-esteem.

How can a person enhance their ability to the point of pursuing new pursuits or by taking training for a present or new job or set goals? The ability to solve problems starts in planning for success. The ability to define your limits is in the ability to use your innate physical and mental abilities, also determined by how well you will do in life. To what degree does **ego** and **pride** play in doing things there is an optimal degree of anxiety as a person seeks to do anything. **Motivation** will propel a person into accomplishing goals. In this sense, the **inner person** is being able to master aptitude that affects themselves and others, either by facilitating or what is interfering with their goals.

This part of the study describes "how to set a goal which is self-imposed concepts and delay "gratification" to the point of self-sacrifice to reach your goal, it is perhaps the most essential part of *self-regulation*:

- The ability to deny impulses in the service of a goal
- Whether it is building or solving problems

- Or pursuing life to the fullest.

To underscore the role of **inner personal** motives look at your Meta Cognitive ability in determining how well or how poorly you have done something did you accomplish your goal? Use your ability to use other mental capacities such how well you get along with others as you help them reach their goals.

Explanation for saying "we have two minds" what does this mean.

1. the emotional mind = has do with a person's feelings
2. the rational mind = how and what a person thinks in a situation.

There are two fundamentally different ways of knowing how interactions work the emotions drive the mental and psychic phenomena. At the same time, knowing impulses are defined as emotional responses and prejudices have to be taken into account as the rational mind kicks in. The emotions charge the make-up in the different sections of the brain and they create activity or a response.

There is a distinction between the heart and the mind, knowing something is right in the heart and the conviction is thinking with the rational mind something is right.

The more intense the feelings the more dominate the mind-set becomes and the more ineffective the rational mind will be able to evaluate and function well.

Self-actualization and motivation go hand in hand when you are determined to get something done, often you feel motivated to make things happen, rather than to wait for things to happen.

In psychological terms, self-determination presses toward motivation and the processes involve people who strive on three basic needs. Those needs are relatedness, autonomy, and above all else, competency. Others may think of self-determination as inspiration that embellishes the person to react to their needs and how to satisfy those needs and compromise things at the same time. The autonomy of self-determination is the process of building independence, sufficiency, self-rule, and so on. People often build determination on trust, confidence, reliance, faith, hope, beliefs, and needs.

The world leads us into many struggles, which makes it harder for us to fulfill basic human needs let alone build self-determination. In order to accomplish a task, however while battling through situations and dealing with one's self and their need for success can get in the way of accomplishing their goal.

Self-Actualization starts with exploring the different aspects of self-esteem. When people feel rewarded they often feel contentment and joy as well. Their interest in activities often improve, because rewards make people more apt to function when they get rewarded for what they have done, or feel rewarded because they have succeed or at least think they have done something.

While the questions presents thoughtful suggestions for various aspects of living, such as parenting, labor/working, and school. There are still other variant aspects to consider before any true resolutions are apparent. The question is to create a child's interest in a given subject and the expectation of rewarding the child with good things to develop and increase their interests.

The controversy comes when a person sends mixed signals that are contrary to their expectations that are in accord with how to reward themselves and how they are able to interact with others. The common theory of self-actualization suggests that relatedness, autonomy, and competence can inspire motivation without rigid penalties that accompanies the other it only compromises the entity and autonomy. The development of competence through rewards and at other times threats could cause a person to feel pushed into doing something they ordinary did not want to do. Rewards are often determined by the individual who views the results and they reward themselves if it seems good. If someone innate ability, determination, or actualization was compromised when they did not get what they wanted or expected; it could be a lack of self-actualization. If the entity views use praise as a reward or something other than a bribery or threat, thus the person would likely feel motivated to perform.

This entity within a person should build the self-actualization of parents, teachers, and others to encouragement, support, and praise them for their efforts. The idea is to encourage self-actualization and have a greater emphasis on their competences rather than a child's ability to perform for rewards they need both to build on their self-esteem.

Based on the knowledge we see self-esteem is also the process of building self-actualization. When you combine the two, it builds more productive skills, which ensures that they will succeed in almost every endeavor.

Available Observations

Such opinions are based on assumptions formulated on generalities, but over use of these strategies form false solutions even when it is clear a person should not do something. In other words, we fall prey to the *representative* strategies of assuming that each solution is representative of their own assumptions, because others may not assume it to be true. Reliance on Meta Cognition means there is a need for awareness it may not be evident when someone offers an opinion or is persuaded by another person's argument.

"What do you mean that cigarettes cause cancer?" I have an aunt who smokes cigarettes, and she's was perfectly healthy at age eighty-two!" Such arguments are often presented in defiance of a viewpoint, and even use this logic because they have a forceful point of view, or to generalize a single statement and accept their view. We act as though the speaker's aunt is representative of all cigarette smokers, even though there is ample proof to support there are other reasons why she lived to be eighty-two.

In other words hearing about an eight-two-year old ant that smoked might not be enough evidence to convince a person that smoking is not hazardous, but hearing it from "The American Cancer Society might carry more evidence of how bad smoking can be to your health."

In some settings, we do seem to realize that a member of a particular category is typical, and some would hesitate to draw conclusions about the entire category based on one observation or just a few instances is not good evidence. That is why we don't expect you to accept our studies without proof.

However, a different arguments work against such self-corrections. This is called *confirmation bias*; it actually takes several different forms.

1. When people are given an opportunity to seek out new information, they tend to seek information that will confirm their beliefs, rather than from information that might challenge their beliefs and why they should do things.
2. If people are given the right kind of evidence that is consistent with their beliefs and information that is inconsistent, they tend to take the belief more seriously and discount those beliefs they don't agree with.
3. A person may not be influenced by the new evidence even if it doesn't support their views and beliefs.
4. A person maybe impressed if it the evidence strengthens and supports their views and beliefs.
5. In contrast they can be skeptical and critical if the evidence does not support their views and beliefs or they ignore the argument altogether.

Confirmation bias may be genuinely helpful in many ways it may also disconfirmation and can be more helpful in search of the true about one's self. One the confirmation may show a hypothesis is true, but countless confirmations may seem to prove something to be true. Never-the-less confirmation bias is a powerful argument in favor of your beliefs and views, but scientific evidence is only one evidence, there could be stronger arguments in the defense of your learning, more about what a person believes people become more alert both by dealing with their problems and drawing a conclusion based on the experience.

Now let's see if the proof comes from the assessment of self-worth is valid; however, a person that has positive results are more likely to believe in themselves. The point I am making, if it doesn't inflate their pride, and when they believe there are good solutions to their problems they are more likely to make better decisions in the future.

As a clinical counselor, I must confront the real issues in a person or couples life. I may or may not need to take the position as a mediator, I am a problem solver, and I want you to become a problem solver. A person's needs to know more about their backgrounds including their family, social, economic, has a bearing on what or how (he or she) thinks, or believes.

At this point one or both should be able to state what is bothering them and the problems involved. At this point a person should look back at why things are still bothering one or both of them. There are always two sides to be considered and to be fair I must look both viewpoints.

The real problem is when you have not been able to solve these problems before you came to me. There is usually more than one solution or alternatives to any problem, as we will discuss now I want to help you solve problems in this part of our study. If two people can't agree, I will have them think it through again, and come back with what they think is wrong, and why; or why the problem can or cannot be solved at this point. There is hope as long as a person or persons are willing work on the problem.

The best way is to be able to talk about your problems I believe in taking on small problems that are solvable and by taking them one-step at a time, and then see how you have gone about selecting the alternatives.

Next, see how you are able to communicate with each other person during this time and together find the points of disagree and the best way to solve the problem that both of you feel good about.

Later on you must be able to define what are the under lying problems within yourself that you need to worked on, at the same time you must confront the deeper feelings and your self- actualization needs. A determination is how you relate or go about your methods in getting things done; if there is faulty reasoning that might be the reason you are not able to solve the problem. Then think of what has worked or has not work it may be a matter of a sin or some faults in your own life, how you relate to the problems, and what can be done.

Now, let's try to understand the mental and spiritual aspects in your relationships and how it is affecting both of you. This can only be done when each person learns to face their responsibility in solving a problem and still help them to meet their needs. You must be true to your own feeling and beliefs at the same time in order to solve any problem or relationship. If you have not dealt anyone of the two aspects properly, a person will have problems with each segment of their life and their relationships. If a person has hurt someone, how people relate to God and forgiveness is the paramount in the healing process.

This brings us to one of the primary reasons why problems aren't solved. The human element of putting off things and not taking on the challenge of doing something about the problem. The problem will hinge on wanting to get even or revenge, hatred or any of those types of feelings, while taking on the new challenges you should be able to forgive the other person, put it behind you, or at least to some degree.

Conclusion in terms of self-esteem

I have spent a great deal of time dealing with emotions, motivations, and how to deal with what is known as interactions within your relationships and life. There is the personal feelings and the need to be able to reason things out in your mind and how a person deals with their logic and reasoning. How a person tries to meet their needs regardless of their wants and desires and self- actualization. Now that we've look at the reasoning process. We want to explain how we use an hypothesis to present an idea we believe to be right, or by using reasoning and common sense. We are going to deal with several basic premises as we have dealt with self-esteem let's define hypothesis as a method reasoning.

Definition of Hypothesis: *noun* {15}
Etymology: **Greek**, from *hyposthenia to put* under, suppose, from *hypo- + tithenai* to put
    1 a:an assumption or concession made for the sake of argument
     b: an interpretation of a practical situation or condition taken as the ground for action
    2 : a tentative assumption made in order to draw out and test its logical or empirical consequences
    3 : the antecedent clause of a conditional statement

Definition of Logic: *noun* {16}
Etymology: Middle English *logik,* from Anglo-French, from Latin *logica,* from Greek
logike, from feminine of *logikos* of reason, from *logos* reason -- more at LEGEND
Date: 12th century
    1 a: (1) a science that deals with the principles and criteria of valide of inference
    and demonstration : the science of the formal principles of reasoning
    : (2) a branch or variety of logic <modal *logic*> <Boolean *logic*>

:   (3) a branch of semiotic; *especially :* SYNTACTICS
:   (4) the formal principles of a branch of knowledge
b: (1) a particular mode of reasoning viewed as valid or faulty
:   (2) RELEVANCE, **PROPRIETY**
c: interrelation or sequence of facts or events when seen as inevitable or predictable
d: the arrangement of circuit elements (as in a computer) needed for computation; *also :* the circuits themselves
http://www.merriam-webstercollegiate.com/cgi-bin/Eleventh?book=Dictionary&va=theory   1/24/2005

I will use other references to support my logic, there are two (2) broad classes of representations as found by some psychologists, next I will deal with **analogical** and **symbolic reasoning.** I'm going show you how to understand and evaluate the true in other ways if there is faulty argument you will need to be able to know if you have come up with a good solution, the same is true in a personal argument. My purpose is to help you determination if one or both of you are at fault and why? There is usually a reason why you don't come up with a good solution.

Restructuring Methods

Simple reaction tools such as deep breathing and relaxing can help calm down angry feelings. There are books and courses that can teach you relaxation techniques, and once you learn them you can call on them in any situation. If you are involved in a relationship where both partners are hot-tempered, it might be a good idea for both of you to learn these techniques.

Simply put means changing the way you think. When you're angry or upset, your thinking can be exaggerated and overly dramatic. Try replacing these thoughts with more rational thoughts. For instance, instead of telling yourself; how awful it is, instead it's just terrible, even if everything's ruined, tell yourself; it's frustrating, and it's understandable that I'm upset about it, but it's not the end of the world and it doesn't help me to get angry it is not going to fix it anything.

Be careful of the words like 'never' and 'always' when talking about yourself or someone else. These kinds of thoughts never work or help, "if feel you're always forgetting things" it maybe miss leading in the way you

177

think, put things in groups that you understand they will also serve to make you feel better there are ways to solve the problem. When people alienate and humiliate people, others who might otherwise be willing to work with you on a solution.

Remind yourself that you want to help them fix the problem, when you do that you will feel better and you may actually make others feel better rather than worse.

Think logically and don't justify your feelings, remind yourself that the world is not against you, you maybe just experiencing a rough day and it is really not that bad. Do this each time you feel bad or don't let things get the best of you, and it will help you have a more balanced perspective.

People tend to demand things: fairness, appreciation, agreement, or if you are unwilling to do things their way. As part of our cognitive restructuring, people need to become aware of their demanding nature and translate their expectations into desires for others. In other words, saying I would like something is healthier way, "I demand something" or "you might say would you like to do something else for a change."

When you're unable to get what you want can you turn the experience into more normal experience rather than frustration, disappointment, don't get angry. Some people use other ways to avoid feeling that hurt them, they tend to hurt people if things don't go their way and they can quickly become irrational.

Problem Solving

Sometimes, our frustration is caused by the fact it is an inescapable problem. Not all feelings are misplaced; often it's a healthy natural response to most difficulties. There is also a cultural belief that every problem has a solution, and it adds to the frustration when we can't find out what caused it and for what season if there isn't any good answers pick one of the best solutions. The best thing in that kind of situation is not to force things, but find the best solution, but it is important how you handle and face the problem.

Make a plan, and check your progress along the way understand the things that up-set you people who have trouble with planning things might find a good guide is to organize things. Companies use a time management evaluations. Resolve to give it your best, but don't punish yourself if an answer doesn't come right away. If you approach it with your best intentions and efforts, and make a serious attempt to face the problem, be patience and don't fall into the trap of do-nothing thinking, even if the problem does not get solved right away.

Better Communications skills

Angry people tend to jump to conclusions, it is better to think things through before coming to a conclusion. The first thing to do in a heated discussion, slow down and think through your response don't say the first thing that comes into your head, but slow down and think carefully about what you want to say. At the same time, listen carefully to what the other person is saying and take your time and think it through before answering.

Listen, too, to what is they are saying. For instance, do you agree with what they are saying let them have their personal option, and you should have a connection with what they are saying. If (he or she) starts complaining about what is wrong, don't retaliate by painting yourself in a corner as a know it all or find fault with what they are saying, or want to be an albatross around someone's-neck. It's natural to get defensive when you're criticized, but don't fight back instead, listen to what is the underlying problem the person might feel neglected and unloved. It may take a lot of patient when it comes to asking questions on your part, and it may require some breathing space if things are not going well, but don't let things get to the breaking point in a situation let the discussion continue, but don't let it get out-of-control. Keeping your cool head keep the situation from becoming a disastrous situation.

Humor is an antidote can help diffuse a situation for one thing, it can help you get a more balanced and perspective to what is going in a person. This usually happens when a person calls someone a name or refers to them in some negative way, stop and picture what you are saying to the other person literally think about what you've said. If you're at work and you think of a coworker as a 'dirt bag' or a 'single-cell life form,' for example, picture a large bag full of dirt (or an amoeba) sitting at your colleague's desk, talking on the phone, go to the meeting with a humorous ideate. Do this whenever you see a person you don't like think of a mental image that comes into your mind about another person if you can, draw a mental picture of what the actual thing might look like. This will take a lot of the edge off the situation; and humor can always be relied on to help unknot a tense situation.

The underlying message *'things ought ta go my way!'* people tend to feel that they are morally right, that are things blocking or changing a person's way of thinking or plans, but when things get unbearable and they feel they should NOT have to suffer this way. Maybe other people do, but-not-them! When you feel that urge, that suggests something is wrong, picture yourself as a store owner that owns a store or office space, striding alone and having their way in all situations. I hope this is not a picture of you dealing with a failing business, in business the more chances you take, think, maybe you are being irresponsible. You'll also realize how unimportant the things you thought were imposable are possible, don't overlook the consequences.

There are two cautions in any thing you do. First, don't try to 'laugh them off' any problem needs attention; rather, use good judgment to help you to face them more constructively. Second, don't give into others who make remarks, sarcastism; that's just another form of an unhealthy expression.

What have these techniques taught you or what do they have in common may be its a refusal to take yourself too seriously, but it's often accompanied by good ideas, if you examine things and they work, it helps to laugh instead of crying over spilt milk.

SELF-ESTEEM & DEDUCTIVE REASONING?

In *deductive reasoning,* the person tries to determine whether certain conclusions can be drawn from *deductive reasoning* a set of initial assertions or *premises.* According to logical reasoning, the validity of the deduction depends on a small number of rules, framed in terms of certain logical support systems that helps in building a conclusion, do you follow these rules?

A classic example of deduction involves the analysis of *syllogisms,* a reasoning process that goes back as far as Aristotle. Each syllogism contains two premises and a conclusion, and the question is whether the conclusion follows logical reasoning that forms the premises. Two examples of such syllogisms (you need three valid arguments, if one is invalid) then some of the reasoning is false both premises have to be true to form a good conclusion that not always true in arguing a point of view:

All A and *B* have to be true for C to be true.
B is true in C.

Therefore, all A's are C. (which is valid in one point only)
All A's are *B*.
Some *B's* are C if C is true, but not necessarily valid point.

Therefore, all A is C. (C is invalid unless A & B are true)
Here are the same syllogisms, but are framed in concrete terms:
All artwork is beautiful.
All beautiful things should be cherished.

Therefore, all artwork should be cherished. (valid)
And:
All artwork is beautiful, but does not fit that they are cherished.
Some beautiful things are costly.

Therefore, all artwork is costly. (Invalid because it breaks one of the premises, if one is wrong it breaks preemies sought to be right)

Notice: that the validity of these (or any) syllogisms depends only on whether the conclusion *follows logical* forms the premises. The truth of the premises must have two to be true, and the plausibility of the conclusion must be true but if the premise is flawed any of its premises then the conclusion is false, even if the conclusion is right they are irrelevant to whether the syllogism itself is logical. Thus, the following syllogisms are observed as logically and valid:
All artwork is made out of beans.

All items made out of beans can be turned into clocks.

Therefore, all artwork can be turned into clocks. (Invalid)

That is why people use faulty arguments and expect people to except their conclusion. Some clocks could have beans as a part of the clocks borders, but that does not have anything to do with working parts of the clock.

WHAT IS INDUCTIVE REASONING?

In deductive reasoning, it must be reasoned from the general to the particular statement, as a general rule (All people are mortal) ask how it applies to a particular case (Pat Smith is a person therefore she is a mortal person). It is important understand the type of reasoning one is *inductive reasoning,* in this case the process is reversed reasoning it comes from the particular to the general. Consider a number of different instances where things went wrong and try to determine why, the general rule covers the overall assumption is true and if not then there is no inductive reasoning.

Inductive reasoning is at the heart of any reasoning, because the object of the argument is to determine what common principles underlie the premise. To do this, formulate a *hypotheses tentative* assertions about the world being round and then they seek to prove their point. But, many hypotheses are developed by false methods, they seek to understand (and thus predict and influence a conclusion) such as an argument / the conclusion may be right. It is hard to accept the conclusion if a person has availed point rather than argue with someone, instead give a good reason why their point of view is right.

By observing the behavior of a person when they are in an argument largely depends on (his or her) mood at the time. Say for instance you can't get the car to start, to seek a hypotheses you will look at what could be wrong and why it won't start. The hypotheses you come up with may not be correct, but nonetheless if you attempt to comprehend what is wrong by subjugation under a more general rule the conclusion is right something is wrong because it won't start and you is could be wrong and then you come up with a conclusion the car won't start, but the problem is why it won't start.

How do we form hypotheses about the behavior of a person, and then compare it to the misbehavior of an automobile, there is correlation in each deduction when we come up with a deduction something is wrong, we are strongly influenced by the past evidence of what is wrong.

How often has the politician kept his promises?

How frequently has lack of sleep been the source of a person's bad mood?

How often has the car's performance been improved by getting better gas?

How often has a person *failed*?

The same pattern is also evident in studies in which people have been asked which is the more common comparison.

Death by homicide or death by stroke?

Death from car crashes or death from stomach cancer?

People generally identify with the first clause in each pair statements as to the more common; although the opposite is the case (Death by a stroke is ten times more likely than death by homicide.) Estimates in these cases are clearly influenced by the Meta Cognition of awareness of the subject matter: murders and car crashes make front page stories and are common encounters and those that are easily identified. This provides an available advantage and in turn forms the biases for a person's opinion.

The availability of reasoning is based on a wide range is based on the information, including cases in which a person is trying to make decisions of considerable importance. It is troubling when opinions are based on generality rather than on facts this form of reasoning can on occasion lead to an error in precipitation. The same can be said for another common strategy, one that we employ when seeking to generalized forms of information.

This is has been one part of a major study on human reasoning that has to do with a person's self-esteem and determination; I hope it has helped you understand the person inside of you. I have individualized our studies based on a person's needs and that is why I created (**SOS**) self-help studies and information.

Regardless of your faith or even if you do not consider yourself a Christian, there is someone out there that will be able to share your views there is a common bond as we share our experiences, and that is what brings us closer together. Our goal is to help you deal with the mental, physical and your **self-esteem**. There should be something in our programs to help you regardless of what you believe we believe in knowing *who you are* or what you have done no matter how bad the situation. The important thing is turning your life around we want you to make that decision. Even if you have failed in the past please give (**SOS**) self-help studies and study guides a chance and try our methods of help. We are going to deal with other facets in this study on **Self-Esteem.**

Also, nothing can happen until *you* move and do something for *yourself. You* hold the key that unlocks the doors, and there are three keys to unlock those prison doors in a *person's life*.

Sometimes going in the right **direction** didn't seem right because my life seemed so wrong for so long. There were times when I was wrong, and I knew it, but "I did things my way", as the song title by Elvis Presley, even when it seemed the worst I believed the best was yet to come. In that case I was living in hope, when hope didn't seem possible. In my life I found that it is important to be true to *yourself,* "pride comes before a fall" is right, also low self-esteem "is a down fall", and there were other factors that go into my decisions and choices. I have dealt with the **primary** and **secondary influences** I do not consider myself a failure, but I do believe I have made some bad choices, and yet I have turned my life around.

I went through some valleys and there was a time of low self-esteem. Any one of these experiences can bring about a devastating effect on a person's life and how they deal with a situation. There were certainly a lot of different emotions to deal with consequently it affected the way I use to think and react.

As I look back over my life there were some special times, but there is no doubt in my mind they were the toughest times, I had to dig down inside and face the storms in my life. As I look back at those obstacles and health problems, it brought out the best in me. I stopped and took a look at myself, and listened to what was going on inside. In those days there was the agony of defeat in my life.

SETTING GOALS, CHANGE THINGS, TRY SOME THING NEW, DO YOU REALLY WANT CHANGES?

Chapter 8

PROBLEM SOLVING & SELF-ACHIEVEMENT

I want reemphasis the importance of self-esteem if you put your mind to it and put some effort to the extent you are able to deal with the amount of success and the reason a person fails will depend on if you want to accomplish anything, that is also true in solving a problem. There is more to life in regards responsibility.

- Human needs
- Human relationships
- Human boundary's in life

I want you to redefine some of our new guidelines in your life this is very important if you want to deal with your responsibility. The love and hate are at opposite ends of the spectrum. It is hard to believe we can love someone so much and things go so bad to the point of how much a person dislikes or hates at sometimes. How we relate to each other will play a significant role in your life. It is important as you look at your responsibility and why you're past relationships with other things have gone wrong there are reasons why I had failed in my relationships. More than anything else this will determine how I am able to deal with others and to what degree my prejudices and hurt feelings were involved and how they have affected me and my present relationships, it will show up in the situations I am dealing with now.

You should look for some joy in your life and relationships. That is a starting place in how to accomplish things.

Now we are going to deal with other contributing factors, there are reasons why people fail; this affects a person their pride which is the nerve center of a person as it relates to loving people and so on. We have problems dealing with our failures and that is why it is so hard to know *who you are* and what is the best way to deal with our failures, I hope by now you understand *who you are* in relation to your self-esteem. The way to measure your life is by *knowing what is going on in your life* and that means dealing with your responsibility in a situation.

Then what is your attitude is very important of course, but more importantly is how you take on the challenges in the circumstances. A person can get out-of-control the pressures could be causing a person to lose control at work and that can affect their home. That is why a person needs "Meta Cognition Awareness and Personal-Attention" as a person deals with their situations and relationships.

The way we do this is seeing the way you get things done, and how you can help yourself at the same time. Your needs may vary if you are a (women or man) how you meet the challenges in your life regardless of your sex. In part of our study we have dealt with the different things a person incorporates into their thinking process.

What you think of yourself (self-esteem) and how you relate to that person will determine your value your (self-worth). How a person sees things has a lot do with how they think. The eyes of a person are like the soul they see things, but are they as they seem or look; let's see how the five senses affect a person's thinking. All of them have triggering mechanisms that triggers another sense and puts all of them into action, not so fast how do these other four inner actions work the other senses such as taste, smell, feel, and touch.

I don't think we can study the person without giving some credence to another sense that is just as vivid we are going to focus on a person's responds to adversity. I have given two examples of people who were blind and how they used their other senses in unique ways, the other senses kick in and activate other response to help the body and mind to function and have a productive life as we have just experienced in the lives of Ray Charles and Fanny Crosby story.

The Self-Control:

We are going to expand on our responsibility and how a person deals with what happens and what a person's does in their walk and talk, next will be your accountability in your relationships.

There is evidence that testifies to the fact people who know how to manage their own feelings well, who read, and deal effectively with other people **feelings** are at an advantage in life. Whether its romance, and they usually have intimate feelings for others. People who are **emotional stable** govern themselves and are will organized in handling their **emotional skills** they are successful in their personal life and in their vocation. They are more likely to be content and happy, mastering their mindset, plus being productive. People, who cannot master at least to some degree **self-control** over their fear, anxiety, battling their ability to focus on life, job, etc.

Self-Control may mean delaying self-gratification and stifling impulsiveness that underlie accomplishments. And being able to get into the "flow" this is a state of mind which enables an outstanding performance. People who have this skill tend to be more highly productive and effective in whatever they undertake.

Dealing with core emotions, guilt and remorse / depression

We will deal with two basic negative emotions; I believe **love** is the core emotion in the primary sense of emotions. There are stronger emotions as a person relates to their negative feelings.

Another aspect is **fear** I feel that these two emotions will show-up in a person and learning the truth about themselves. Although, there is that core **"emotion"** in terms of the negative dimensions, taking the endless nuances in our **emotional life** there are others which brings about **emotions** like **depression"**.

There is another way to look at fear and the terms of being fearless, "In the case Andrea's parents Gary and Mary Jane Chauncey, who performed a heroic act of saving their child's life they saved her life by pulling her out of an "Amtrak Train", after the bridge had collapsed crashing into a river in the Louisiana Bayou Country. "Thanking first of their daughter, the couple saved Andrea as the water rushed into the sinking train; somehow, they managed to push Andrea through a window to rescue her." There is no doubt that this kind of story has been repeated countless times.

This act of self-sacrifice reflects the purpose and the role and the love of parents; these high emotions can be felt at certain times in any situation. It was certainly an impulse, but the urgency of the situation out weighted their fear in part this is a different kind of **emotional feelings putting** life and death above everything at the time above personal survival they saved their child. This story certainly proves a higher motivation that can come from any **emotional situation**.

The argument for the core **emotions** hinges to some extent on the discovery that specific expressions of (**fear, anger, sadness, enjoyment**). When we think of **negative emotions** in terms of **anger, sadness, fear, shame,** and **guilt**, as it has to do with the endless nuances of our **emotional experiences**.

An increase in the brains activity center can bring about **positive feelings** an increase in available energy, and quieting anxiety. There is likely going to be a physiological shift caused by an **emotional upset**, the mind, body, and spirit should deal with it, but always. The body and mind needs general rest and well-being to handle the tasks ahead with enthusiasm, vitality and striving to reach a person's goals. The biological makeup of a person has a psychological effect on **happiness, joy, love, surprise,** and again if there are **negative** signs of **fear, sadness, hurt, anger, disgust, bitterness**, and on the other side is **guilt** and **remorse involved**."

Now let's start with a person who gets a gift this sets off an emotion, what do you think? Now let's think of another way which is not as emotional, but just as important how to deal with achievements and goals can cause emotions of a different kind.

Life is about **SELF-ACHIEVEMENT** in a person's life.

The view of IQ is monolithic kind of intelligence it is not crucial for life's successes, but rather a wide spectrum of intelligences are the keys to success there are several keys listed:

- Verbal = communication
- Mathematical-logical = alacrity
- Spatial capacity = outstanding art or architect
- Kinesthetic genius = displayed in the physical fluidity and grace
- Interpersonal skills = like those of a therapist such as Carl Rogers or a world-class leader such as Martin Luther King Jr.

"Intrapsychic" = capacity that could emerge, on the other hand, the brilliant insights of Sigmund Freud, but with less fanfare, in the inner contentment that arises from attuning to one's life to be in keeping with one's true feelings.

Optimism and hope are not like being helplessness and despair; we can learn how to deal them as we deal with our life's experiences in the terms of self-achievement, when people believe in what they are doing they are much more likely to succeed.

The basic belief that leads to optimism, remember the opposite leads to *setbacks* or *failures* that are due to circumstances we cannot do something about or the ability to change them for the better."

Of course hope springs eternal in being optimistic "looking for the silver lining", author *unknown*, is another way of looking at the situations positive ways, it is also another way of predicting to some degree the successes in our lives, as we have just related in our life.

You may get it Wrong before you get right   **Pages 1 of 2 [12]**
     Self-Improvement
"The Purpose of Life is to LIVE

Ray Terris
     "What is success? Success is truly living. Struggling to survive is not living.

You really can take control of your life and succeed. Unfortunately life does not come with a manual. Most people struggle through life and wonder   why   they   never   get-anywhere.

You do not have to be one of them.

Your life should be yours to command. Learn how. I will give you fair warning here, becoming successful is not easy, otherwise more people would be successful.
Some of the content of this site may make you feel uncomfortable, but not as uncomfortable as failure. To achieve success you will have to change. If you are not successful then you are doing something wrong.

One of the hardest things for us humans to do is admit when we are wrong, even to ourselves. So if you are reading one of my pages and it seems like I am pointing a finger at you then grit your teeth and keep reading.

Self-Improvement

Everything in your life starts with you. Self-improvement will lead to life improvement. You are the foundation of your life, the decisions that you make, the actions that you take, they are what create your life. If your life is not the way you want it to be then only you can change it. Yes you can get help from other people, but only if you accept their help.

It is often difficult for a person to accept the fact that they are totally responsible for the condition of their life. I mentioned this briefly in but I will expand on it here.

Laying blame and shame on other people or things is the fastest route to losing control of your life. When you place blame outside yourself you have said that somebody else has more control than you do. Essentially you act like a leaf in the wind, blown all over the place by other people's desires and whims. How can you change your life if you give control to outside sources?

Accepting Control

This does not mean that you never let others control you, of course you do. When you get a job your boss will tell you when to work, police officers will control your actions, so will traffic signals. In fact when you look at it a large part of your life is controlled by other people and things. You are still responsible, it is still your decision whether to accept their control or not. Most of the time these controls are good and you accept the control for the benefit of yourself and others.

One time I was stuck in traffic, there had been an accident and a police officer was directing traffic onto a different route. When I came up to him he waved for me to turn left, I refused to accept that control. He started to get annoyed and waved even harder. Then I pointed to the nurse who was pushing a wheelchair across the intersection, he understood.

What if I had blindly followed his control and hit those pedestrians, who would have been responsible? But your honor, he made me do it, ha! If someone was having a heart attack and you were driving them to the hospital would you sit and wait at stop lights?

So the first major step in self-improvement is accepting full responsibility for your life. Read Self-Control other self-help (book).

Controlling the Uncontrollable

Are there circumstances that you don't have control over? Apparently so, floods, fires, accidents etc. But you are still in control of your reactions to them. You can let them defeat you, or you can face them head on and handle them.

How about when someone close to you dies, you do not have control over that and you're initial reactions are not likely to be controlled. Then what, do you give up, go into such grief that you stop living your life? You have just ended two lives, maybe even dishonored their memory by blaming them.

Wouldn't it be so much better to thank them for the time you did have together? Would you give up the memories of those times or say it would have been better to never have known them, of course not. Honor their memory by living your life to the fullest, even do something they always wanted to do.

In another page I will show you how much more control you have over life than you realized, see Creative Visualization. For now let us continue with self-improvement.

Things to Do

There are many obvious steps to self-improvement, exercise, better diet, education and so on. The fact that you are reading this shows that you are on the right track. How about tackling some of the areas that you know you are weak in. I used to be very shy, at social gatherings I would usually sit in a corner hoping that someone nice would talk to me. I would have to know someone for quite a while before I would initiate a conversation. The thought of talking to a crowd of people was terrifying.

Shyness is a very uncomfortable and limiting affliction. I decided to face it head on, I went to auction school. I could have chosen a public speaking course or anything that would put me in front of an audience. It took a little time but after running a few auctions and public presentations I started to enjoy it. Now I love standing in front of a crowd, I even took an acting part in a local play, it was great.

A simple self-improvement technique is to do something new every day or at least once a week. It does not have to be big, take a different route to work, try some different food, shop in a different store. If you continually try new things or change your routines then any fears you may have about making major changes will be reduced.

I am continually working on this website so there will be more pages to help in your self-improvement. See Mind Power, Leadership and Self-Control.

You have already started by reading these pages. Keep going, take control, make some changes and improve your life. Remember your success depends on you."

http://www.what-is-success.com/self-improvement.html 05/29/2010

1. **Pride & Humility:** Can these two work together, sure they can?
2. **Emotional Reactions,** the ups & downs,
   (**Mentally - Emotionally – Physically**) Actions & Reactions
3. **Self-will & Social-Behavior & Personal Problems, Habits, Traits, & Patterns:**

The Challenge in dealing with one's MENTAL **and** EMOTIONAL **aspects in your** LIFE!

Now I am going ask you, how you are handling the different areas and influences, *be honest with yourself and me.* I'm not talking about divorcing a person's feelings from reality that does not mean starting all over again. We tend to make the same mistakes over and over again, (this is human nature at work)!

I'm going to be very honest at this point because I want you understand your self-esteem and personal value, but I feel this maybe the best way to get my point across. Would you like to make some changes or improvements in your life? I didn't want any changes because I thought being dissatisfied was a way of life and thought that was the way life suppose be. I hope I haven't offended anyone up to this point now let's look at our life as it is I believe in (Self-Achievement) in our emotional make-up and divorced from our way of thinking.

How does a person live up to what they believe about their moral values they have set in their life? If you let yourself down in regards to your morals, sometimes we think we're exempt from certain things especially when it comes from doing something wrong. Like saying to their kids "if you cross your eyes the will stay that way" but there are things pasted on to your children, an antidote is what is in a name? Prov. 22:1 says it is important to have "a GOOD name" do children honor their parents?

The idealisms can come into play because the world and society creates a great deal of apprehension and miss trust if you have had a relationship. Whether a person thinks of themselves as perfect and yet have pride I what you are doing. There are those who always think of themselves as a victim and it is even worse if there is abuse involved. If a person thinks they have been hurt (some people make excesses for why they accept the abuse), the driving force in most cases is whether they feel they disserve the abuse.

A person needs to get past those kind of feelings, but if they cannot and they let it dominate their lives and let it dominate their relationships. Even within the failures a person has to live with the other aspects in their life that can seem like a paradox.

I would like to spend a little more time on the subject of pride, and make some applications. If I've hit a nerve let's talk about the need to have pride and to be proud I believe pride builds character and helps improve emotions and feeling.

The need to care and the need to be loved is one our basic needs and drives. This can take on many forms of desire for the right or wrong reasons, and the need can take on different forms of caring and ways to express your love for one another.

I have talked about the need for love in other books it comes from not knowing how to deal with what is love. People can do some pretty crazy things to get another person's attention, whether we're young or old, especially when we need love and when that need is not being met to our expectation and desire. There can be other feelings such as disappointments. The excitement of a new love and romance is one thing and that is why some feel the need for extra sexual relationships, but the excitement and challenge of an affair turns them on; there are other factors why a person takes on extra marital relationships.

How to "Develop ACHIEVEMENTS, & Motivation".

Again, self-achievement starts with balancing of your goals needs to be dealt understanding the negatives in a positive way. The anxiety and depression a person maybe dealing with things negatively. When this happens a person's nerves are on edge, anxiety can lead to a stressed-out feeling. Anyone can get caught up in what they are doing, if things don't happen or they have high stress levels at times we overload the mind and body with too much, or when a person sets the wrong kind of goals, that is to be "**human** and to err is doing something counter-productive, it may cause a problem in reaching your goal.

When dealing with a person's pride/ego it can get in their way, this is a dangerous,

Especially to those who are unable to show their achievements and are critical of others for their success. A person may not need and want attention (May I reemphasize something wrong when a person does things for the wrong reasons, whether they're an adult or child). When, this happens a person has an "improper balance" in their self-image. At this point we want a person to establish **Self-Control** there needs to be a **Proper Balance** between the right kind of **pride** and **humility** about themselves and *who they think they are* as a person, and in what they have accomplished as a person.

We need to feel good without having to be praised, or needing pats on the back, or they can come in the form of flattery. It is nice when someone says or does something nice, and people should appreciate others for what they have done, but a person should not let it go to their head. We should spend time encouraging others.

This is another good way to accomplish proper **Control** and **Balance** in a person's life by using **Self Control Factors**.

Control Factors

ATTITUDES: Hurt – Anger – Hostility - Bitterness
AUSE: Controlled – Controlling – Co-dependences
ANXIETY: Burnout – Conflicts – Guilt –
DEPRESSION: Disappointments – Stress – Panic attacks

Here are some common manipulative characteristics.
1. Destroying & under mining someone's confidence.
2. Pushing the envelope.
3. Deliberately stressing to the point it up-sets a person.
4. Controlling to the point that you're always right.
5. Mentally over loading, and holding others hostage.
6. Emotional black-mail.

Balance & Control in your goals
1. Using Damage Control
2. Proper balance = Proper control
3. To be happy with one's self-esteem in whatever they do.

Are we dealing with proper balance and control?
Life is balancing act & →
who we think we are →
→between family &
→"the real you".

Basically everyone thinks their OK as long as everything is going fine it can seem like a balancing act. Meeting our needs and despairs in the (Right) way. But, feeling good about ourselves is something a person may not really understand and consider when it comes to *"knowing who they are and what they want to be"*.

This is not a difficult concept to grasp in fact it maybe much easier for a person to know their true feelings, even if they are struggling and especially when they do not understand their inner feelings:

1. *What do you see in yourself*? But probably more important is,
2. *What do you see in others*?

Another perplexing QUSTION of the day is "*are you able to find out who you really are*? You may say I want to know more about your studies and information about self-control as you know more about yourself. I believe there is a middle ground watch for the balance and be truthful with who you are because if not why? Let me say this I don't have all the answers to life's questions? We want to look at the BIGEST QUSTION WHICH IS *YOU*? Next is your accountability?

(Author unknown)

"To appear wise, one must know where they are going;

To be wise, one must be a listener.

To do good things, one must be busy;

To do well, one must know when to stand aside.

To appear to lead, one must put others first;

To lead, one must put oneself last.

To appear caring, one must give advice and be able to

To be caring, one must give space for others to take advice;

    achievements.

To appear to love, one must know how to give love;

To love, one must know also know how to receive love.

To appear happy, one must smile;

To be happy, is be free with their tears and caring.

Poem

What do You Mean to Me

You turned my darkness into light;

You made everything alright.

You picked me up when I was down;

You turned my life around.

If I didn't have you, what would I be?

A blessing is what you are to me.

When I needed you the most, because you were there;
Even if it seemed like you didn't care.
When I didn't think I could make it another day,
You chased all my doubts away.
If I didn't have you, what would I be?
A treasure is what you are to me.

The world is full of many people, it's true;
But there is only one of you.
You fill my heart with love;
You're a God-sent gift from above.
If I didn't have you, what would I be?
An angel is what you are to me.

Lost and alone, I will no longer be;
Because you are here with me.
There is no reason to be sad;
You've taken away all the bad.
If I didn't have you, what would I be?
A best friend is what you are to me!"

12 Reasons Why Budgeting can improve your life
Pages 1-2 of 1 [13]
Why Budget? Here are twelve good reasons:

A. "A budget is a guide that tells you whether you're going in the direction you want to be headed in financially. You may have goals and dreams but if you don't set up guidelines for reaching them and you don't measure your progress, you may end up going so far in the wrong direction you can never make it back. Can you imagine the government or a major corporation operating without a budget? No, and neither should you.

B. A budget lets you control your money instead of your money controlling you. A budget will tell you if you're living within your means. Before the widespread use of credit cards, you could tell if you were living within your means because you had money left over after paying all your bills.

C. The use of credit cards has made this much less obvious. Many people don't realize they're living far beyond their means until they're knee deep in debt.

D. A budget can help you meet your savings goals. It includes a mechanism for setting aside money for savings and investments.

E. Following a realistic budget frees up spare cash so you can use your money on the things that really matter to you instead of frittering it away on things you don't even remember buying.

F.A budget helps your entire family focus on common goals.

G. A budget helps you prepare for emergencies or large or unanticipated expenses that might otherwise knock you for a loop financially.

H. A budget can improve your marriage. A good budget is not just a spending plan; it's a communication tool. Done right, a budget can bring the two of you closer together as you identify and work towards common goals and reduce arguments about money. That's got to be good for your sex life!

I. A budget reveals areas where you're spending too much money so you can refocus on your most important goals.

J. A budget can *keep* you out of debt or help you *get* out of debt.

K. A budget actually creates extra money for you to do use on things that matter to you.

L. A budget helps you sleep better at night because you don't lie awake worrying able how you're going to make ends meet."

http://www.financialplan.about.com/cs/budgeting/a/12ReasonsBudget.html   2/20/05

Steven C. Rockefeller, *John Dewey: Religious Faith and Democratic Humanism* [14]

"There is one other aspect **emotions, empathy,** which in turn can enable true character development and a foundation for societies, is to consider some of the ways **emotional stability** helps build this foundation. The bedrock of character and personality is *self-discipline*;

(…), as philosophers since Aristotle observed, is based on *self-control*. A related keystone of character is being able to motivate and guide oneself, being honest with one's self whether it's doing homework, to finishing a job, or getting up in the morning. The ability to control gratification and channel one's urges, to act properly in the situation is a basic **emotional skill**, one that in a former day was called will. "We need to be in control of ourselves, our appetites, our passions, and to do right by others. It takes *will-power* to keep **emotions** under the control of reason."

Steven C. Rockefeller, *John Dewey: Religious Faith and Democratic Humanism* (New York: Columbia University Press, 1991).

Think things through before taking on problem solving.
Resourcefulness describes how well a "goal-is-directed, dealing gratification", is the essence of *self-regulation*:

1. The ability to deny impulses in achieving a goal
2. Whether it is building or solving problems
3. Or pursuing life to the fullest.
4. *Negotiating solutions*—the wisdom in being able to prevent conflicts, resolving problems or dealing with flare ups. People who have the ability excel in deal making, in arbitrating or mediating disputes; they might have a career in diplomacy, in arbitration or law, or as middlemen or managers.

The ability to have compassion with each other should be the **hope** for both parties, involvement in both should be each other's **well-being,** if both are to have a good relationship. People need to work together if there is any chance in solving the problem or a situation. The ability to achieve and being in control depends on the outcome of any decision, / settling arguments before they get out-of-control, not fighting over trivial things, but more importantly is deciding what is right or wrong.

Remember if one person is wrong both suffer.
1. Is the give and take and being able to compromise to get things done?

2. What if you are a 100 percent right and the other person is wrong? What then?
3. If both people feel good about the relationship or problem both will be happier.
4. Love each other with all your heart, soul, and mind.
5. By not being overly critical and judgmental
6. In problem solving keep the argument under **control**
7. By giving alternatives, rather than fighting, if one withdraws or quits that is a problem.
8. Talk about the situation and how it makes you feel.

Think of ways to solve the problem or problems
1. What are the consequences and what might happen if no solution is found;
2. Pick solutions and execute them—be an adult grown-up.
3. By using pro-strategies for interpersonal problem-solving
4. By improving your social cognitive behavior skills,
5. By controlling emotions, recognition and understanding the problem.
6. A person needs self-control and being able to take control of their emotions,
7. A person needs to plan how to go about solving bad behaviors.

A person will do better when they think before acting
1. A person can be more effective when they are under control in a conflict.
2. A person does better when they control their impulses,
3. There needs to be improvements in interpersonal effectiveness.
4. A person needs to work on enhanced coping skills,
5. A person can always improve interpersonal conflicts and problems.
6. A person needs better coping skills when dealing with anxiety and depression,
7. The need to deal with behaviors and find resolutions that work,
8. Some are better at conflict-resolution skills.

Results
1. This should lead to less arguments,
2. There should be fewer verbal put-downs,

3. This will lead to a more-caring atmosphere.
4. Then people are more willingness to cooperate,
5. People have more empathy.
6. They need to improve their communication skills,
7. They are more sensitive to others' feelings.

They have a higher self-worth
1. They are more pro-behavior oriented,
2. They are better able to handle the transition from one situation to another.
3. They are less antisocial, self-destructive, in disordered behavior, even when followed up,
4. They are better at self-control, social awareness, and decision-making.
5. They are better at understanding the consequences of their behavior,
6. They have increased ability to "size up" interpersonal situations and plan appropriate actions.

Cognitive Skills
1. *Self-talk*—conducting an "inner dialogue" as a way to cope with a topic or challenge, or reinforce one's own behavior.
2. ***Interpreting social cues***, recognizing social influences and behaviors, and seeing oneself in the perspective of the larger picture.
3. ***Using steps for problem solving and decision-making*** controlling actions, setting goals, identifying alternative actions, and anticipating consequences.
4. ***Understanding the perspective of others.***
5. ***Understanding behavioral norms*** (what is and those that are not acceptable behaviors).
6. ***A positive attitude toward life.***
7. ***Self-awareness*** cognition developing realistic expectations about oneself.

We all know when we are feeling bad and if a person is being controlled, whether it is a fleeting annoyance or a full-fledged argument or fight.

If it is normal feeling a person should feel in-control that is sign of a healthy emotion, the Bible says "don't let your anger get out-of-control." But, when it gets out-of-control and turns destructive it can lead to problems in your personal relationships, and in the overall quality of your life. That is what we want to discuss, it can make you feel as though you are at the mercy of an unpredictable powerful force. This is meant to help you understand and get a handle on controlling other aspects of your life.

A person's emotional state may vary in intensity from mild to irrational actions, to intense fury and rage. Like other feelings it is accompanied by physiological and biological changes in the body your heart rate and blood pressure go up, as the level of your energy, hormones, adrenaline, and non-adrenaline.

Both internal and external emotions are specific and each person is governed an event such as an accident (a traffic jam, a canceled concert), anther it can cause a person to worry needlessly about their problems. Like memories of traumatic events of the past and can also trigger other feelings.

The biological functions of the brain

An intrinsic episode brings out the miss faring of the neural transmitters or by expressing why a person may respond aggressively and it can also be a passive response which is an internal feeling of despair. Anger is a neural adaptive response when perceived as a threat; it brings out powerful psychological responses in light of how a person responds to aggressive and passive behaviors it will show up their positive or negative emotions. Which allows a person to want to defend themselves when they have been attacked or hurt by someone? A certain amount of aggression is necessary to defend one's self and puts a person in a survival mode. For instance when someone hits you how do you respond; there is usually two ways to respond, either by a passive or an aggressive response. When a person says, "I will get even with you for what you've done" which can either be done by hitting the person or because they hit them, that is known as being physically aggressive. Another approach, which is just as bad, "when a person doesn't care what happens to them and they respond by not doing anything," that is known as acute passive aggression.

On the other hand, we know a person should not lash out at every little thing or personal insult, or object because it irritates or annoys them. There are social norms that are acceptable and common-sense limits. We should allow for a person to respond to others appropriately and it should not take on the form of retaliation.

People use a variety of reasons for not understanding the conscious and subconscious processes of what happened a person needs to learn how to deal with their emotions. The three main approaches are *expressing, suppressing*, and *calming*.

Expressing your feelings in an assertive way – nor in an aggressive manner it is not the healthiest of ways to express your feelings. To do this, you have to learn how to make clear what your needs are and how to get them under control without hurting others. Being assertive doesn't mean being pushy or demanding; it means being respectful of yourself and others rights. *Suppressing* your emotions is just as bad and there is a need to convert or redirect those feelings. This happens when you hold on to those bad feelings; that is a passive response, and when you can't stop thinking about it, it is always good to focus on something else in a positive way. The aim is to suppress your feelings and convert them into a more constructive behavior. The danger in this type of response means it hasn't allowed you to use other kinds of expressions. The problem is when it turns outward by fighting or arguing, or when it turns inward in many cases it causes emotional and psychological problems.

Unexpressed feelings can create other problems; it can lead to pathological feelings, in feeling bad about yourself leading to a passive aggressive behavior. (When a person wants to get back at a person in an indirect way, without telling them why they did something to them. Rather than confronting them and or talking about why a person is angry with them). This can stem from a personality disorder known as manic depression or perpetual cynical remarks and hostility and it will affect every situation. People who are constantly putting others down, criticizing everything, and making cynical comments haven't learned how to constructively express their feelings. They are more likely to have unsuccessful relationships.

Finally, a person should *calm down* this means not only controlling your behavior, but also controlling your internal feelings, taking steps to lower your heart rate, calm yourself down, and let those feelings subside, but when none of these three techniques work, that's when someone has not been able to control their emotions.

Controlling Your Emotional Feelings

The goal is to control your emotions and to reduce both your emotional bad feelings and the physiological arousal that causes those feelings. People try to get rid of things by avoiding them that is why we use reconstructive techniques to help people and have them engage in trying to find ways to control those feelings. A person can't change things if they don't try, but they can learn to control their reactions by controlling their emotions.

Are you too angry there are psychological tests that measure feelings, how pronged a person is to anger, and how well people handle things? If you find yourself out-of-control or a person feels frightened, a person might need help finding better ways to deal with those emotions.

Why are some people more angry than others psychologists have come up with methods for control management it is a good way to deal those emotions, some people really are more 'hotheaded' than others; they get angry easily and are more intense than the average person, we feel they can be helped by our methods. There are also those who don't show their anger it shows up in their temperament, but it shows up in other ways they are usually chronically irritable and grumpy and it could be they release their tension by throw things; sometimes they withdrawn, sulk, and it can lead to certain types of illnesses.

People who argue generally have what some psychologists call a *low tolerance for frustration*, meaning simply that they feel they could be subjected to other people's frustration, inconvenience, or annoyances.

While others take things in stride, and while others are particularly infuriated when the situation seems to go wrong or something doesn't happen the way they want somehow they justify their feelings; for example correcting others for a minor mistake.

What makes people this way? There are a number of reasons; it may be genetic, biological, or physiological. There is evidence that some children are born irritable, touchy, and have a temper, and that can be trace back to the third generation, these signs are present at a very early age. Another may be their social or cultural background that has caused those behaviors. Negative emotions; we're taught that it's alright to express anxiety because people have frustrations, but when it leads to depression, it is a stronger emotion, but to never express anger is usually a result of a passive behavior; people need to learn how to handle or channel constructive techniques.

Research has also found that a family's background and genetics plays a major role in behaviors. Typically, people who are easily upset come from families that are disruptive, chaotic, and not skilled at emotional communications.

Psychologists now say some people use their bad behaviors as a license to hurt others. Research has found that people say and want to '*let it rip*' which actually escalates aggression and does nothing to help them in controlling their anger or gives them a resolve to settle a situation.

It's best to find out what triggers the anger and then develop strategies to keep those triggers from tipping a person over the edge.

STRESS, CRISIS, AND DEMAND

Now let's see how you are dealing with these three factors I put them in that order for a reason, usually stress is the first indicator, if you are dealing with a crisis, the demands increase how do these affect your personal experiences and your **self-esteem**. The stress point is the way I measure a reaction and how you react to stress is one of the most common tell-tale signs in how problems are affecting you. When there is a crisis we want you see the amount of stress or what is the stress point, how much stress is involved, and how you react is very important. That will determine whether it is a major or minor problem, you are dealing with. There are so many demands in life that you will not be able to count all of them. Emotional experiences are in some ways the easiest to see because a person has feeling and some never show any sign of stress because they keep it inward, but on the other hand some are more likely to feel anxiety if it is an inward stress, others will show more emotions when there is a lot of stress. If the stress is too high, how can you lower the stress?

Definition stress: *noun* {17}
Etymology: Middle English *stressed* stress, distress, short for *distress* - - more at DISTRESS Date: 14th century
1:   constraining force or influence:
:   a force exerted when one body or body part presses on, pulls on, pushes against, or tends to compress or twist another body or body part; *especially*
:   the intensity of this mutual force commonly
   expressed in pounds per square inch
b: the deformation caused in a body by such a force
c: a physical, chemical, or emotional factor that causes bodily or mental tension and may be a factor in disease causation
d: a state resulting from a stress; *especially*
:   one of bodily or mental tension resulting from factors that tend to alter an existent equilibrium <job-related *stress*>
e: STRAIN, PRESSURE <the environment is under *stress* to the point of collapse – Joseph Shoben>

Again, there is another factor because of the way a (male and female) approach their emotional experience, in that case there are two different views of the same situation. Then you have two different sets of emotions and sensitivity levels, any two people will have different stress levels, and at the same time both are not approaching or looking at a situation in the same way.

There is such a thing as too much stress and what caused the crisis, and the emotional demands are not the same. Also, when you think of the word stress you should have a good understanding how your stress is effecting you. The next word you see is a crisis and most can define a crisis, some believe every stressful situation is a crisis that is not a good sign.

Definition of crisis: *noun*   {18}

Inflected Form(s): *plural* **cri·ses**

Etymology: Middle English, from Latin, from Greek *krisis,* literally, decision, from *krinein* to decide -- more at CERTAIN

Date: 15th century

1a: the turning point for better or worse in an acute disease or fever

  b: a paroxysmal attack of pain, distress, or disordered function

  c: an emotionally significant event or radical change of status in a person's life <a midlife *crisis*>

2 : the decisive moment (as in a literary plot)

3a: an unstable or crucial time or state of affairs in which a decisive change is impending;

especially

  : one with the distinct possibility of a highly undesirable outcome <a financial *crisis*>

  b: a situation that has reached a critical point <the environmental *crisis*>

The demands in your life are when someone expects you to do something or tells you what to do about something, but there are other demands such as meeting your financial needs.

Definition of Demand – Merriam-Webester Dictionary
                  Pages 1 – 4 {19}

¹de·mand

noun \di-ˈmand, -ˈmänd, dē-\

  : a forceful statement in which you say that something must be done or given to you

  : a strong need *for* something

  : the ability and need or desire to buy goods and services

  1 *a*:an act of demanding or asking especially with authority <a *demand* for obedience>

  b: something claimed as due <a list of *demands*>

2 *archaic* : QUESTION

3 *a*:   willingness and ability to purchase a commodity or service
<the *demand* for quality day care>

  b: the quantity of a commodity or service wanted at a specified price
      and time

    <supply and *demand*>

4 *a*:a seeking or state of being sought after <in great *demand* as an
entertainer>

  b:urgent need

  5: the requirement of work or of the expenditure of a resource
      <equal to the *demands* of the office> <*demands* on one's time>
      <oxygen *demand* for waste oxidation>

  on demand

      : upon presentation and request for payment; *also*

      : when requested or needed <video *on demand*

Examples of *DEMAND*

  1. The committee is considering her *demand* that she be given more
      time to complete the study.

  2. The workers said they would not end the strike until their *demands*
      were met.

  3. The *demand for* low-income housing is increasing as the economy
      gets worse.

  4. We are seeing an increased *demand for* hospital beds.

  5. The company increased production to meet *demand*.

²demand *verb*

      : to say in a forceful way that something must be done or
        given to you

      : to say that you have a right to (something)

      : to say or ask (something) in a very forceful way

      : to require (something)

Full Definition of *DEMAND*

intransitive verb

  :   to make a demand : ASK

      transitive verb

1: to ask or call for with authority: claim as due or just *<demanded to see a lawyer>*

2: to call for urgently, peremptorily, or insistently *<demanded that the rioters disperse>*

3*a*: to ask authoritatively or earnestly to be informed of
<demand the reason for the dismissal>

  b: to require to come : SUMMON

4: to call for as useful or necessary *<etiquette demands a handwritten thank-you>*

  — **de·mand·able** \-'man-də-bəl\ *adjective*

  — de·mand·er *noun*

Examples of *DEMAND*

    1. The customer *demanded* a refund.

    2. Parents have *demanded* that the teacher resign.

    3. The reporter *demanded* to see the documents.

    4. I *demand* to know what is going on here!

    5. "Come here at once!" he *demanded*.

    6. "Why won't you answer me?" she *demanded*.

    7. The situation *demands* immediate action.

Synonym Discussion of *DEMAND*

DEMAND, CLAIM, REQUIRE, EXACT mean to ask or call for something as due or as necessary. DEMAND implies peremptoriness and insistence and often the right to make requests that are to be regarded as commands *<demanded payment of the debt>*.

CLAIM implies a demand for the delivery or concession of something due as one's own or one's right *<claimed the right to manage his own affairs>*.

REQUIRE suggests the imperativeness that arises from inner necessity, compulsion of law or regulation, or the exigencies of the situation *<the patient requires constant attention>*.

EXACT implies not only demanding but getting what one demands <*exacts* absolute loyalty>.
http://merriam-webester.com/dictionary/demand?show=0&t=1412785627 10/8/2014

One of the best ways to define demand is by the amount of demand put on the relationship and the emotions a person deals with in the relationship. There is more to what happens in a personal relationship as we look at the normal reactions in your life and in your relationships. I find people using the quick fixes. Does your life go back to normal quickly after a demand or crisis is there a prolonged time of bad feelings in a situation?

There is one outstanding thing there are both positive and negative reactions causing stress.

At this point, we are going deal with the well-being of a person in relation to self-esteem; there are different kinds of self-determination, the two wells the mind and conscience, and I will not, I can't do this anymore. This is a defiantly a conflict of wells when no one will give in and your heart says one thing and your mind says something is wrong. This does not mean that life does not go on.

PRESSURE-RELIEF / COPING

Pressure-Relief is letting the air out of the situation and taking the pressure off of the situation or relationship. We use the word COPE! Let me say this I do not condemn any person for using something to help them COPE, but there are things that make things worse rather than help or relief the pressure. Without some kind of **pressure-relief,** life can become impossible to deal with at times. A person has to be able to COPE at every level, and in every aspects of your life. (What do we mean by perfect, but people are not perfect.) As you can see, there are many dangerous areas and the same is true with the wrong kind of pressure relief.

This is one of the things I learned; I tried to find ways to COPE, and keep my prospective and keep a balance and I felt I did not over react, every relationship has these kinds of problems.

This goes back to our study on ATTITUDE I want you to look at COPING a person can lose their BALANCE. How do you deal with the stress then what kind of pressure-relief can you use? It sounds harmless enough when I say it, but it can become a hot issue if a person is not careful.

There are some bad things to look for in **finding a pressure-relief** and sometimes a person overlooks the significance of why things happen and what they can cause. When a situation is too much for a person they tend to over react in some way. A very good way to know when something is wrong, a person goes in the opposite direction to far or they go into denial. These are some of the warning signs.

Thus when someone is observed to be talkative and sociable (the so-called "extravert") (he or she) can be described as "expressive" in contrast people who are quiet and private (they are called "introverts") they can be described as "reserved." Interestingly, a reserved persons tend to hold back on their verbally expressions, they tend to listen carefully to what others say, while an expressive person tends not to listen very well, they are eager to express themselves and they want to tell others what they know and what they have on their mind. In general, the expressive person is usually quick to speak and slow to listen, while the reserved person is true to others they are quick to listen and slow to speak.

Of course everyone is expressive in some way, but not in the same ways. Those who are more expressive appear more comfortable in groups of people, thus, they can also be thought of as socially gregarious or outgoing. On the other hand, those who are more reserved seem to be more comfortable when alone, rather than when they are in a crowd, in extreme cases they can be thought of as unsocial.

Remember these distinctions are not clear-cut: each individual varies from time to time in (his or her) desire to be expressive in a group or reserved in seclusion.

Outgoing people are quick to approach others, even strangers, they find ways to be pleasant when there is something they want to do or say. Apparently, such interaction charges their batteries and makes them feel alive. Thus, they might well be ready to go on to another encounter their batteries are almost always overcharged from the social interaction. They resort to feelings of loneliness when they are not in contact with others. For example, if an expressive person goes to a library to do research and (he or she) after fifteen minutes can feel bored and tired, and have to exercise strong willpower to keep from taking a short brain break and striking up a conversation with the librarian.

On the other hand, the reserve person is true they can draw energy from different sources. They prefer to pursue solitary types of activities, working quietly alone on their favorite project or hobby, they enjoy isolated activities that charge their batteries. Indeed, the reserved person can remain alone in contrast their energies come from doing things like hobbies. If required by their job, family, or social responsibilities they can be expressive or outgoing to make interpersonal relationships better. If the reserved person goes into a noisy place they may stay a while then they are ready to go home. They enjoy socializing with others for a while, but at large social gatherings or professional meetings they tend to seek a quiet corner where they can chat with one or two other persons.

There is some social bias toward expressive social life, the reserved person does not feel there is anything wrong with them, and they enjoy quiet times to themselves.

I identify with the extraversion or introversion by observing others because introverts will appear extraverted when they are expressing their viewpoints that interest them. This "activation" of the introvert can be extraverts at times, this is the definition of extraversion, when an introvert is like an extravert they are interested in something, however when it becomes prolonged socializing they must retreat from people to fully be recharge.

Thus a "sensation" may be used synonymously with words pertaining to external attention," observations", and "externalization."

In contrast, two emerging metaphors convey the word intuition is "listening to the inner voice" or "heeding the promptings from within." The word intuition literally means "internal attention." We don't always pay attention to what is going on in the mind our mind can be the ear of conscience; these promptings come through as feelings. Thus, "intuition" can be used synonymously with three other terms pertaining to internal attention, "inner perception," and "internalization," we can contrast "interaction" with "observation," "internalization" with "externalization."

For the purposes of describing personality types, I have found the easiest and most accurate terms to be "introspection" and "observation." Very simply, we observe through what we see in others. Thus, we look at objects and identify them to be true, but when it comes to thought, we listen to sounds we hear, touch surfaces to feel them, sniff odors to smell them, and we put in food in our mouth to taste them. We can observe what is present; we may have a problem when we don't understand the present senses, what do I mean by interpersonal reasoning.

Both observation and introspection, but it is a rare when individuals do an equal amount of each. The vast majority, spend most of their waking hours looking, listening, and touching objects in our immediate presence, very little of our time introspecting our thoughts, that is imagining, daydreaming, or wondering about things.

The point I'm making these things are happening simultaneously. When we observe what's going on around us, and at the same time we can't observe what's going on within us without an introspective sense of one's self-esteem. We may alternate our attention from one thing to another, but we cannot divide ourselves. Some people live in an infancy world; they seem to be more attentive to inner promptings, rather than outer promptings. The reason for this difference there is not enough attention to the facts around them; it is a matter of conjecture as to how a person thinks or why they do certain things at certain times of the day. If they pay attention and observe why they are doing things, and how they look at the consequences of what could happen. Those of us who attend inwardly learn our strengthens from within their beliefs are in one' self and given to their inner thinking, but when things become louder a person has clearer feelings about themselves, in that instance, their inner promptings become more vivid. Likewise, those of us who heed the external reasoning and begin to see and obtain objective motives in more detail and with greater specificity.

This does not mean we don't observe things, this doesn't mean these types are without inner feelings far from it, but simply that their introspection takes a back seat to their observation. Nor does this mean that inner personal types are unaware of things around them not at all, but simply that they are more inclined to become absorbed in their ideas.

To put this another way people need to look at the concrete down to earth things and they tend to keep their feet on the ground. These People see what is in front of them and are usually accurate in catching details. It is said that "they don't miss much" people who observe facts, trust facts, and remember facts, and as they deal with the facts in a situation as they are, things in the here and now. They focus on what is happening, or what has happened, we want people to anticipate what might happen, another way of saying what if, or what might occur in the future.

In contrast, inner personal people might look at abstract things with their head in the clouds, who wonder about the curiosities of the earth. They might become absorbed in the internal world and how it works, they tend to miss a great deal of what's right around them or in the current reality of a situation. They may observe things as a mere problem to be solved, or a stage of development toward some future ideal. Not only can they miss details, they can also lose track of where they are and for instance drive right past their turn-off. "Their reality is sometimes clouded, and unable to register their relative disinterest in the concrete. But, more than disinterest, they can be discontent with reality, even bothered by it, and look at other possible ways of improving things.

Because of their tenuous grasp of reality a person can appear to observer things as being flighty, impractical and unrealistic, a dreamer or like the absent-minded professor who can't be bothered with the everyday things in life. For their part, some people can seem unimaginative, concerned only with trivial pursuits, exasperatingly slow to consider implications and possibilities, both views are exaggerations. Indeed, both kinds of people are capable of creative things in their own way it's just that they attend to very different sides of life, with the other side getting short-changed.

Thus, observers can manage the material world with skill they have promptings from within, these promptings can gradually fade away, and they may end up with undeveloped introspective abilities. They may now and then be introspective, but not for long and they spend time doing things for pleasure, as a penalty they pay for this with their realities being undeveloped.

Regret and remorse are some of the hall-marks of such emotional reactions.

A person is usually left with such thoughts as to why they did or said something, or say why I got so angry. A sense of bewilderment of an unconscious act of not knowing what came over them at the time. If this is a repeated behavior, something could be very wrong!

When was the last time you "lost your temper" or "blowing up over something or someone?" The key is how often and how sever are the emotional out-breaks, are you really sorry, or just saying I'm sorry is not enough if a person doesn't mean it. The real problem may lie in the fact a person can't control their temper, usually; such irritation and name-calling should subside.

We have finished one part of this study on self-esteem and how it has an effect on a person's feeling. Many become fascinated and entertained by the people who have their differences, further studies finds a person making allowances for themselves in (his or her) own way. Some can actually come to see that the two styles are complementary when it comes to turning in a job well done: these people spot opportunities and lay out alternatives, and schedule their time and press for closure."

I do not imply that their changes will not last. I encourage them to make sure the changes do last. This positive expectation helps the couples then act confidently in expressing their new behaviors as indications of real love for each other.

If the couple does relapse, however, I talk with them about the usual progress of counseling. To enhance their belief that this is a regular happening, I point out that not every couple relapses because each couple is unique. Relapses are to be viewed as another challenge to be conquered rather than an indication that the couple can't progress. I want to stress that each couple will have some degree of a relapse will vary of on the amount of effort put forth in settling arguments and conflicts. Some plunge even below where they were before things get better. Some can arrest the relapse quickly. Positive lessons from the relapse are stressed.

SELF-ACHAVEMENT

Controlling You

&

You're

Environment

Applying SELF HELP PRINCIPLES to SELF-WORTH & CONTROL

Chapter 9

RESPONSABLITY & SELF-DEVELOPEMENT

Controlling You & Your Environment

Sometimes it's our immediate surroundings that give us cause for irritation and not getting along. Problems can weigh on you and make you feel angry at the 'tip of a hat' you seem to have fallen into trap and all people do, look for things that formed that trap and being accountable for what happens.

Give yourself a break make sure you have some 'personal time' schedule a special time of the day that is yours. One example is the working mother who has a standing rule that when she comes home from work, she takes the first 15 minutes to unwind "nobody talks to mom unless the house is on fire." After this quiet time, she feels better prepared to handle demands from her kids without blowing up at them.

Some other tips for easing up on yourself as follows.

Timing. If you and your spouse tend to fight when you discuss things at night - perhaps you're tired, or distracted, maybe it's become a habit not a discussion; try changing the times when you talk about important matters so these talks don't turn into a routine or arguments.

Avoidance. If your child's chaotic room makes you furious every time you walk by it, shut the door don't make yourself look at what infuriates you. Don't say 'well, my child should clean the room clean so I won't have to be angry!' That's not the point. The point is to keep yourself calm and remind yourself how much nicer it would be if it were clean.

Finding Alternatives. If you're daily commute through traffic leaves you in a state of rage and frustration, give yourself a project map find a different route, one that's less congested or more scenic. Or find another alternative, such as a bus or commuter train.

If you feel that your anger is really out-of-control, if it is having an impact on your relationships and on important things in your life, you might consider counseling learn how to handle it better. A psychologist or other licensed mental health professional can work with you in developing a range of techniques for changing your thinking and your behavior.

Life is about motivation in a person's desire, wants, and needs

I cannot solve this problem, I want too, but maybe it's too messed up, I am driven to think it's hopeless, I feel trapped, and act in a way that produces hopelessness, fear, frustration, and feelings of doubt. I will activate the most constructive centers of my mind and the innermost feelings of my being and let them move me into the thought process that is what a person needs to have at any given moment to realize there is a solution. At any given moment there is the need to put your thoughts into action and realize your feelings are dragging you down, I need to be productive and get something done.

I can let it go and let it be - if not I must let the mind do its work. The will of a person can and does in the process of thinking things through. You may think all you have to do is think positive, NOT in the way you think everything thing goes through the brain the problem the brain stores all the baggage. To be in step you have to activate your **motivation** you have to take on the everyday challenges or you can get lost and over whelmed by life.

The process I just described is obviously not a one-time and final action. Although, at that moment the action has taken place, in the beginning you may feel that way, you may pull yourself together and follow through on the action and indeed experience the most favorable results. But, then you must assume you can do it, and no further steps are going to be needed, wrong. Of course that method does not always suffice because most any problem is on a continuous basis. For some of you it may be a negative response this will be degrading if you don't understand the self-concept. No thought comes to fruition without a conscious effort.

You must work through the process of activating, formulating, and conceiving a plan of what needs to be done, using the proper thoughts in relation to the spirit and will. This process is repeated each time you have a problem the thinking process doesn't work unless you put it into action. Each juncture in the problem may present different roadblocks, (walls) which have to be recognized and eliminated. Each time difficulties and negativities things appear you must halt the magnetism that seems so strong, if you are not carful you will give in; it is hard to believe that you must fight to contact the inner being, why? Because there are **two natures**, this may be hard to believe; it really is rather easy if you think about a solution there is always more than one way to do something in principle that is life in nut shell.

Each time you do something there is going to be some positive or negative reactions, another aspect is tarring down the (walls) of disbelief by conquering your self-determination and utilizing the inner spirit to removed doubts and fears. One way is motivation and understanding more about the situation eventually you will feel this power as it moves you and *empowers* you. You will feel a oneness of spirit then finally use the inner self, and this is the balancing of the inner feelings, I call this a manifestation by taking a deliberate action, but did the "thought process" help or hinder.

It will no longer seem as though a second consciousness existed in you, but a oneness of the mind and spirit. Nor will it be as though the results in your life had nothing to do with it. You will be connected both with the positive and negative causes in ways that you have not seen before, and with the *positive powers* you never dreamed possible. This will result in filling you with productive thoughts and a wider vision and leave you with all kinds of possibilities. Each situation will offer many possibilities for desirable results for solutions, and for "creative thinking and growth".

Let your mind help you

You cannot come out of any difficulty if you trust the outer influences to control the mind exclusively. Let the mind be filled with the inner spirit and well-being, and then can you find the solution for each specific problem.

There-for-establish the balance regarding controlling the mind don't let it run a way and take you with it, balance can best be demonstrated by the following.

Examples:

Each human has needs, wants, and desires, whether it's from a (man or women's) point of view. When you are separated from the inner person you have lost your approach to deal with your feelings, the way to do this is by controlling your feelings when there is a proper balance and controls exists, you are more likely if you:

- Give of yourself freely and fearlessly.
- At the same time, you give your love freely.
- Focus on issues, you do not want to be possessive,
- You do not need to own someone else to be happy,
- You do not need to be an expert or take control and pressure someone else.
- Therefore (he or she) cannot be owned or controlled by other influences.
- Hence, (he or she) needs not to fear their love and being loved.
- (He or she) must realize in the frame work of the mind/brain, that love is the greatest freedom.

Love Poem Quoted Poem

"HOW do I love thee? Let me count the ways.
I love thee to the depth and breadth and height
My soul can reach, when feeling out of sight
For the ends of Being and ideal Grace.
I love thee to the level of every day's
Most quiet need, by sun and candle-light.
I love thee freely, as men strive for Right;
I love thee purely, as they turn from Praise.
I love thee with the passion put to use
In my old grief's, and with my childhood's faith.
I love thee with a love I seemed to lose
With my lost saints, -I love thee with the breath,
Smiles, tears, of all my life! - and, if God choose,
I shall but love thee forever."
By: Elizabeth Barrett Browning

Self-confidence and Self-worth

That love must come to (him or her) if (he or she) lets their spouse have freedom and let them be a free gift of themselves, so that the spouse can feel free to go back and forth, that (he or she) does not have to fight for (his or her) commitment. (He or she) can let others be free in their expression of love because (he or she) knows that they have received it. True love is not blocked; (he or she) does not fear or resist it. Love is a continuum of the person, it has no beginning and no end, it endures and cannot fad, but it can never be taken away from (him or her) as long as they do not take it away from themselves. There is no end to it as long as (he or she) does not end it. It is utterly safe, there is no danger and no conflict attached to it. Therefore, to give of one's self is the best gift, and to contribute to someone else's well-being does not imply a loss of control. (He or she) is in the true sense of the word, self-evolved and not self-propitiated. In the best sense a person should control to some existent (his or her) own destiny without having to fight or be afraid to live. This must truly please the heart of God as He made us, when we come to Him with our problems.

But, there is an opposite effect, when false controls are put on a person's life and when you and your relationship is mess (bondage) is the result in this case:

- (He or she) constitutes the false version of life the false version is not letting a person be free.
- To live life in a distorted way is a type of martyrdom, sacrificing, in a sense it is self-in- flicking submission, and self-destructive if it were not for the sake of the living life.
- To live can become distorted, to possess someone by controlling their life.
- A person yearns for life, yet they are afraid of it, and therefore they only resist.

The individual who abuses someone, or feels they have to own and control another person to the point of exclusive control, it is sad when they believe it to be necessary to control the other person. Being controlled (a person losses their value for life), and fear of losing someone or being able to control someone leads to the false perversion of letting someone be free. Which in return brings about withdrawal such as indifference, non-involvement, non-commitment, and numbness of feelings, separation, and a refusal to value life.

When a person is involved in this distortion of values of what life should be, they cannot see the true picture of life and the freedom to live what life has to offer. They have associated life with the lack of freedom. Even if intellectually (he or she) knows better, emotionally (he or she) cannot experience what life has to offer.

Such a struggle cannot be resolved without understanding how the mind works, knowing the spirit of a person. We activate the heart of the person by letting them express their gift of themselves fearlessly, without fear of being controlled. Express your desire to feel and experience the oneness of two people as you grant it to each other let the experience grow and flourish. This can happen in personal relationships and especially as a person lets God into their heart.

We have tried to get you ready for the next part of this study, by establishing the necessary sense of integrity and self-acceptance. You will discover the more you love the more freedom you have and selfhood you have. WOW isn't that great news if you express this possibility as a formulated thought, and then activate the inner powers to help you experience it, you must come out of a problem better than when you came into a problem because you may find yourself in the real sense of the moment finding real joy and happiness.

Your loneliness, your fears, and your conflicts, in one way or another come down to this: you need to look for purposeful things to do with your life. It is the only real fulfillment if you can live a productive life letting things go and finding a release. The heart and soul of a person can indeed help when a person is trying to solve a problem, if you can only let go and let it happen. It can only help you when you call upon the resources of your inner being, that knows and understands the "process" of living without danger of losing it is being able to give love and the freedom to give of yourself, the second is in receiving love and remaining free in your relationships. You want people to see who you are, but what you want others to see in you, but if you don't understand this concept you are missing what life is all about. You cannot produce a healthy state of mind if you do not truly comprehend freedom of choice your inner-self can help you call upon it.

False control strengthens the (walls of separation). How we go about eliminating these (walls) by contacting the deeper and vaster faculties of the mind; even while the (walls are still present) we want you to tear them down little by little. WOW isn't great to be known as friends; your main concern at this time is opening the keys of the mind which is the (center of all activity in the brain) in whatever area you are dealing with and wherever you feel will govern what happens. You have needs every day and at any given moment of each day, you will have to call on your inner strength to make it. The more resourceful you become in formulating your wants, needs, and desires, your wishes for the inner nucleus to help guide and inspire you, to activate and fill you with understanding, with a constructive outlook and energies, the more perfect the manifestations of the mind you will find peace-of-mind. In so many different ways it will manifest how truly a person is committed to themselves and that it will truly fill you with security and trust within yourself. Trust in yourself as you pursue your "life dreams".

When a person has cancer a person's will is brought out more validly than a cold or flu, I can think of a person who has had to deal with cancer, it is usually the fight of their life. How many times have you seen an older person hang to life until someone comes to see them and then they pass away a few minutes later or few days later after they see them?

Seek these constructive powers this nucleus of the mind prefects the beauty of living in your health and in the wisdom of living. I want to give you some ideas for removing and tearing down (walls) by recognizing the power to overcome, we want to do this by inspiring you with one of the most effective avenues, prayer at any given moment can change things, so that even your inner being can be renewed and put your mind at peace. How can a person make the first step easier by being able to establish contact with the inner-self; this happens when a person understands the power of one's self? Thus the interaction will work both ways the more you cultivate this process, the safer you will feel, and the more you will realize that no problem is too Big or small, and without some form of solution you will likely fail to accomplish your goals.

My friends it lies exclusively in the mind the inner person. This is the way to deal with the truth about yourself with the belief things can get better, but it will never occur unless you go into the deeper recesses of yourself, your heart and mind have to be in tune together, and then the answers will come, enlightenment must be followed by the pursuit of happiness.

For many of you the enlightenment of the knowledge of one's self and the understanding, a glimpse in hope for a new beginning and building on the hope of getting better. This process shows it can be done if you are enter dependent on the inner being, in the way those two powers work to balance and control when submitted to the availability of these powers inside you if not there is confusion. It is a secure feeling knowing "God is there in the time of need" in doing so; you will soon be out of your crisis and your painful confusion. Next, is how to gain the power of **Self-control** and how it works?

The Ingredients in SELF-CONTROL   **Pages 2 – 10** [15]
"A proper balance must be struck between indulgence and severity. However, severity, despite occasional mistakes, is preferable to a lack of discipline."

"Self-discipline is a very powerful tool that can be developed for achieving anything which you can dream. However, there are four key ingredients that must be present in our lives to allow for self-discipline to flourish and exist. Most people have some or all of these key ingredients, but lack the knowledge of where and how to use them. Here are the four key ingredients of self-discipline:

A. *Self-Control* – The act of controlling our emotions, actions, thoughts, words, and personal direction.
B. *Motivation* – The "fire inside" that fuels our efforts and makes accomplishments worth achieving.
C. *Persistence* – The ability to continue through adversity. The ability to brush off failure and stay focused on our goals.
D. *Goals* – Those tangible achievements that breed motivation and form our definitions of happiness and success.

All four of these ingredients must be present in our lives to achieve self-discipline. Every one of us knows a highly motivated person or two that just can't seem to do anything right. A friend or neighbor who has the goal of becoming self-employed, but just can't muster enough courage to take the first step. At one time or another, all of us have been motivated to do something, only to give up after the first failure. How many people go on a diet each year and gain more weight than they originally started with? How often have you created a household budget for you and your family, only to find yourself deeper in debt? These are examples of living without self-discipline. The reason we get depressed and frustrated when we pinch the fat on our midsection or thighs, is not because we lack a proper genetic make-up, but because we have undertaken a task without developing **self-control**.

In order to ensure our success at every endeavor, we must first understand how to strengthen and enhance each of the four key-ingredients needed for **self-discipline**. By understanding and practicing simple techniques that strengthen each ingredient, we open the door to success by eliminating our self-destructive behaviors. Once, we become accustomed to recognizing and implementing these four ingredients, the programmed habit of **self-control** allows us to take control of our lives. Let's begin by examining each key-ingredient and learning simple techniques for enhancing their influence.

A. *SELF-CONTROL*

'I count him braver who overcomes his desires than him who conquers his enemies; for the hardest victory is over self.'
-Aristotle (384 – 322 B.C.)

Learn to say NO to your destructive feelings, uncontrolled cravings, and selfish desires. Our primal and self-satisfying desires constantly demand appropriate control, and if we continue to satisfy the need of urges, we weaken our self-control. The narcotic of having everything all the time can dominate every action of our lives. When we begin to discriminate between what is actually needed and what is truly unnecessary, we develop a powerful sense of personal management.

The ability to control our emotions, actions, words, and thoughts has always been one of man's most difficult tasks. In today's society, we have made even the most outrageous overindulgence accessible by the simple push of a button. It is far more difficult to exert **self-control** over our lives today, than any other time in human history, and it shows!

Once we stop succumbing to every whim, craving, and desire we have, our **self-control** begins to strengthen and create a chain reaction. We become more alert and vigilant towards managing that which is good, and that which is unnecessary or bad. The power of **self-control** becomes strong enough to regulate our mental and physical cravings, society-induced desires, and influenced behaviors.

Once we have awakened **self-control** through the management of urges, we must reinforce it by creating the habit of denying ourselves that which we crave. **Self-control** acts as a filter against the powerful influence of advertising, accessibility, and our own destructive human habits. We live in a society where it is hard NOT to be fat, lazy, unhealthy, drugged up, bankrupt, depressed, or emotionally unstable. We have created so many conveniences, trends, wants, and erratic behaviors through advertising and mass media, that we are brainwashed to crave things.

The first step to gaining **self-control** is one of identifying the areas in our lives that are **out of control**. We have to take a close look:

Once we identify those things we need more control over, we can start small by gaining little victories each day. For example if you smoke you must begin denying yourself one cigarette a day, the extra snack, that extra beer after work, or the satisfaction of indulging your emotional outbursts. If you try to go "cold-turkey" on all of your cravings, habits, and behaviors, you will surely fail.

A technique for gaining self-control over our cravings and habits involves a self-inspection of our daily lives. By performing an inventory of our bad behaviors and habits, we can focus our efforts on controlling them.

Here is a step by step description of this self-control technique:

1. **Personal Inventory** – Find a quiet and private place to sit down with a paper and pen. Begin taking a day by day inventory of your bad habits and destructive cravings.

2. **Start Small** – Begin reducing each habit or craving a little each day. Keep a journal of your progress and talk to yourself about the benefits of eliminating destructive behaviors.

3. **Self-Denial** – Start by denying yourself a certain pleasure each day. Target a daily activity like excessive eating or watching television.

4.**Keep a Schedule** – Make a to-do list and stick to it for a change. Make a commitment to write a daily schedule and accomplish every task.

5.   **Review** – At the end of each day, sit down and critique your performance.

Mentally re-live how you exercised self-control over your cravings and habits.

Another very effective technique is called the power band. This method involves wearing a piece of colored string or rubber band around your wrist to constantly remind yourself of the habit or craving you are going to control today. Take a large rubber band and write the bad habit or behavior that you wish to focus on for this particular day, and wear it around your wrist to constantly remind you of your control. I have personally seen this method change the lives of many people. Visualize in your mind that this rubber band empowers you with self-control that flows through your whole body. Every time you are faced with a certain thought, action, or environment that stimulates this craving or bad behavior, look to the power band for help. Remember that the power of your mind is the most important ally you have in the battle for self-control.

B. *MOTIVATION*

'Rest not! Life is sweeping by; go and do before you die. Something mighty and sublime, leave behind to conquer time.'
-Johann Goethe (1749 – 1832)

Motivation is the fuel that gives our success engine its drive. Motivation is a group of reasons that develop a desire to accomplish, have, act, and perform in a manner that will satisfy a certain desire. Strong motivation is the underlying power behind some of the world's greatest achievements. Motivation is responsible for creating actions, thoughts, and situations that are directed toward a specific accomplishment. There is no use in trying to master self-discipline if you lack the motivation to have it. Every human being has been motivated by something at some point in their lives. The fact that you are reading this book shows that you have a certain degree of motivation to succeed at something.

The problem that most people encounter when trying to motivate themselves to achieve a certain goal, is the problem of false motivators. False motivation is the main problem behind most humans' poor daily performance. For example, the person who wakes up each and every day to go to work because he has to, and not because he wants to, is falsely motivated. The person that goes on a diet because his or her spouse wants them to is falsely motivated. The employee, who is told to perform a certain task because their boss told them to, is falsely motivated. These are all examples of why people perform poorly or experience lackluster results. True motivation is the result of a strong personal desire that focuses a person's thoughts, words, and actions in such a way as to elicit 100 percent effort. Imagine if you could muster the same motivation for performing at work, as you do for personal gain. How strong would your motivation be if you were promised one million dollars for showing up to work every day this week?

The reason that Super-Humans live a life of greatness and success is because they are truly motivated to accomplish their goals. How many people achieve a life of greatness or success in a job that they hate? How financially disciplined is a person who works simply to pay off daily bills and not for the attainment of goals? How many A's did you receive in classes that you were completely uninterested in? When we stop and think about our daily lives, we can easily distinguish false and true motivators simply by looking at our performance in certain areas.

When you truly desire to control certain habits, cravings, and behaviors in your life, you already have one of the key ingredients to self-discipline. Most people know that they want control over certain aspects of their lives, but lack the motivation to bring about true change. One of the easiest methods for strengthening motivation is through pressure. By telling your family, friends, and co-workers of your commitment to control an aspect of your life, you establish the presence of external pressure. Now, the motivation for achieving discipline is embarrassment, self-worth, and challenge. Peer pressure is a very powerful motivator for most people. Tell your family and friends of the commitment you have made to losing weight and exercising. Tell all of your co-workers of your personal challenge, and let everyone at lunch and dinner know of your low-fat diet and see how strong your motivation becomes.

Only through self-discipline can we begin to control and shape the direction of our lives, and only through proper motivation can we experience self-discipline. Always be aware of your level of motivation. Use different techniques and situations to strengthen your motivation in specific areas. Only by focusing on self-control and motivation first, can you expect to open the doors to a life of self-discipline.

C. *PERSISTENCE*

'Endurance is one of the most difficult disciplines, but it is to the one who endures that the final victory comes.'

Persistence is the act of continued action and effort towards an objective or goal, even in the face of multiple failures. Do you remember a time in your life when you kept after something again and again until you finally succeeded? How powerful and glorious did it make you feel to finally achieve your intended goal? How often in your daily life do you accept failure or the answer NO? How about all of your bad habits, cravings, and bad behaviors which now exist in your life, how many times did you give up after failing to control them?

Self-discipline does not come without experiencing failure, and the only way to defeat failure is through persistence and perseverance. All of the civilizations past and present Super-Humans have found success and happiness with a never-say-die attitude. One of our country's most successful Super-Humans was also one of history's most persistent failures. Here is his story:

Abraham Lincoln

1831 - Failed in business - declared bankruptcy.

1832 - Defeated for State Legislature.

1834 - Again failed in business – declares bankruptcy.

1835 - Fiancée dies.

1836 - Has a nervous breakdown.

1837 - Defeated in election.

1843 - Defeated in bid for U.S. Congress.

1846 - Again defeated for U.S. Congress.

1847 - Fails for a third time in bid for U.S. Congress.

1855 - Defeated for U.S. Senate.

1856 - Defeated for office of Vice President.

1858 - Again defeated for U.S. Senate.

1859 - Elected President of the United States of America.

The history books are full of Super-Humans who used the power of persistence to gain control of their destinies. The great Prime Minister of Great Britain, Winston Churchill, once said, "Success is going from failure to failure without a loss of enthusiasm." This is the most common reason for people's lack of self-discipline. It is because they failed once or twice at controlling their life that they become afraid to try again. Well, here is your chance to begin anew. By using the information and techniques found in this chapter, you will become better educated at how to achieve total control of your life. There is no magic formula or ancient Hindu technique for becoming persistent. All the perseverance and persistence you will ever need is deep inside you, waiting to be exercised.

Of the four ingredients required for self-discipline, persistence is probably the most powerful of the four, because without persistence you will never experience success. You must plan to never give up, even before you begin. If you mentally motivate yourself to keep trying no matter what, you will subconsciously program yourself for persistence. If you are motivated, have self-control, and set specific goals to achieve self-discipline, but give up at the first sign of failure, you will never experience self-discipline or success.

Persistence is the one ingredient that must always be present in order to succeed. Begin today by declaring your tenacity and vowing to never give up, no matter how long it takes. Make a point of going that extra mile. Learn to break out of your comfort zone and start testing the boundaries of your physical and mental limitations.

D. *GOALS*

'One should act in consonance with the way of Heaven and Earth, enduring and eternal, the superior man perseveres long in his course, adapts to the times, but remains firm in his direction and correct in his goals.' -I Ching (1150 BC)

Highly successful people, world leaders, great artists, and history's most important Super-Humans all have one thing in common: they use self-discipline on a daily basis to achieve their goals. Clear and specific goals are the essential foundation of not only self-discipline, but also a lifetime of health, wealth, and longevity. Without clearly defining short-term and lifelong goals, you have no use for self-discipline. Learning life mastery and personal discipline will only come about when you set precise goals that you wish to achieve. Self-discipline goals are somewhat different than success-oriented goals, in that self-discipline goals are defined by personal improvement. Once you identify areas of your life that you wish to gain total control over, you have now defined specific areas of improvement.

Self-discipline-oriented goals are essential to generating self-control, motivation, and persistence, the other three key ingredients needed for self-control. Here is an example of setting goals:

1. I want to have total control over when, how, and what I eat for the next 30 days.

2. I am going to gain control of my finances by sticking to my scheduled budget each and every day for the next 90 days.

3. I want my fellow co-workers to look up to me as a leader and example of discipline by the way I speak, act, and dress in 60 days.

4. I will gain control of my emotions by disciplining my anger, depression, and attitude around my family, friends, and co-workers.

5. I am going to set aside one hour every day to work on my goal of being self-employed in one year.

6. I will set aside one hour each day to organizing, maintaining, and cleaning my household, my clothing, and my possessions.

7. I want to dedicate one evening each week to my spouse, and use this evening to improve our relationship and show my love and appreciation.

As you can see from this list of self-discipline goals, the key to having discipline is to clearly define that for which you want to use it. By setting specific goals, you enact powerful mental forces that help you focus your thoughts, actions, and efforts to accomplishing them. Take the time to think about your personal improvement desires and clearly write them down. Make photocopies of your self-discipline goals, paste them all over your office, put them in your car, stick them to your bathroom mirror, and visualize yourself achieving total control. It is one thing to say that you want to lose weight, but it is another to clearly define the amount, how, and when you are going to lose the weight.

You must understand that simply wanting something is not enough, you must define, refine, focus, and schedule specific actions that you will take to have what you desire. The amazing power of self-discipline can alter your life to that of a Super-Human, by simply understanding the process and forces at work in the human body and mind. Remember that the four key-ingredients are specific guidelines by which you will ensure the greatest chance of success in your quest for self-control. Use the powerful techniques that you have learned in this chapter to prepare a personal battle plan for achieving your desires, wants, and goals.

Self-control can surely set you free and change your whole life, but you must pay attention to the four key-ingredients to insure total success. Tomorrow when you go to work, stop and look around at all of the people you see, and think about how a self-disciplined person would act, talk, and look. Use the power of self-discipline to enhance your wealth, happiness, and the lives of your loved ones. Make the commitment to gain total control of your life today, and you will thank yourself tomorrow. Know that it is possible to rise above average human performance, by dedicating time each day to achieve the status of a disciplined person.

TO THE READER:

I hope that you enjoyed this article. This article is taken from my new book entitled, 'POWER LIVING – Mastering The Art of Self-Discipline'. Please don't get the impression that I am trying to give you the answers to all of the world's problems, but rather that I have a few ideas and experiences that have been proven to work –even in life and death situations. We are all trying to improve something about ourselves. It seems that everywhere you turn there is some slick-talking ex-car salesman trying to make a buck off of an instant success formula –there is no such thing. I have spent over 12 years studying and practicing personal achievement and discipline-building tools in the world of special operations. Through it all, I have come to realize that all of the answers to achievement are found right in your pretty little head. The trick is to dig deep and go a little further than then next guy. Remember that whatever you consider to be successful, someone,

somewhere has already done it. Learn how, why, and what he/she did to accomplish it. This is the fastest way to getting what you want. I highly encourage you to read the rest of my book, not because I want your money –but because you have already invested the time to learn a new way of becoming a better person by reading this article."
http://www.self-discipline.8m.com/ingredients_of_self.html 2/24/05

They get to the point that they don't even know who they are and where they are going. There is a real danger at this point, when the other person wants to dominate, control and isolate this person. They don't know who you are in the relationship! You can lose your identity as a person and end up with low self-esteem sets in, they feel inadequate within them self. Also they become a codependent, they can't move without the other person's approval. This person always has to deal with the other person's anger and disapproval, and even worse is their violent out bursts, they are trapped.

The persons themselves are caught up this warfare of who's right and who's wrong and the custody of the kids. In most cases each person thinks they are RIGHT and each person has their own point of view. Each one has their own prospective of what has happened or who is RIGHT and who is WRONG.

They have created a real problem to deal with, there has to be a certain amount of parental control because of the children. Especially if they don't want to destroy the emotional stability of the children! But, in most cases they are under mind by the circumstance! In some cases the parents are so bitter that they don't realize what they are doing to the children. They are more concerned about getting even, this is one of the ways of getting-even with the other person, and make them pay for the suffering and pain they caused.

ARE YOU GOING BACK TO THE OLD PATTERNS OF ANGER

Chapter 10

MEETING YOUR DEMANDS

Assessment III - ACCOUNTABILITY in a person's life.

No one is an island reflecting a cultural understanding of connectedness and responsibility between people. We were designed to be interconnected and complement to each other.

What does accountability actually mean: Reckoning?

Computation.

: A statement explaining one's conduct. *(Webster's Dictionary)*

Accounting denotes certain theories, behavioral assumptions, measurement rules and procedures for collecting and reporting useful information concerning the activities and objectives of a person or organization.

Accountability looks back to some deed done or attitude held. Obligation looks forward to normal demands that need to be met in relationships. Our cultural understanding suggest that accountability is best designed when it encourages desirable performance. This process is served by the discipline and classifying of data and activities in order to measured standards and expectations. It is organic in nature and expressed through relationships, networks and systems.

Reflective questions can be helpful when people self-audit even when dealing with others. Accountability is demonstrated through concern for others. Rewards and penalties will be mastered in light of whether we construct our lives on a good foundation. *(Encyclopedia Britannica)*

HOW TO DEAL WITH ANGER

"Anger is a healthy emotion when it is expressed appropriately. When it is not, it can have devastating effects.

One out of five Americans has an anger management problem. It is a major cause of conflict in our personal and relationships. Child abuse, spousal abuse, divorce, stormy relationships, addiction, workplace violence and crime are just a few examples of what happens when anger is mismanaged.

Anger also affects our physical health. For example, it has been shown to contribute to headaches and migraines, severe gastrointestinal symptoms, hypertension, depression, anxiety and heart disease.

Symptoms of Anger
Symptoms of Anger Out of Control

Anger becomes out of control and destructive when a person responds to their angry feelings by attacking someone, with the intention to harm them. It can be a verbal attack – insults, threats, sarcasm – or it can be physical punishment or restriction.

The following are unhealthy responses to anger:

Direct behavioral signs:
- Assaultive: physical and verbal cruelty, rage, slapping, shoving, kicking, hitting, threaten with knife or gun.
- Aggression: overly critical, fault finding, name-calling, accusing someone of having immoral or despicable traits or motives, nagging, whining, sarcasm, prejudice, flashes of temper.
- Hurtful: malicious gossip, stealing, trouble-making
- Rebellious: anti-social behavior, open defiance, refusal to talk

Direct verbal or cognitive signs:
- Open hatred and insults

- Contempt and disgust

- Critical: 'If you really cared about me, you'd…'

- Suspicious: 'You haven't been fair…'

- Blaming: 'They have been trying to cause me trouble.'

- Revengeful: 'I wish I could really hurt them.'

- Name calling

Research has found that 'flying off the handle' or 'letting it rip' with anger actually escalates anger and aggression and does nothing to help you resolve the situation. In fact, none of the responses listed above do anything to help solve a problem. These unhealthy responses to anger serve only to destroy your personal relationships, undermine your work life and job effectiveness and damage your physical and emotional health.

The chances are good that if you do have a problem with anger, you already know it. If you find yourself acting in ways that seem out of control and frightening, if you recognize the negative impact it is having on your personal relationships, at work, or other important areas of your life, it is time to learn better ways to deal with anger. Through counseling, you can learn how to manage your anger and learn how to express anger in constructive – rather than destructive – ways."

Dealing with Self-Control

Are you famous for your short temper? Do you have a short fuse or find yourself getting into frequent arguments and fights? Anger is a normal, healthy emotion. But it's unhealthy when it flares up all the time or spirals out of control. Chronic, explosive anger has serious consequences for your relationships, your health, and your state of mind. The good news is that getting anger under control is easier than you think. With a little insight into the real reasons for your anger and some effective anger management tools, you can learn how to express your feelings in healthier ways and keep your temper from hijacking your life.

Understanding Anger

The emotion of anger is neither good nor bad. It's perfectly healthy and normal to feel angry when you've been mistreated or wronged. The feeling isn't the problem—it's what you do with it that makes a difference. Anger becomes a problem when it harms you or others.

If you have a hot temper, you may feel like it's out of your hands and there's little you can do to tame the beast. But you have more control over your anger than you think. You *can* learn to express your emotions without hurting others—and when you do, you'll not only feel better, but you'll also be more likely to get your needs met. Mastering the art of anger management takes work, but the more you practice, the easier it will get. And the payoff is huge. Learning to control your anger and express it appropriately will help you build better relationships, achieve your goals, and lead a healthier, more satisfying life.

Myths and Facts about Anger

Myth: I shouldn't "hold in" my anger. It's healthy to vent and let it out.

Fact: While it's true that suppressing and ignoring anger is unhealthy, venting is no better. Anger is not something you have to 'let out' in an aggressive way in order to avoid blowing up. In fact, outbursts and tirades only fuel the fire and reinforce your anger problem.

Myth: Anger, aggression, and intimidation help me earn respect and get what I want.

Fact: True power doesn't come from bullying others. People may be afraid of you, but they won't respect you if you can't control yourself or handle opposing viewpoints. Others will be more willing to listen to you and accommodate your needs if you communicate in a respectful way.

Myth: I can't help myself. Anger isn't something you can control.

Fact: You can't always control the situation you're in or how it makes you feel, but you *can* control how you express your anger. And you *can* express your anger without being verbally or physically abusive. Even if someone is pushing your buttons, you always have a choice about how to respond.

Myth: Anger management is about learning to suppress your anger.

Fact: Never getting angry is not a good goal. Anger is normal, and it will come out regardless of how hard you try to suppress it. Anger management is all about becoming aware of your underlying feelings and needs and developing healthier ways to manage upset. Rather than trying to suppress your anger, the goal is to express it in constructive ways.

Why learning to control your anger is important

You might think that venting your anger is healthy, that the people around you are too sensitive, that your anger is justified, or that you need to show your fury to get respect. But the truth is that anger is much more likely to damage your relationships, impair your judgment, get in the way of success, and have a negative impact on the way people see you.

- **Out-of-control anger hurts your physical health.** Constantly operating at high levels of stress and tension is bad for your health. Chronic anger makes you more susceptible to heart disease, diabetes, high cholesterol levels, a weakened immune system, insomnia, and high blood pressure.

- **Out-of-control anger hurts your mental health.** Chronic anger consumes huge amounts of mental energy and clouds your thinking, making it harder to concentrate, see the bigger picture, and enjoy life. It can also lead to stress, depression, and other mental health problems.

- **Out-of-control anger hurts your career.** Constructive criticism, creative differences, and heated debate can be healthy. But lashing out only alienates your colleagues, supervisors, or clients and erodes their respect. What's more, a bad reputation can follow you wherever you go, making it harder and harder to get ahead.

- **Out-of-control anger hurts your relationships with others.** It causes lasting scars in the people you love most and gets in the way of your friendships and work relationships. Chronic, intense anger makes it hard for others to trust you, speak honestly, or feel comfortable—they never know what is going to set you off or what you will do. Explosive anger is especially damaging to children."

Anger control and management tip

1: Explore what's really behind your anger

If you're struggling with out-of-control anger, you may be wondering why your fuse is so short. Anger problems often stem from what you've learned as a child. If you watched others in your family scream, hit each other, or throw things, you might think this is how anger is supposed to be expressed. Traumatic events and high levels of stress can make you more susceptible to anger as well.

Anger is often a cover-up for other feelings

In order to get your needs met and express your anger in appropriate ways, you need to be in touch with what you are really feeling. Are you truly angry? Or is your anger masking other feelings such as embarrassment, insecurity, hurt, shame, or vulnerability?

If your knee-jerk response in many situations is anger, it is very likely that your temper is covering up your true feelings and needs. This is especially likely if you grew up in a family where expressing feelings was strongly discouraged. As an adult, you may have a hard time acknowledging feelings other than anger.

Clues that there's something more to your anger

- **You have a hard time compromising.** Is it hard for you to understand other people's points of view, and even harder to concede a point? If you grew up in a family where anger was out of control, you may remember how the angry person got his or her way by being the loudest and most demanding. Compromising might bring up scary feelings of failure and vulnerability.

- **You have trouble expressing emotions other than anger.** Do you pride yourself on being tough and in control, never letting your guard down? Do you feel that emotions like fear, guilt, or shame don't apply to you? Everyone has those emotions, and if you think you don't, you may be using anger as a cover for them.

- **You view different opinions and viewpoints as a personal challenge to you.** Do you believe that your way is always right and get angry when others disagree? If you have a strong need to be in control or a fragile ego, you may interpret other perspectives as a challenge to your authority, rather than simply a different way of looking at things.

If you are uncomfortable with many emotions, disconnected, or stuck on an angry one-note response to everything, it might do you some good to get back in touch with your feelings. Emotional awareness is the key to self-understanding and success in life. Without the ability to recognize, manage, and deal with the full range of human emotions, you'll inevitably spin into confusion, isolation, and self-doubt.

To learn more, visit <u>Emotional Awareness: Managing and Dealing with Emotions and Feelings</u>.

Some Dynamics of Anger

- We become angry when we are stressed and body resources are down.
- We are rarely ever angry for the reasons we think.
- We are often angry when we didn't get what we needed as a child.
- We often become angry when we see a trait in others we can't stand in ourselves.
- Underneath many current angers are old disappointments, traumas, and triggers.
- Sometimes we get angry because we were hurt as a child.
- We get angry when a current event brings up an old unresolved situation from the past.
- We often feel strong emotion when a situation has a similar content, words or energy that we have felt before.

Anger control and management tip
2: Be aware of your anger warning signs and triggers

While you might feel that you just explode into anger without warning, in fact, there are physical warning signs in your body. Anger is a normal physical response. It fuels the 'fight or flight' system of the body, and the angrier you get, the more your body goes into overdrive. Becoming aware of your own personal signs that your temper is starting to boil allows you to take steps to manage your anger before it gets out of control.

Pay attention to the way anger feels in your body

- Knots in your stomach
- Clenching your hands or jaw
- Feeling clammy or flushed
- Breathing faster
- Headaches
- Pacing or needing to walk around
- "Seeing red"
- Having trouble concentrating
- Pounding heart
- Tensing your shoulders

Identify the negative thought patterns that trigger your temper

You may think that external things—the insensitive actions of other people, for example, or frustrating situations—are what cause your anger. But anger problems have less to do with what happens to you than how you interpret and think about what happened. Common negative thinking patterns that trigger and fuel anger include:

- **Overgeneralizing.** For example, "You always interrupt me. You NEVER consider my needs. EVERYONE disrespects me. I NEVER get the credit I deserve."
- **Obsessing on "should" and "must."** Having a rigid view of the way things should or must be and getting angry when reality doesn't line up with this vision.
- **Mind reading and jumping to conclusions**. Assuming you "know" what someone else is thinking or feeling—that he or she intentionally upset you, ignored your wishes, or disrespected you.
- **Collecting straws**. Looking for things to get upset about, usually while overlooking or blowing past anything positive. Letting these small irritations build and build until you reach the "final straw" and explode, often over something relatively minor.
- **Blaming.** When anything bad happens or something goes wrong, it's always someone else's fault. You blame others for the things that happen to you rather than taking responsibility for your own life.

Avoid people, places, and situations that bring out your worst

Stressful events don't excuse anger, but understanding how these events affect you can help you take control of your environment and avoid unnecessary aggravation. Look at your regular routine and try to identify activities, times of day, people, places, or situations that trigger irritable or angry feelings. Maybe you get into a fight every time you go out for drinks with a certain group of friends. Or maybe the traffic on your daily commute drives you crazy. Then think about ways to avoid these triggers or view the situation differently so it doesn't make your blood boil.

Anger control and management tip 3: Learn ways to cool down

Once you know how to recognize the warning signs that your temper is rising and anticipate your triggers, you can act quickly to deal with your anger before it spins out of control. There are many techniques that can help you cool down and keep your anger in check.

Quick tips for cooling down

- **Focus on the physical sensations of anger.** While it may seem counterintuitive, tuning into the way your body feels when you're angry often lessens the emotional intensity of your anger.
- **Take some deep breaths**. Deep, slow breathing helps counteract rising tension. The key is to breathe deeply from the abdomen, getting as much fresh air as possible into your lungs.
- **Exercise**. A brisk walk around the block is a great idea. It releases pent-up energy so you can approach the situation with a cooler head.
- **Use your senses.** Take advantage of the relaxing power of your sense of sight, smell, hearing, touch, and taste. You might try listening to music or picturing yourself in a favorite place.
- **Stretch or massage areas of tension.** Roll your shoulders if you are tensing them, for example, or gently massage your neck and scalp.
- **Slowly count to ten.** Focus on the counting to let your rational mind catch up with your feelings. If you still feel out of control by the time you reach ten, start counting again.

For more rapid cool-down techniques, see Quick Stress Relief: How to Manage and Relieve Stress in the Moment.

Give yourself a reality check

When you start getting upset about something, take a moment to think about the situation. Ask yourself:

- How important is it in the grand scheme of things?
- Is it really worth getting angry about it?
- Is it worth ruining the rest of my day?
- Is my response appropriate to the situation?
- Is there anything I can do about it?
- Is taking action worth my time?

Anger control and management tip 4: Find healthier ways to express your anger

If you've decided that the situation is worth getting angry about and there's something you can do to make it better, the key is to express your feelings in a healthy way. When communicated respectfully and channeled effectively, anger can be a tremendous source of energy and inspiration for change.

Pinpoint what you're really angry about

Have you ever gotten into an argument over something silly? Big fights often happen over something small, like a dish left out or being ten minutes late. But there's usually a bigger issue behind it. If you find your irritation and anger rapidly rising, ask yourself "What am I really angry about?" Identifying the real source of frustration will help you communicate your anger better, take constructive action, and work towards a resolution.

Take five if things get too heated

If your anger seems to be spiraling out of control, remove yourself from the situation for a few minutes or for as long as it takes you to cool down. A brisk walk, a trip to the gym, or a few minutes listening to some music should allow you to calm down, release pent up emotion, and then approach the situation with a cooler head.

Always fight fair

It's okay to be upset at someone, but if you don't fight fair, the relationship will quickly break down. Fighting fair allows you to express your own needs while still respecting others.

- **Make the relationship your priority.** Maintaining and strengthening the relationship, rather than "winning" the argument, should always be your first priority. Be respectful of the other person and his or her viewpoint.

- **Focus on the present.** Once you are in the heat of arguing, it's easy to start throwing past grievances into the mix. Rather than looking to the past and assigning blame, focus on what you can do in the present to solve the problem.

- **Choose your battles.** Conflicts can be draining, so it's important to consider whether the issue is really worthy of your time and energy. If you pick your battles rather than fighting over every little thing, others will take you more seriously when you are upset.

- **Be willing to forgive.** Resolving conflict is impossible if you're unwilling or unable to forgive. Resolution lies in releasing the urge to punish, which can never compensate for our losses and only adds to our injury by further depleting and draining our lives.

- **Know when to let something go.** If you can't come to an agreement, agree to disagree. It takes two people to keep an argument going. If a conflict is going nowhere, you can choose to disengage and move on.

- **Therapy for anger problems.** Therapy can be a great way to explore the reasons behind your anger. If you don't know why you are getting angry, it's very hard to control. Therapy provides a safe environment to learn more about your reasons and identify triggers for your anger. It's also a safe place to practice new skills in expressing your anger.

- **Anger management classes or groups.** Anger management classes or groups allow you to see others coping with the same struggles. You will also learn tips and techniques for managing your anger and hear other people's stories. For domestic violence issues, traditional anger management is usually not recommended. There are special classes that go to the issue of power and control that are at the heart of domestic violence.

When to seek help for anger management

If your anger is still spiraling out of control, despite putting the previous anger management techniques into practice, or if you're getting into trouble with the law or hurting others—you need more help. There are many therapists, classes, and programs for people with anger management problems. Asking for help is not a sign of weakness. You'll often find others in the same shoes, and getting direct feedback on techniques for controlling anger can be tremendously helpful.

If you're loved one has an anger management problem

If your loved one has an anger problem, you probably feel like you're walking on eggshells all the time. But always remember that you are not to blame for your loved one's anger. There is never an excuse for physically or verbally abusive behavior. You have a right to be treated with respect and to live without fear of an angry outburst or a violent rage.

Tips for dealing with a loved one's anger management problem

While you can't control another person's anger, you can control how you respond to it:

- Set clear boundaries about what you will and will not tolerate.
- Wait for a time when you are both calm to talk to your loved one about the anger problem. Don't bring it up when either one of you is already angry.
- Remove yourself from the situation if your loved one does not calm down.
- Consider counseling or therapy for yourself if you are having a hard time standing up for yourself.
- Put your safety first. Trust your instincts. If you feel unsafe or threatened in any way, get away from your loved one and go somewhere safe.

Anger isn't the real problem in abusive relationships

Despite what many people believe, domestic violence and abuse is not due to the abuser's loss of control over his behavior and temper. In fact, abusive behavior is a deliberate choice for the sole purpose of controlling you. If you are in an abusive relationship, know that couples counseling is not recommended—and your partner need specialized treatment, not regular anger management classes.

What Your Anger May Be Hiding / Psychology Today
Pages 1-3 [16]

"The heading above (which, half-seriously, I've contemplated submitting to various quotation dictionaries) aptly sums up my professional experience working with this so very problematic emotion. In the past 20+ years I've taught well over a hundred classes and workshops on anger management, and delivered many professional presentations on the subject.

When I first became interested in exploring this typically destructive emotion, the clinical literature devoted to it was curiously scant. But times have changed dramatically since then. With the increasing occurrence of such phenomena as road rage, drive-by shootings, high school and post office killing sprees—in short, with the prevalence of violence in America today—the attention given to acting-out, out-of-control anger may never have been greater. Probably no fewer than 50 books on anger geared toward the layperson have emerged in the past 15 years or so. And in 1995 a much overdue professionally-oriented book, entitled *Anger Disorders: Definition, Diagnosis, and Treatment* (ed. Howard Kassinove), finally proposed a comprehensive set of diagnostic categories to deal with anger as itself a clinical syndrome—rather than an emotion linked to other mental disorders.

As a psychologist, however, what I've learned about anger has come as much from my efforts as a therapist to better understand its dynamics in my clients as from examining the various writings focused on it. In what follows, I'll try to highlight some of the insights I've gained from trying to make coherent sense of the self-defeating behaviors I've seen in scores of-challenging-cases.

Anger as Freud's Forgotten Defense

If to Freud all defense mechanisms exist to protect the personality from an intolerable attack of anxiety when the ego is under siege, it's strange that he never considered anger as serving this pivotal psychological function. But to regard an essential human emotion as mainly designed to safeguard an individual from *another*, much more distressful emotion, is hardly a line of reasoning Freud might have been expected to follow. Still, in my own clinical experience, anger is almost never a primary emotion in that even when anger seems like an instantaneous, knee-jerk reaction to provocation, there's always some other feeling that gave rise to it. And this particular feeling is precisely what the anger has contrived to camouflage or control.

The simplest example of my admittedly unorthodox relegation of anger to secondary, 'reactive' status might relate to the universally frustrating situation of being cut off while driving. Virtually everyone I've ever asked has responded emphatically that their immediate reaction to such an event is anger. But when I further inquire as to what being 'cut off' typically involves—namely, the very real threat of an accident—they realize that in the fraction of a second before acting successfully to avert a collision, their emotion must certainly have been one of apprehension or fear. Cycling from the heightened arousal level of fear to an equally intense anger happens with such breathtaking speed that almost no one can recollect that flash of trepidation preceding the anger—or even rage. (And rage itself seems mostly a more potent, or desperate, form of anger created to fend off an even more serious threat to one's ego or sense of personal safety--whether that threat be mental, emotional or physical.)

The internal dynamic depicted in this illustration is the same with a whole host of emotions that, as soon as they begin to surface, can be effectively masked, squelched, or preempted through the emergence of secondary anger. And just as other defenses hinder healthy psychological coping (by hiding the underlying reality of anxiety that needs to be dealt with), so does anger belie the fragility of the ego that must depend on it for shielding and support.

Anger as Freud's Forgotten Defense

If to **Freud** all defense mechanisms exist to protect the **personality** from an intolerable attack of anxiety when the ego is under siege, it's strange that he never considered anger as serving this pivotal psychological function. But to regard an essential human emotion as mainly designed to safeguard an individual from *another*, much more distressful emotion, is hardly a line of reasoning Freud might have been expected to follow. Still, in my own clinical experience, anger is almost never a primary emotion in that even when anger seems like an instantaneous, knee-jerk reaction to provocation, there's always some other feeling that gave rise to it. And this particular feeling is precisely what the anger has contrived to camouflage or control.

The simplest example of my admittedly unorthodox relegation of anger to secondary, 'reactive' status might relate to the universally frustrating situation of being cut off while driving. Virtually everyone I've ever asked has responded emphatically that their immediate reaction to such an event is anger. But when I further inquire as to what being 'cut off' typically involves—namely, the very real threat of an accident—they realize that in the fraction of a second before acting successfully to avert a collision, their emotion must certainly have been one of apprehension or **fear**. Cycling from the heightened arousal level of fear to an equally intense anger happens with such breathtaking speed that almost no one can recollect that flash of trepidation preceding the anger—or even rage. (And rage itself seems mostly a more potent, or desperate, form of anger created to fend off an even more serious threat to one's ego or sense of personal safety--whether that threat be mental, emotional or physical.)

The internal dynamic depicted in this illustration is the same with a whole host of emotions that, as soon as they begin to surface, can be effectively masked, squelched, or preempted through the emergence of secondary anger. And just as other defenses hinder healthy psychological coping (by hiding the underlying reality of anxiety that needs to be dealt with), so does anger belie the fragility of the ego that must depend on it for shielding and support.

Anger as a Neurochemical Way of Self-Soothing
If to **Freud** all defense mechanisms exist to protect the **personality** from an intolerable attack of anxiety when the ego is under siege, it's strange that he never considered anger as serving this pivotal psychological function. But to regard an essential human emotion as mainly designed to safeguard an individual from *another*, much more distressful emotion, is hardly a line of reasoning Freud might have been expected to follow. Still, in my own clinical experience, anger is almost never a primary emotion in that even when anger seems like an instantaneous,

knee-jerk reaction to provocation, there's always some other feeling that gave rise to it. And this particular feeling is precisely what the anger has contrived to camouflage or control.

The simplest example of my admittedly unorthodox relegation of anger to secondary, 'reactive' status might relate to the universally frustrating situation of being cut off while driving. Virtually everyone I've ever asked has responded emphatically that their immediate reaction to such an event is anger. But when I further inquire as to what being 'cut off' typically involves—namely, the very real threat of an accident—they realize that in the fraction of a second before acting successfully to avert a collision, their emotion must certainly have been one of apprehension or **fear**. Cycling from the heightened arousal level of fear to an equally intense anger happens with such breathtaking speed that almost no one can recollect that flash of trepidation preceding the anger—or even rage. (And rage itself seems mostly a more potent, or desperate, form of anger created to fend off an even more serious threat to one's ego or sense of personal safety--whether that threat be mental, emotional or physical.)

The internal dynamic depicted in this illustration is the same with a whole host of emotions that, as soon as they begin to surface, can be effectively masked, squelched, or preempted through the emergence of secondary anger. And just as other defenses hinder healthy psychological coping (by hiding the underlying reality of anxiety that needs to be dealt with), so does anger belie the fragility of the ego that must depend on it for shielding and support.

Anger as Freud's Forgotten Defense

If to **Freud** all defense mechanisms exist to protect the **personality** from an intolerable attack of anxiety when the ego is under siege, it's strange that he never considered anger as serving this pivotal psychological function. But to regard an essential human emotion as mainly designed to safeguard an individual from *another*, much more distressful emotion, is hardly a line of reasoning Freud might have been expected to follow. Still, in my own clinical experience, anger is almost never a primary emotion in that even when anger seems like an instantaneous, knee-jerk reaction to provocation, there's always some other feeling that gave rise to it. And this particular feeling is precisely what the anger has contrived to camouflage or control.

The simplest example of my admittedly unorthodox relegation of anger to secondary, 'reactive' status might relate to the universally frustrating situation of being cut off while driving. Virtually everyone I've ever asked has responded emphatically that their immediate reaction to such an event is anger. But when I further inquire as to what being 'cut off' typically involves—namely, the very real threat of an accident—they realize that in the fraction of a second before acting successfully to avert a collision, their emotion must certainly have been one of apprehension or fear. Cycling from the heightened arousal level of fear to an equally intense anger happens with such breathtaking speed that almost no one can recollect that flash of trepidation preceding the anger—or even rage. (And rage itself seems mostly a more potent, or desperate, form of anger created to fend off an even more serious threat to one's ego or sense of personal safety--whether that threat be mental, emotional or physical.)

The internal dynamic depicted in this illustration is the same with a whole host of emotions that, as soon as they begin to surface, can be effectively masked, squelched, or preempted through the emergence of secondary anger. And just as other defenses hinder healthy psychological coping (by hiding the underlying reality of anxiety that needs to be dealt with), so does anger belie the fragility of the ego that must depend on it for shielding and-support.

Anger as a Neurochemical Way of Self-Soothing

With very few exceptions, the angry people I've worked with have suffered from significant **self-image** deficits. Many have been quite successful in their careers but far less so in their relationships, where anger triggers abound. Regardless of their professional achievements, however, almost all of them have been afflicted by an 'I'm not good enough' program (and some with an additional 'I'm a fraud' script as well).

In effect, whether individuals are confronted with physical or psychological pain (or the *threat* of such pain), the internal activation of the anger response will precipitate the release of a chemical expressly designed to *numb* it. This is why I've long viewed anger as a double-edged sword: terribly detrimental to relationships but nonetheless crucial in enabling many vulnerable people to emotionally survive in them.

Symptomatic anger covers up the pain of our 'core hurts.' These key distressful emotions include feeling ignored, unimportant, accused, guilty, untrustworthy, devalued, rejected, powerless, unlovable—or even unfit for human contact (cf. John Bradshaw's 'shame-based identity'). It is, therefore, only reasonable that if the self-elicitation of anger can successfully fend off such hurtful or unbearable feelings, one might eventually become dependent on the emotion to the point of addiction. The psychological concept of self-soothing is unquestionably relevant here. For we all need to find ways of comforting or reassuring ourselves when our self-esteem is endangered—whether through criticism, dismissal, or any other outside stimuli that feels invalidating and so revives old self-doubts. If we're healthy psychologically, then we have the internal resources to self-validate: to admit to ourselves possible inadequacies without experiencing intolerable guilt or shame. But if, deep down, we still feel bad about who we are, our deficient sense of self simply won't be able to withstand such external threats.

The remedy in this case? Paradoxical as it may seem, anger—even though it destroys any true peace of mind or sense of well-being—can yet help us to soothe ourselves. For our anger potently serves to *invalidate* whoever or whatever led *us* to feel invalidated. In adamantly disconfirming the legitimacy of the menacing external force, we self-righteously proclaim the superiority of our own viewpoint. Thus is our critical need for emotional/mental security restored.

Although we're hardly left in a state of inner harmony—and may actually be experiencing substantial turmoil—our defensive anger still permits us to achieve a certain comfort. After all, *we're* not wrong, or bad, or selfish, or inconsiderate; it's our spouse, our child, our neighbor, our coworker. Granted, this desperate reaction may be self-soothing of the last resort, but it's a kind of self-soothing nonetheless. In short, if we can't comfort ourselves through self-validation, we'll need to do so through *in*validating others. And people who suffer from chronic depression typically have not learned how to avail themselves of this potent, though ultimately self-defeating, defense.

Anger as the Low Road to Self-Empowerment

If anger can help us self-medicate against all sorts of psychological pain, it is equally effective in helping ward off exasperating feelings of powerlessness. And here again Not only does our brain secrete the analgesic-like norepinephrine when we're provoked, it also produces the amphetamine-like hormone epinephrine, which enables us to experience a surge of energy throughout our body—the adrenaline rush that many of my clients have reported feeling during a sudden attack of anger.

How ironically 'adaptive'!—and seductive as well. A person or situation somehow makes us feel defeated or powerless, and reactively transforming these helpless feelings into anger instantly provides us with a heightened sense of control. As the title of this article suggests, if anger can make us feel powerful, if it's the 'magic elixir' that seemingly is able to address our deepest doubts about ourselves, no wonder it can end up controlling us. In a sense, it's every bit as much a drug as alcohol or cocaine. And it's my strong belief that many, many millions of people worldwide are addicted to anger because of its illusorily empowering aspects.

Although almost nobody appreciates their proclivities toward anger as coping strategies calculated to disarm, denigrate, or intimidate 'the enemy,' I'm convinced that anger is employed universally to bolster a diminished sense of personal power. Contrary to feeling weak or out of control, the experience of anger can foster a sense of invulnerability— even invincibility. The movie *Raging Bull*ing is possibly one of the most compelling examples of how anger can *physically* fortify an individual, powerfully compensating for various personal deficits (particularly in the realm of relationships).

Anger as a 'Safe' Way to Attach in Intimate (Read, Vulnerable) Relationships

I would like to briefly to explore--also paradoxically—anger's function in ensuring safety in close relationships by regulating distance. It's only logical that if a child's caretakers proved distressingly unresponsive, unreliable or untrustworthy, the 'adult child' is likely to be gun-shy, or defensively cultivate a certain emotional detachment, in intimate relationships. While such individuals may desperately yearn for the secure **attachment** bond that eluded them in **childhood,** they will be wary of openly expressing such needs and desire. Doing so that a partner who might respond negatively to them could reopen ancient wounds.

The primal fear of these individuals is that if they let their guard down and made themselves truly vulnerable—freely revealing what their heart still aches for—a disapproving or rejecting response from their mate might lead them, almost literally, to bleed to death. And so (however ultimately self-defeating) the protective role of anger in non-disclosure and distancing can feel not simply necessary but absolutely essential.

Repeatedly, I've heard spouses complain that when their relationship seemed to be going better than usual, their partner—apparently beginning to experience some trepidation about 'getting too close for comfort'—would, with little or no provocation, pick a fight. Psychologically wounded from parental insensitivity, disregard, or worse, their profound distrust of intimate connections would compel them to disengage through self-protective anger.

Contrariwise, anger also has the effect of pushing the other person away, of getting *them* to withdraw. In my anger classes I've many times suggested that if you want a lot of space in your life, just be a very angry person . . . and you'll get all the space you could ever desire. After all, if there's really been no precedent in our life for relational intimacy, getting really close to another—or having another get really close to *us*—can begin to feel hazardous to our emotional equilibrium, thereby setting off a self-insulating reaction of anger.

Yet feeling *too* detached from our partner can also revivify old attachment wounds and fears, so at times the dance changes and the distance becomes the pursuer. The main point here is that anger, however unconsciously, can be employed in a variety of ways to regulate vulnerability in committed relationships. Not only can it be used to disengage from the other when the sought-after closeness starts to create anxiety, it can also, ironically, be a tactic for *engaging* the other—but at a safe distance. To corrupt Descartes, the assumption here might be: 'We fight, therefore we exist [as a couple].'

If our attachment bond with our original caretakers was tenuous or insecure, it's only reasonable that one of the least perilous way to 'attach' to another would be through a distance-moderating anger that helped control our sense of risk about such ties. Uncomfortable about getting too close, yet apprehensive about a *total* break in our attachment, our being easily provoked by our partner may become the only viable solution to our dilemma—however dysfunctional and unsatisfying this solution might be.

To conclude, in devising an appropriate treatment for a client's anger problems, what I've learned to ask myself is not simply, 'What anger control skills does this person need to learn?' but rather, 'What is this person's anger enabling, protecting against, or symptomatic of?' For if there is such a thing as a tip-of-the-iceberg emotion, surely it is anger—the feeling that can conceal so very much below it—that best fits the bill."

Psychology Today

Next we want to deal with:

Applying SELF HELP PRINCIPLES to SELF CONTROL

I want to help a person control their conflicts / environment and if a person is not in control of their situations, the next question are others controlling you. How to deal with the different aspects self-control? I know I would not be where I am today without being a disciplined person. How was I able to deal with the anger and how can a person manage one self and control the situations in their life? When you are able to do this you will have to control your mind and master your environment and the way to do this is using self-help principles.

This part of this study I will clearly define some of the basis in one's beliefs about self-control and this will include your own self-control. Personal discipline is ultimately controlling ones' self-will, sacrifice, and gratification.

I will take into consideration a person's ability to control their desire to overcome personal failures and yet that is another aspect of overcoming in a person's life.

How can I refuse other people's demands without making enemies?

Another basic element is assertiveness and wanting e4verything your way or the other person wants everything their way creates **demands**. There are training methods a person learns the right to say no to certain **demands**, and not feel guilty. You do not have to meet everybody's needs, or agree to help everyone who asks for help. Saying no can be a great **stress** reducer by preventing a person from becoming overcommitted. Here, there are five points to remember:

1. Saying no does not reject or put down the other person. It simply means you are refusing a specific request. If you can keep the relationship with the other person and a person may say yes to other requests in the future.

2. When saying no, be brief and direct.

3. Do not diminish your refusal with elaborate explanations, apologies, or excuses. You can give a brief reason, such as "I'm really too busy this time and will be glad to help later or maybe next time." A good reason is not an excuse and don't let it provides the other person with ammunition for trying to make you change your mind.

4. If you really mean to say no, stick to it. Don't be swayed or coerced by the other person, who may plead, compliment you, or make you feel guilty, particularly if you have been manipulated into saying yes in the past. Remember, although the other person has (needs, wants, and desires), so do you. And you have a right not to meet all the needs of others. A person is not obligated if they can't do it.

5. When saying no, use assertive body language. Make direct eye contact, speak clearly and distinctly, have good posture, and use appropriate gestures for emphasis. Avoid whining, slumping, and looking away.

People who get caught in this trap of **overwhelming demands** are likely to become prisoners of the routine of saying yes, and meaning it. They may not take time to notice other opportunities, and their habitual routine prevents them from taking the first step necessary toward harnessing their will to say no.

Most people are overwhelmed by the **demands** put on them, even in a work situation, but it is more important how they deal with those situations. How does a person know whether there's a problem with the way they approach life? Some deem other aspects of life more important than others and that is natural, but a person has a problem when they never find time to really see what is going on in their life and relationships. Or they might feel under constant pressure from all of the above. The danger sign is when a person believes they are indispensable, and have problems developing the capacity to dream an idea into existence and transforming it into a concrete intention.

People who fall into the trap of **overwhelming demands** typically do so because they fail to actively influence those **demands**, and they let them take them under. There are some people who take **demands** for granted, or simply don't respond to them.

DR JOHN BARRETT

Self-Discipline

Self-Improvement Methods?

Chapter 11

SELF-DISCIPLINE CHECKS & BALANCES

Self-Controlling Techniques

Assessment III. Life is about **DISCIPLINE** such as in self-correction
  (Discipline)
  Mind = Personal, Social, and Human Behaviors
  Spirit = Emotions, Reactions, and Self-Will
  Body = Stress, Health, and Genetics

You can do this:
Definition of discipline: *noun*   {20}

Etymology: Middle English, from Middle French & Latin; Middle French *discipline, discipline,* from Latin *discipline,* literally, teaching, instruction, alteration of *discipline,* from *discipulus* pupil -- more at DISCIPLE

1 *obsolete* : TEACHING, INSTRUCTION, TUTORING
2 :   a subject that is taught : a branch of learning : field of study
<such traditional *disciplines* as history, literature, political science – W.R.Steckel>
3 :   training or experience that corrects, molds, strengthens, or perfects especially
the mental faculties or moral character
<will submit willingly to severe *discipline* in order to acquire some coveted
knowledge or skill – Bertrand Russell>
<the valuable intellectual *discipline* of close research into a limited topic>

<needs the *discipline* of hard work and early rising>
<to learn to dance is the most austere of *disciplines* -- Havelock Ellis>

4 : PUNISHMENT

: as **a** : chastisement self-inflicted as mortification or imposed as a penance or
as a penalty

b : an instrument of chastisement; *specifically* : WHIP, SCOURGE

c : punishment by one in authority especially with a view to correction or
training

<schoolboys kept in line by floggings and other severe *discipline*>

5 a : control gained by enforcing obedience or order (as in a school or army)

: strict government to the end of effective action

<maintained the strictest *discipline* in the barracks and the field>

b :behavior in accordance with the rules (as of an organization)
: prompt and willing obedience to the orders of superiors

: systematic, willing, and purposeful attention to the performance of assigned tasks

: orderly conduct <commended the *discipline* of these veteran troops>

<lack of *discipline* was made plain by the students' listless, apathetic recitation

: behavior (as of students or soldiers) regarded in terms of its conformity with an ideal or actual code or set of rules

<poor *discipline*>

<good *discipline*>

c : conduct in accordance with a self-imposed rule or set of rules

: SELF-CONTROL, SELF-RESTRAINT

<with a remarkable *discipline* she avoided all reference to this incident in the pages of her diary>

<the sixty-six-pound free luggage allowance ... forces me into a *discipline* in selecting what to take along -- Richard Joseph>

6 : a rule or system of rules governing conduct or action : system of regulation

<in these revolutions the *disciplines,* such as food rationing, either collapsed

or near-collapsed -- Herbert Hoover>:

a :   a body of laws relating to conduct and church government

   :   practical rules as distinguished from dogmatic formulations

<to introduce the Presbyterian polity and *discipline*>

b :   a body of purely ecclesiastical laws or practices that may be altered to meet new conditions

<changes in the Roman Catholic *discipline* relating to fasting>

7 a :an orderly or regular pattern of behavior

<watching the *discipline* of the tides, with their evident rhythm – Clare Leighton>

b :   METHOD, APPROACH

<argued that the *discipline* of science differs from that of the humanities>

Self-Discipline
1) How can a person "Develop Self Control & Balance while maintaining a disciplined life.
2) There are two aspects and inner connecting
3) The inner-being spirit and will
4) The inner power of God and the Holy Spirit.

Maintaining a Disciplined Life
1) Self-Control & Anger management
2) What are some secrets for happiness and a successful Life?
3) What is happiness?
   a. What are the secrets to happiness,
   b. How to become happier,
   c. How to deal with personal happiness,
   d. How does happiness and well-being fit into your life.
4) What is success?
   a. What is the definition of success,
   b. What is success?

Effective Planning

Plans tend to be less effective when they are not thought out thoroughly; wise planning encourages active participation from a variety of views.

However, when a person is rushed to get something done they are more likely to make mistakes bypassing or ignoring advice or missed details. That invariably leads to problems—sometimes catastrophic problems, because hasty planning is rarely effective. Although, many details fall through the cracks when a person cannot remember everything that is said by the other person talking with others can increase the possibility of overlooking crucial factors in a person's decisions.

Another reason for including others rather than excluding professionals in different areas will help in the decision-making process at some point a person must carry out the plans that need to be and carried out. To the extent, a person is involved in formulating those plans they must implement, but if things don't go according to plans, other decisions will need to be made.

Another problem is when a person tries to control things when things go wrong; the way to change this is by bringing your positive traits into play; personal characteristics such as patience, cheerfulness and a sense of humor are very valuable in helping you to react properly.

Learn to "count to 10" before responding wait until you are in control of your negative emotions. You must depersonalize the situation and not let things "get under your skin," or bother you. Try to view the bright side of every situation. Learn to laugh at yourself and your mistakes.

The techniques above may sound very simple, but in actuality they are not easy to put into practice. A person may think they are patience when in reality they are not and they feel they have made a conscious effort to become well-adjusted while learning from past experiences. Determine your shortcomings and then try to improve on them decide upon specific ways in which you need to change your behavior and then implement those changes. Self-Control is based upon mental discipline and personal will power.

You must develop a plan of action to achieve your goal of eliminating an undesirable action. The following steps will guide you in developing your own personal self-control plan.

   1) Identify the undesirable behavior.

2) Begin self-observation the behavior and include the following information:

3) Use the self-control techniques previously listed to control bad behaviors,

4) Monitor your progress.

5) *Self-observation* - examining yourself, your thinking, and your behavior,

6) *Self-judgment* - comparing yourself to a standard of good behavior,

7) *Self-response* - reacting to your good judgment through self-administered rewards and punishment.

All behavior is learned, any given behavior shows up in a given situation and is influenced by what a person has learned from their experiences in similar situations. Thus, your ability to control your emotions is a learned response.

In order to achieve self-control, you need to learn new behaviors appropriate in the situation. It is possible to develop techniques to decrease undesirable behaviors.

The following techniques can be utilized to help develop appropriate behaviors:

1. *Self-Observation*-In order to change a behavior, you must monitor yourself and collect information about your problem. It is very helpful to keep a chart or a notebook and record in the situation and the results when your control is tested.

2. *Reward Technique*-Reward yourself when you exhibit the desired behavior. Make sure the reward is meaningful to you, it is readily available to you, and provides a strong incentive for you to maintain self-control.

3. *Punishment Technique*-Penalize yourself each time you exhibit a loss of control. It is so easy to get caught up in the problem and this can create an imbalance don't give priority to bad behaviors, it should truly matter to you how you behave.

If a person doesn't consciously choose how they spend their precious time, a person loses it and they are more likely to take on mundane tasks. Another is when they don't see things through or not meeting the other people's expectations. Your own dreams stay dreams and never see the light of day make your dreams happen and make them meaningful in your life they are the worthwhile goals you want achieve.

4. ***Extinction***-State by providing a reward for the desirable behavior. For example, if you lose your temper, don't pamper yourself face your incorrect response and deny yourself the pampering.

5. ***Alternate Behavior***-Train yourself to turn to an alternate behavior when you are confronted with a problem, when you behave poorly find a better way, and so that you perform normally under the same circumstances.

6. ***Stimulus Control***-Learn to recognize the stimulus which triggers your negative behavior. Then try an alternate behavior, each time the stimulus appears. Also, use rewards or punishments as an incentive to do better eventually this will help bring your behaviors under control.

FEAR AS YOUR ALLY

FEAR AS YOUR ALLY   .   **Pages 1 of 3** [16]

1.   "A recent study conducted by a well-respected organization in the United States determined that in 80% of attacks on women (I would even extrapolate this to men as well), the predator frightened his victim into submission simply by using verbal intimidation. The mind guides the body. The street predator knows that if he is able to paralyze your mind through fear, your body will freeze also, no matter how much physical training you have.

    What is fear? Most people view fear as an extremely negative feeling which causes one to totally freeze and panic, and as a result get hurt. Although this is a common belief, it is not quite accurate.

2.   Fear is both a physical and an emotional response to a perceived threat or danger. The physical reactions prepare us to confront and survive a dangerous situation, by readying autonomic functions for self-preservation and trauma. Heart rate increases; adrenaline and blood clotting enzymes are released to

make the body stronger, faster and less likely to feel pain. Although the biological response to fear does not differ from person to person, the emotional response will, based upon one's perception of threat. It is this perception of threat that can, and will, differ from person to person based upon training and learned past experiences in how to deal with the specific threat encountered. What may seem to be a threatening situation to one person may not be to another.

3.   This emotional response to fear is both learned and voluntary. A learned experience is generally taught to you. For instance, if you are a parent who has arachnophobia, and you see a spider crawling across the floor, your first reaction may be to scream and jump on a chair. Your small child will soon begin to 'model' his behavior in the same way. Seeing the spider will trigger the learned fear response.

The voluntary reaction is what we choose to do when faced with a dangerous situation. Unfortunately, many people use fear in a self-defeating, negative way rather than with a challenging positive attitude.

4.   Perceived threats trigger our learned and voluntary responses and any three will occur: fight, flight, or hypervigilance. A lot of us know about the fight or flight response, but not many of us know about hypervigilance. Hypervigilance (freezing in place or taking irrational actions) is something that we are all inbred and programmed with from the cave man days, at the 'reptilian brain' or 'frog brain' level. For those of you that have seen Jurassic Park the movie, what do the experts in the move yell to those people who were running from the Tyrannosaurus Rex? Why? Because it was 'hypothesized' that dinosaurs hunted via movement. Now, let's bring this to the tear 2002. Let's say you are traveling mach factor ten down a deserted highway in the middle of the night with your high beams on, when all of a sudden a deer jumps out in front of your car. What does the deer do? It freezes. Why? Does it see the car as a car? No, it sees the car as a threat. What does Bambi do when it sees or senses a threat in the bush? It freezes, in an attempt to not be seen by that which is potentially hunting it. Like

Bambi, we have this same response programmed into us as well. Once caught in a state of hypervigilance, it is a downward spiral that once caught into, is very difficult, if not impossible, to get out of. Why is this important? Because the mind guides the body. If the brain freezes, so will the body!!!!! Allowing yourself to become stuck in a state of hypervigilance, both mentally and physically, will most certainly allow the attacker to succeed, or will prevent you from becoming proactive in dealing with the situation at hand.

5.   The emotional response to fear, need not be mental immobility; it can be trained and utilized as a voluntary, positive force. An analogy can be drawn by comparing the fear emotion, with electricity. When used positively and appropriately, electricity runs our lives; when used negatively and carelessly, electricity can kill. The emotion of fear is the same way; used in a positive way, the emotion of fear is a 'powerizer' and an 'energizer'. Used in a negative way, the emotion of fear can cause one to panic, freeze, get seriously injured, and in the worse cases, even killed. What you choose to do with the emotion of fear – don't allow it to control you, or harness the energy – is left up to you to decide, it is a conscious choice, but the decision you make could mean the difference between winning or losing.

6.   So now we know that fear is simply an 'emotion', just like any other emotion that the good Lord gives us. We also now know that although the emotion of fear is triggered based upon one's perception of the threat, which could differ from person to person, biologically it reacts the same in each and every one of us. We also now know that when the emotion of fear hits, one of three responses; fight, flight, or hypervigilance, will take place. Based upon what I just shared with you about the hypervigilant state, I think you will agree that we want to pick the 'fight' or 'flight' response. How do you choose fight or flight and not the hypervigilance response? The answer is simple in concept; ask yourself: 'Am I threatened or am I challenged?'

To understand this concept, place yourself in the following scenario: 'You are in an office building that has thirty floors, and wanting to go to the top floor, you decide to use the elevator. When the elevator arrives, with no one inside, you enter and start your ascent. Arriving at the tenth floor, the door opens and standing in front of you is an unknown male, 6'5", 250 ponds, built like a Mac truck, brandishing a knife and saying, 'shut up and I won't hurt you, if you scream, you're dead." Now ask yourself, 'Am I threatened or am I challenged?' Most people, when faced with this situation, will say they are threatened.

The brain makes decisions for the future based upon past experience and training; it guides the body. No matter how much physical training you have to deal with an attacker who is about to assault you, if you stay in the "threatened" mindset, you will go into hypervigilance mode, come to a paralytic standstill, and be at the mercy of the attacker. Because off this fact, you need to get 'CHALLENGED.' (…)

The powerful word 'BUT' challenges the brain and allows it to work and think. When I give do seminars on how the brain works I use this kind of illustration to get my point across, I always lead my audience up to the point where I ask them this question: 'There is one little three letter word that will change your mindset from threatened to challenged, do you want to know what that word is?' At this point I pause for about three seconds, and then I say the word 'BUT'. It is amazing to see the expressions on people's faces. I then share with them that as soon as I said the word 'BUT' most of the audiences' brains asked themselves, 'BUT what?' As soon as the brain goes 'But what', the brain now begins to work. It can now find answers to the questions it is being faced with, such as, 'How am I going to get out of this situation as quickly and safely as possible.' Once the brain is allowed to work, the training and experiences you may have can now be applied. In other words, instead of freezing into a complete standstill, you begin to take some action to protect yourself.

A good self-protection program should be 'realistic' a scenario based training is beneficial not only in teaching you strategies, but in helping you realize that you CAN use fear to your advantage. However, even if you do not have the self-protection training or life experiences to deal with a specific threat, the 'CHALLENGED' brain will begin to adapt, overcome, and improvise to find a way for you to stay safe. There are hundreds of instances in which men and women with no prior self-protection training have resisted their attackers and 'won.' Why? They CHALLENGED themselves.

As previously stated, in 80% of attacks on women, the predator used only verbal intimidation to scare his victim into a submissive state of hypervigilance. To overcome this, you must allow the brain to work, challenge it to mentally figure a way out of the dangerous situation, and to physically release the 'internal warrior' that the emotion of fear can stimulate. Decide to focus and direct the mental and physical forces into a powerful attack of your own, and allow the full impact of the fear response to propel your mind, body, and soul against your attacker. Fear can be your greatest ally in a dangerous situation, but it can also be your worst enemy. THE CHOICE IS ULTIMATELY YOURS TO MAKE !!!!!!

What I have just shared with you, you can practice in your everyday life. I share with you, this personal experience to demonstrate this fact:

I was one of the youngest sergeants ever to be promoted in my police department. While in the promotional process, the last stage was an interview in front of a panel consisting of the Chief of police, the Deputy Chief, a Police Board member, and a City Counselor. My interview was set for 2pm, so I was there at 1:45pm. The panel knowing of my early arrival, waited until 2:30pm to call me in. Why? They wanted to sweat me!!!! As I was waiting for my interview, I noted that my heart rate and breathing had increased, I was sweating, my mind was racing a mile a minute, at which time I asked myself; 'Am I threatened or am I challenged.' I immediately identified the fact that I was 'THREATENED.' Upon comprehending this fact, I knew that if I went into this interview in this mindset, I would choke (go into a state of hypervigilance)!!!! How many of you have heard of this happening to someone, or experienced this yourself. Immediately upon recognizing my state of mind, I said that magical, but very powerful word.

Why did I share the above noted experience with you the reader? Because in my 15 year career as a police officer, I have been attacked with an edged weapon on four separate occasions. In each one of these edged weapon encounters, the biological effects of fear that I felt were no different than those I experienced during my sergeant interview.

Strength and Honor

Darren Laur
Integrated Street Combatives
http://www.members.shaw.ca/tmanifold/fear.htm   5/30/2010

Conclusion of Self-Worth

A summary of chapters 6 – 10 the value of one's self the summation of self-image and self-esteem. We have dealt with mental disorders, self-control issues, responsibility, accountability, and resiliency. The final evolution is about controlling you and your environment being self-sufficient knowing who you are. I hope you find our books helpful! What books do you go to over and over again? What's your favorite anger management book?

SELF CONTROL & MOTIVATION & COPING WITH CONFLICTS

Chapter 12

CONTROLLING YOU & YOUR ENVIRONMENT

Requires Self-Control & Motivation
Self Help Values & Principles
Knowing the real you, and facing the real influences inside and out!

Anger Management is a part of controlling you & Your Environment

Self-Improvement & Self-Discipline

I want to help a person understand how to use discipline in their life there are two types. One relates to the family if their family is out-of-control it affects other situations. Two is how does a person deal with the different aspects self-discipline?

I know I would not be where I am today without being a disciplined person. The important thing have you been able to deal with your past hurt feelings, how can a person manage one's self and control the situations in their life and family? To do this you must be able to control your thinking and master your role in the home, the way to do this is using self-help principles.

I will clearly define some of them based in one's beliefs about self-control and this will include your own self-control in any given situation. Personal discipline ultimately controlling ones' self-will, sacrifice, and controlling self-gratification.

I will take into consideration what is known as basic social behaviors a person's ability to control their desire and meet social expectance to be able to overcome social failures and yet that is another aspect of overcoming in a person's life.

One way to this is by using self-improvement methods that is the foundation to build on, the decisions you make, the actions you have taken have influenced your life up to now. If you are not socially accepted this is another way of knowing how you get along with other people, but only if you accept who you are and how well you accept your role in society.

It is often difficult for a person to accept the fact that they have some responsible for the problems in a family. I mentioned this briefly because this is one of the problems in families they don't spend quality family time together, that is why children feel alone, and it can lead to other social problems I will expand on this in **Assessment III**.

We can lay some of the blame on the family for what is going wrong in our society shame on us for letting this happen. This is another way to lose control in the family by letting other people control you and your home by letting things control you. This is the fastest route to losing control of your life and family. When you place the blame outside yourself, you have said that somebody or something else has more control over you and your family. A good illustration is like a leaf in the wind, blown all over the place and yet it hangs on why people do the same thing by letting others things control them or let their desires and whims control them. How can you change your life if you can't control your life?

This does not mean you never let others be a part of your life; you don't let them control you. When you get a job your boss will tell you the hours to work, and so will the traffic signals tell you when you can go or stop. In fact when you look at it a large part of your life is controlled by other people and things. You are still responsible, and you may say how can I control my life?

The first major step in motivation is accepting full responsibility for your actions and how it will affect others. (Right) Take your life back and expand new possibilities.

I will show you how much more control you have over life than you realized, for now let us continue with this study on self-discipline.

There are obvious steps in **self-discipline**, exercise, better diet, education and so on. The fact that you are reading this information shows you may be on the right track.

How about tackling some of the areas that you are weak in I used to be very shy at social gatherings I would usually sit in a corner hoping no one would notice me. I would have to know someone before I would initiate a conversation. The thought of talking to a crowd of people was terrifying, but I enjoy doing it now.

Shyness is a very uncomfortable and limiting behavior I decided to face it head on; I went to college I chose public speaking courses or anything that would put me in front of an audience. It took a little time, but after teaching and public presentations, I started to enjoy it. Now I love standing in front of a crowd, I am even better at one to one communication because of my degree in counseling taught me good communication skills.

Some simple motivation technique is to do something new every day or at least once a week. It does not have to be anything big, take a different route to work, try some different kinds of food, shop at different store, and expand your view and do something for yourself.

Romans 12:2, 3

"And do not be conformed to this world, but be transformed by the renewing of your mind, that you may prove what the will of God is, that which is good and acceptable and perfect." For I say, through the grace given unto me, to every man that is among you, not to think *of himself* more highly than he ought to think; but to think soberly, according as God hath dealt to every man the measure of faith.

1 Corinthians 8:2 (KJV)

And if any man think that he knoweth any thing, he knoweth nothing yet as he ought to know.

2 Corinthians 3:5 (KJV)

Not that we are sufficient of ourselves to think any thing as of ourselves; but our sufficiency *is* of God;

Galatians 6:3 (KJV)

For if a man think himself to be something, when he is nothing, he deceiveth himself.

Ephesians 3:20 (KJV)

Now unto him that is able to do exceeding abundantly above all that we ask or think, according to the power that worketh in us,

Philippians 4:8 (KJV)

Finally, brethren, whatsoever things are true, whatsoever things *are* honest, whatsoever things *are* just, whatsoever things *are* pure, whatsoever things *are* lovely, whatsoever things *are* of good report; if *there be* any virtue, and if *there be* any praise, think on these things.

When you feel like a loser, you act like a loser!

SELF-IMROVEMENT, & SELF-CONTROL

Willpower is defined as "the ability to control and determine of one's actions."

Self-improvement is the result of a conscious choices to do what ought to be done people have been given the power of choice. If you fail to achieve goals in your life it is because a person fails to do something or they are unable to make things right. Another is being able to fulfill the desires of your heart at the same time. Personal improvement is the result of a conscious choice and deliberate action.

Add **self-control** to self-improvement it is easier when a person is engaged in helping others and the willpower to do the right thing.

Here are several guidelines, which may be helpful as you attempt to avoid situations which test your **self-control**.

Identify your vulnerabilities try to learn your own weaknesses once you know your weak points, you can begin to confront them.

Avoid obvious temptations do everything in your power to minimize your encounters with temptations, temptations usually come when a person yields to something wrong the same circumstances may be successful in avoiding other problems take control of your weaknesses.

A = *Self-awareness* means recognizing your strengths and weaknesses, and seeing yourself in a realistic light and avoiding the common pitfalls in light of a person's **self-esteem**.

B = *Managing-emotions*: realizing that behind your feelings as an example look at the hurt that triggers anger, and learning ways to handle anxieties, anger, and sadness. Still another emphasis is taking on the responsibility for your decisions and actions, and following through on the commitment.

C = *Empathy-understanding:* is the key to *social abilities* and feelings for others, looking at it from their perspective, and respecting their differences of opinion in how they feel, and think about how it is going affect you. Relationships are a major force in your life, including learning to be a good listener and asking good questions; distinguishing between what someone says or does. What they meant to say, your own reactions and don't judge; be assertive but not pushy, while not being angry, upset, or not being too passive at the same time, while caring at the same time. Then the art of learning cooperation, without conflicts, but resolutions that are negotiable, without compromising your-self ideals and values.

D = *Personal decision-making:* examining your actions and knowing their consequences; knowing if your thoughts and feelings are ruling your decisions; applying these insights to issues such as addictions.

E = *Managing feelings:* monitoring "self-talk" to catch negative messages such as internal put-downs; realizing what is behind a **feeling** (e.g., the hurt that under lies anger); finding ways to handle **fears anxieties**, **anger**, and **sadness.**

1. *Handling stress*: learning the value of exercise, guided imagery, relaxation methods.
2. *Empathy:* understanding others' **feelings** and **concerns**, and taking their perspective; appreciating the differences in how different people feel about things.
3. *Communications:* talking about **feelings effectively**: becoming a **good listener** and ask questions that don't affined; distinguishing between what someone does or says, and your own reactions or judgments about things; sending "I" messages or instead of placing some of the blame on yourself, taking off on someone else.
4. *Self-disclosure:* valuing openness and building trust in a relationship; knowing when it's safe to risk talking about your **private feelings** or **putting off an argument until both have com-down.**
5. *Insight:* identifying patterns in your **emotional up-sets** and **reactions**; recognizing similar patterns in others.
6. *Self-acceptance:* **feeling pride** in the right way and seeing yourself in a positive light; recognizing your strengths and weaknesses; being able to laugh at yourself.
7. *Personal responsibility:* taking responsibility; recognizing the consciences of your decisions and actions, **accepting your feelings** and **moods**, be willing to change following through on commitments.
8. *Assertiveness:* stating your **concerns** and **feelings** without anger or being passive

9. *Self dynamics:* cooperation; knowing when and how to lead, and when to follow.
10. *Conflict resolution*: how to be fair with others; the win/win model for negotiating compromise.

The First Step

I want you to read these five statements what made you like you are.
1. Have you developed good or bad behaviors over the years
2. I believe people have these beliefs firmly fixed in their mind because of all the things they have experienced in their life.
3. The apostle Paul urged us to avoid the world's bad influences.
4. We should not be conformed to the pattern of this world because it shows us the way the world would have you go,
5. I would have us look at ourselves.

These false beliefs are so much a part of a person's thinking; this can cause them to react to life situations in harmful ways. Have you ever found yourself saying:

"Why in the world did I do that?"

"Wow, that just goes to show what a dummy I am,"

"I feel like a real loser,"

"I'll never be able to do that correctly,"

"Nothing in my life ever turns out right"?

You may not have said these remarks out loud, but you may feel that in some way or said to yourself in response to an unpleasant situation and you found yourself confronting or trying to fix something that went wrong. (Great)

Personal Strengths and Weaknesses Pages 1-7 / 1 thru 7 [18]

Developing Your Strengths while Managing your Weaknesses

"Many are painfully aware of weaknesses that hold them back. Yet, surprisingly, they are unaware of their many strengths. Focusing on our weaknesses while ignoring our strengths can be a source of discouragement and failure. And glorifying our strengths while ignoring our weaknesses can be equally unproductive. It is only when we give equal weight to your strong points and faults that we can realize our potential. Also note that you must choose friends carefully because each relationship nurtures your strengths and weaknesses. That is, we will grow better or worse, depending on whom you spend your time with. Considering how they affect your life and we seldom see the big picture, I will try to share some helpful ideas about our strengths and weaknesses.

THE BIG PICTURE

We all want to be powerful. By powerful, I don't mean ruling over others, but ruling over ourselves. How can we reach our dreams unless we first master ourselves? This is why understanding and managing our weaknesses is so important. The first lesson is to remember that weakness means the absence of power. The question we have to ask is not 'Do I want to overcome this weakness?' but 'Do I want to be powerful or powerless?' Weakness is nothing to be ashamed of; it is part of human nature. We are not dealing with a moral issue, but a practical one. That is, do you want to know how it works?

What will help you reach your goals? It is not weakness but strength that will take a person where they want to go. So, we need to identify our weaknesses and overcome or manage them. Yet, we also have to realize that we will never overcome ALL our weaknesses, nor should we want to. For weaknesses are important. They help each of us to become a unique individual. You see, it is not only the strengths of others that make them appealing, but their weaknesses as well. We relate to their flaws and root for them because we, too, are imperfect. And as we open up and expose our weaknesses to friends, we develop intimacy, strengthening our relationship. In fact, weaknesses contribute to our greatest relationship, our love life, as well. For as Francois Mauriac (1885~1970) wrote, 'Human love is often but the encounter of two weaknesses.' Although we are painfully aware of some of our weakness, we fail to acknowledge others. Yet, the first step in overcoming any weakness is to become aware of it. So, how do we detect character flaws that are hiding in the background? A good way to start is by monitoring our negative emotions. Are we angry, vengeful, resentful, jealous, envious...? They all point to weaknesses that we can work on.

279

WHAT SHOULD WE DO AFTER
FINDING OUR FAULTS?

1.   Change those you can. The important thing is not overcoming them, but the strength we gain in doing so.
2.   Accept those you cannot change.
3.   Regularly come back to the ones you can't change, for what you can't do today, you may be able to do tomorrow.
4.   Embrace those you cannot change because it is what makes you unique. If everyone were perfect, everyone would be the same, and we would live in a dull world.
5.   Use your weaknesses to develop compassion. Since others have to tolerate your faults, it is only fair that you tolerate theirs. Also use your flaws to learn new coping skills and strategies. In other words, use your weaknesses to find new strength.

EXAMPLE WEAKNESSES

1.   Envy. If you envy (or admire) someone, that is useful information. It points to the person you would like to become. So make that your goal. You can even ask the person you admire how you can become more like them. They may not only be happy to help, but may develop into an important friend.
2.   Anger and resentment. Here is useful advice from August Wilson (1945~2005), 'Confront the dark parts of yourself, and work to banish them with illumination and forgiveness. Your willingness to wrestle with your demons will cause your angels to sing. Use the pain as fuel, as a reminder of your strength.'
3.   Ingratitude. Failure to be grateful for what we have prevents us from being happy, weakens relationships, and blocks more good from entering our lives. Live with a grateful heart and you will live a long, happy life.
4.   Arrogant. People who think they know it all weaken themselves because they stop learning. They are also easily hurt by the criticism of others. The paradox is they become weak because of their fear of appearing weak.

5. Gullibility. To accept as true whatever one reads or hears without questioning the facts may leave one misinformed, ignorant, or open to manipulation by others.

6. Insecurity. To be uncomfortable with insecurity is to be uncomfortable with life, for insecurity is the nature of life. If you need to satisfy your hunger for security, rest with the assurance that although you cannot count on others or the world, you can always count on yourself. So, use your feelings of insecurity as a catalyst to develop self-reliance.

7. Failure. Failure is not possible unless one stops trying. Its cures are perseverance, patience, commitment, flexibility, creativity, and solution-oriented thinking. As Kin Hubbard (1868~1930) wrote, 'There is no failure except in no longer trying. There is no defeat except from within, no really insurmountable barrier save our own inherent weakness.'

8. Boredom. Boredom is a lack of interest in doing anything. Its equivalent to feeling life isn't interesting. Whenever you are troubled with boredom, rather than asking yourself why you don't feel like doing anything, ask what you SHOULD be doing.

Why? Because what you SHOULD be doing is what you really WANT to do. The reason why you're not doing it is not because it isn't interesting, but because your subconscious has created a wall of resistance that is blocking you. To learn more about this problem and how to easily overcome it, see the 'GAINING CONTROL OVER OUR LIVES' section of this article:

PART TWO: OUR STRENGTHS THE BIG PICTURE

We all have strengths. But we cannot just smugly sit self- satisfied like a Cheshire cat. Rather we need to further develop our strong points because it's a matter of using them or losing them. Dwight D. Eisenhower (1890~1969) explains, 'Our real problem, then, is not our strength today; it is rather the vital necessity of action today to ensure our strength tomorrow.' As a military commander he knew we must never run from, but squarely face adversity, for we gain the strength of that which we have overcome. How strong is an ant?

Scientists in Krakow, Poland were astonished to see an ant holding a dead bird in the air weighing 500 times more than the ant. That would be equivalent to a 200- pound man holding 50 tons in the air (National Geographic, December, 1996)! You, too, have enormous power at your disposal, but it is often overlooked and neglected. I'm referring to the power of commitment. With it you can make the 'impossible' possible. People do not lack strength; they lack commitment. And if you cultivate it, you will be laying a-firm-foundation-for-success. It is a sign of strength to be weak, to know it, and to manage it, but a sign of weakness to be unaware of our faults and mistakenly believe we are strong. Oddly enough, many people are unaware of their many strengths. It is important to recognize our inner resources, for until we do, we will fail to use them. The sad fact is a strong person unaware of his strength is no more-useful-than-a-weak-person. How can we make sure we are not overlooking our strengths? A good way to identify personal strengths you have overlooked is to ask yourself a series of questions, such as the following.

Do I hunger for success? Do I set goals and am I eager to take action to realize them? Am I excited by life? Am I curious? Do I love adventure? Do I live courageously? Do I like to support others, lead others, or both? Am I patient? Am I a risk taker? Do I get along with others? Do I look at the pros and cons before acting? Can I depend on myself? Do I encourage others and offer praise where it is due? Do I respect and learn from others? Do I see the potential in others and in myself? Do I control my emotions or do I allow them to control me? Do I balance work and recreation? Do I look after my general well- being or do I neglect myself? Am I organized? Am I a visionary and see what others miss? Do I have a positive outlook? Am I a peacemaker? Do I empathize with others? Am I interested in what works and what doesn't? Do I embrace change or do I prefer the status quo? Do I love to learn and apply new things? Am I a thinker, planner, and doer? Do I always strive to do my best? Am I gentle and kind? Am-I-generous? Am-I-understanding-and-accepting?

THE DANGER OF OUR STRENGTHS CHANGING TO WEAKNESSES

Once we become aware of our strengths, we need to regularly monitor them, for unless we are careful, they could turn into weaknesses and halt our progress. Here are some examples of-what-I-mean.

1. Self-confidence is good, but when we are too confident, we stop learning.
2. When we are overly concerned about personal problems, we become blind to the problems of others.
3. It is good to be prudent, but unless we are willing to take risks, we cannot go very far in life.
4. Decisiveness is a strength, but guard against stubbornness.
5. Striking while the iron is hot is a positive trait, but acting rashly can lead to a downfall.
6. Self-discipline can lead you to expect too much of others.
7. Thoroughness is good, but it can turn into perfectionism.
8. It's good to be supportive, but not when you conform to every wish of others.
9. If you are too patient, things may never get done.
10. Diplomacy helps, but not when you allow others to take advantage of you.
11. Self-starters sometimes have problems working harmoniously with others.
12. Decisiveness is a strength, but not when you fail to consider other viewpoints.
13. Determination is a strong point, unless one is headstrong, one-sided, and aggressive.
14. Being a good speaker is an asset, unless one talks too much.

EXAMPLE OF STRENGTHS

1. Faith, trust, and confidence. Unshakeable faith in ourselves and the world create a **launching pad for success, for as William James** (1842~1910) taught, 'Pessimism leads to weakness, optimism to power.'

2. Excited by life. Or, as Vincent van Gogh (1853~1890) said, 'Love many things, for therein lies the true strength, and whosoever loves much performs much, and can accomplish much, and what is done in love is done well.'

3. Living Courageously. After all, this is the bedrock of a happy life. Rabindranath Tagore (1861~1941) prays, 'Let me not pray to be sheltered from dangers but to be fearless in facing them. Let me not beg for the stilling of my pain, but for the heart to conquer it. Let me not look for allies in life's battlefield but to my own strength. Let me not cave in.' Arnold Schwarzenegger continues, 'Strength does not come from winning. Your struggles develop your strength. When you go through hardship and decide not to surrender, that is strength.'

4. Getting along with others. The Dalai Lama fills in the details, 'In my own limited experience I have found that the more we care for the happiness of others, the greater is our own sense of well-being. Cultivating a close, warmhearted feeling for others automatically puts the mind at ease. It helps remove whatever fears or insecurities we may have and gives us the strength to cope with any obstacles we encounter. It is the principal source of success in life. Since we are not solely material creatures, it is a mistake to place all our hopes for happiness on external development alone. The key is to develop inner peace.'

5. Self-motivation (self-leadership). Self-discipline is an essential ingredient of success, and, therefore, a major strength. Judith Viorst aptly explains the true meaning of strength, 'Strength is the capacity to break a chocolate bar into four pieces with your bare hands -- then eat just one of the pieces.'

6. Follow-through. The greatest idea and the finest intention are utterly worthless unless we follow through. If you need some help in this area, I recommend, 'FOLLOWING THROUGH, A Revolutionary New Model for Finishing Whatever You Start,' by Steve Levinson, Ph.D. and Pete Greider, M.Ed., Unlimited Publishing, 2007.

7. Compassion. Compassion is love in action. The more of it we give away, the more of it comes back to us. Here's something to keep in

mind; if we are not compassionate toward others, how can we be compassionate toward ourselves?

8.RESPONSIBILITY. We all have challenges, but when Tom prayed for a helping hand to solve his problems, God said, 'I already gave you a helping hand. It is attached to your arm.' When we accept responsibility, we realize that God helps those who help themselves. Sure, there are always excuses available if you are weak enough to use them, but wouldn't you rather be strong?

A wise man admits his weaknesses I would admit mine if I had any. Ha! Ha! That is supposed to be funny. Now that I've made a point, let's get serious again. I'm going to end with three relevant quotations, followed by two more books for recommended reading." *Those who gave thee a body, furnished it with weakness; but He who gave thee Soul, armed thee with resolution. Employ it, and thou art wise; be wise and thou art happy.' --Akhenaton (King of Egypt, 14th century BC)*

'A true friend knows your weaknesses but shows you your strengths; feels your fears but fortifies your faith; sees your anxieties but frees your spirit; recognizes your disabilities but emphasizes your possibilities.' -- William Arthur Ward (1921~1994) 'When I dare to be powerful - to use my strength in the service of my vision, then it becomes less and less important whether I am afraid' --Audre Lorde (1934~1992)"

http://www.personal-development.com/chuck/strengths-weaknesses.htm

4/8/2012

The psychology of man/women is not complete in their nature or in the make-up of their character, but the very nature of our creation by God, who left us with choices in life.

Therefore, there are defiantly conflicts in our relationships especially when it comes to the will of two people. You can hardly get two people with the same **values** and **morals** even in the same family let alone two people with the same viewpoint about society and life in general. Of course, there are two viewpoints from the male and female because we are two different emotional creations. There are different beliefs about God's creation. There are also spiritual applications to man's will and the will of God.

Do you think that the development of **character** comes from God, or lack of it has any significant influence on any generation? There is a central role in cultivating **character** by including self-discipline and empathy for others, which in turn enables true commitment to civic values, **morals,** and the need to practice them. Which happens as we teach and build on essential **emotional social skills,** in that sense **emotional literacy** goes hand in hand with good **morals**; also morals develop **character**, and thus becoming a better person.

Illustration of Life!

For the most part, people are looking for the easy-way-out, or quick-fixes for *their* problems and situations. Life is usually much more complicated when dealings with the problems in the situation and how a person relates to *their* life.

The brain is a receiver like a television set which picks up a signal and it's amazing the signal is in the same room we walk in and the air we breathe the spirit works in the same manor. The information comes from a person's spirit, some call it the soul, (the conscience) and it sends and receives a signal like the television station and the brain is also like a computer it stores information. Does the brain actually think?

No! in the same sense the spirit of a person functions quite independently and it communicates the feeling to the brain, the information is stored and then a person makes a decision they can recall the information at any time, I think of the soul and spirit as the inner being, not the brain. The (conscience and sub-conscience) make judgments according to a person's feelings. If they are up-sets guess what it's probably going to be a bad decision.

This is never more evident when a person recognizes the hindrances, or upsetting the harmony in a person's life. There could be many reasons why things happen. Something needs to be done in those kinds of situations! There is a saying, "when things get tough, the tough get going". Some people fall apart when things happen or something doesn't go their way or what they want, or sometimes they shut down and can't function.

The same is true in life and relationships if they have no self-control over their own thoughts or without knowing their own limits, and knowing how to deal with the consequences.

If a person is not **paying-attention** to others feelings, the danger comes when others are more likely to do things because they feel they can get by with it, they may not have paid attention to the warning signs in their life.

Watch for the **warning signs,** they may come in the form of everyday situations building up over time. The bases for our self-help studies is to help a person look for the **warning signs** by **measuring** their **emotions,** and understand the role **demands** plays in their life. A **crisis** is an **alarm signal,** and is much more severe as it relates to extreme **emotions** that affects a person's life. **Emotions** are the interactions within the situation, **demands** involves every aspect of a person's life and situation.

How do different emotional feelings relate to:
shame, embarrassment or unworthiness?

The **feeling** of belonging equates with social acceptance, peer pressure and all of them play a role in **strong belonging behaviors** and needs.

If a person can or may not recognize any or all of these personal characteristics, if they can they will better understand their **emotions** in regards to relationships with others in a better way.

- How can a person manage their **emotional feelings**?
  - o **Emotions** can signal (drives, needs, and desires).
- o **Emotions drive** the nervous system and the **emotions** may be characterized by (yelling / screaming / shouting)
  - o **Emotions** cause impulsive reactions like (hitting, slapping / retaliation / out of control)

Control Management Means Controlling the Uncontrollable

There are circumstances that you don't have control over, floods, fires, accidents, health issues etc.? But you are still in control in how you deal with them your reactions can defeat you as I implied earlier, or you can face them head on, but it is how you handle them.

Definition of anger ad More from Free Merrian Webster Dictionary

Page 1 {21}

verb \\'aŋ-gər\\

: to make (someone) angry

an·geredan·ger·ing\\-g(ə-)riŋ\\

Top of Form

Full Definition of *ANGER*

transitive verb

: to make angry <he was *angered* by the decision>

intransitive verb

: to become angry

Examples of *ANGER*

1. They were shocked and *angered* by the company's arrogance.
2. He was *angered* to learn that he had been fired.
3. It *angered* me that she would say something like that.
4. He's a gentle man who's not easily *angered*.

First Known Use of *ANGER*

13th century

Related to *ANGER*

Synonyms

ENRAGE, INCENSE, INFLAME (*also* ENFLAME), INFURIATE, IRE, MADDEN, OUTRAGE, RANKLE, RILE, ROIL, STEAM UP, TICK OFF, get one's goat, rub the wrong way

Antonyms

DELIGHT, GRATIFY, PLEASE

Near Antonyms

ALLAY, ASSUAGE, RELIEVE; COMFORT, CONSOLE, SOOTHE; APPEASE, CONCILIATE, MOLLIFY, PACIFY, PLACATE; CALM, LULL, QUIET, SETTLE; BEGUILE, BEWITCH, CAPTIVATE, CHARM, DISARM,

anger *noun*

: a strong feeling of being upset or annoyed because of something wrong or bad

: the feeling that makes someone want to hurt other people, etc.

: the feeling of being angry

Full Definition of *ANGER*

: a strong feeling of displeasure and usually of antagonism

: RAGE

Examples of *ANGER*

1. He couldn't hide his *anger* with us.
2. You could hear the *anger* in his voice.
3. The group expressed its *anger* over the company's arrogance.
4. He said that he had no *anger* towards the person who shot him.

http://www.merriam-webster.com/dicionary/anger   9/29/2014

Definition of anger: *noun* Etymology: Middle English, affliction, anger, from Old Norse *angr* grief, sorrow; akin to Old English *enge* narrow, Old High German *engi,* Old Norse *öngr,* Gothic *angwus,* Latin *angor* strangling, anguish, *angere* to strangle, distress, Greek *anchein* to strangle, Sanskrit *amhas* anxiety

   1 *now dialect England* **:** inflammation especially of a wound or sore

   2 : a strong feeling of displeasure and usually of antagonism
     <an outburst of >

   3 : a cause or manifestation of anger
     <or if thy mistress some rich *anger* shows – John Keats>

   4 : something resembling the state, appearance, or behavior of an angry person

© 2005 by Merriam-Webster, Inc.

http://unabridged.merriam-webster.com/cgi-
bin/Third?book=Third&success   9/10/2005

PRACTICE + SUCCESS = MOTIVATION

\

Chapter 13

RESILIENCY & COPING-SKILLS

Assessment IV. MOTIVATION in how a person lives their life
MOTIVATION – DETERMINTION

Motivation and determination includes managing your life in a positive way. It is our goal to help people and lead people to direct their lives in a positive insight and gain sufficient autonomy with one's self. To be able to motivate them in new ways that changes things in their life. We will emphasize personal (**resiliency**). *Teaching* Self-Motivation and Coping-Skills which include self-monitoring, self-reward, self-contracting and stimulus-control by that we mean some level-of-control. Eventually, it is hoped that people will use some kind of training skills as they deal with any solution. This is something people can do on their own when it comes solving their problems a person needs to implement self-help skills that helps them.

In order to deal with procrastination, you must begin with self-observation of one's physiological needs, cognitive and manageable responses to motivation indicators. Then you need to determine what course of action is needed. We have shown you how to evaluate and cope with why you are not getting things done. One of the priorities is to set goals and practices in coping strategies. Later, after you have done an evaluation you should set out to accomplish the task through self-monitoring techniques like a behavioral journal. In the process, a person should learn ways to control their motives as they deal with the situation, to defiantly talk with someone who cares and be able to deal with those reactions. It is also very important that each person use self-reinforcement tools / by rewarding good behaviors and look at the consequences of (his or her) actions / now there should be accountability for wrong doing.

I want to help a person have a better understanding of their motives the one thing a person has to understand how to deal with their goals and reaching them. Some of these methods have to with motivation, which are in fact in the principles I use every day. I want to challenge you to take control, and balance your goals with your everyday responsibilities.

I will present some keys that will unlock the door to why a person doesn't get things done. A person must want to change their goals if they need to and to do this it will take a changed heart and mind, and living a life to the fullest and the way you look at the world around you. There is a strong correlation between self-motivation, personal goals and achievement. In order to get properly motivated it helps to spend some time thinking about your personal goals and what you want to achieve in your life.

In there simplest form you can think about these two types of motivation as:

- **Intrinsic** = love, because we want to.
- **Extrinsic** = oblations, because we have to.

A more detailed definition is:

- **Intrinsic:** To perform an action or task based on the expected or perceived satisfaction of performing the action or task. Intrinsic motivators include having fun, being interested and personal challenge.
- **Extrinsic:** To perform an action or task in order to attain some sort of reward, including money, power and good marks or grades.

"If you want to achieve **greatness** stop asking for permission."

"Good things come to people who wait, but better things come to those who go out and get them."

It is up to the person to identify with their needs and don't let your problems pull you down, but more than that if you do not know how to control self; I want you to make a list you want to do and the way you can do that is through self-control, a person will not be able to help themselves if they don't take advantage of their own abilities. Nor is anyone else going to able to help you because in reality if you are unable to help yourself.

You do this by being realistic I found it harder live to up to what was expected of me rather than give up on my expectations of myself. There is so much more to living than just saying, I want to be successful and live a better life, but the challenge comes when a person learns to control what they want to be.

We are not puppets on string; we have spent time exploring a person's intelligence, we are to ruler over our own lives in regards to our achievements and we are not to be deceived by other people and devices. I believe to do that a person has to deal with self-control and motivation.

So, you can say a person can do whatever (he or she) wants, but not really some feel they can get by with anything, but in most cases it is only for a while, some believe they can get by with things if they are not caught, if they are willing to pay the price for what they have done. A person has to deal with control issues does that rule apply to everybody? (Yes) the best alternative for a person is to define and understand things before they do them and are they willing to pay the consequences for what happens, but there is advantage if you do things for the right reasons?

We have studied how (Accountability) is important now we add (Responsibility) and works hand in hand in a person's life. Now we will study a person's motives fit into the picture before and after changes are made. I don't want to take anything away from the experience it's yours to enjoy. That is one of the most important steps in the process of helping yourself; looking back at what has happened and why things didn't get done? It is a good way to understand why something has happened and think about what is going to happen before you do it.

The importance of this study deals how a person feels about themselves and others, what drives *your* emotions. What does motivation have to do with *your* thoughts and thinking? The question comes down to how do *you* "Control the Brain Functions"?

I found the motivation came when I wanted to change my life it came because of my life treating heart problems. Then I used these principles to help me in understanding how to deal with my health problems. How does this fit into the human aspect of motivation I learned if it didn't fit into good heath guide lines, I knew it was wrong for me.

I would like to explain how these skills work, when applied and used in the RIGHT way. Then, show *you* how important motivation and determination is in the interaction with these methods.

If you are technology available, you can learn how to cook, use tools, make clothes, and use a computer. You can learn to do anything you really want to do. All you need is the motivation and commitment. You can learn to fly an airplane, drive a truck, scuba dive, fix a car--name it.

I like to think this is the glue that holds a person together (Passion, Motivation, & Desire), and **I want *you* to evaluate the use of these 3-D's Dedication, Determination, & Discipline**. A person's feelings are influenced by their emotions, attitude, and motivation. This in return brings out how character influences such as genetics, and environment influences what a person does.

In a nutshell, a good mind with a positive attitude and some good problem solving skills will go far in solving any problem. Interest in and commitment to the problem is the key. Motivation--a willingness to expend the effort--is more important than a laboratory. And remember that you can always do something. Even if you cannot totally eradicate the problem from the face of the earth, you can always do something to make the situation better.

It is another thing to talk about dealing with the (ME) in this instance, which means I had to make some changes in my life; I had to learn to live with my health as it is, I had to create a healthy mind-set. The problem I had seemed to be making the same mistakes over and over in dealing with my health I would get to feeling better, then I would over do things. I had to pick the pieces and undo what I had done wrong.

I will use this metaphor before but it fits, "*I was going around my mountain*", not "*climbing the mountain*", another metaphor "*I was going in circles*", I hope this is a way to identify with how a person does things. That can be good if a person can look up and change their life at that point, a person needs to take advantage of their well and determination.

We cannot deal with any of these aspects without first understanding *who we are* as a person, but a person should try to do the best they can with their ability and use those skills taught them. Our studies are about building not tarring down a person's life, we have provided tools and we are going to try and teach a person how to use their knowledge and skills in many ways.

Most of us will agree that the tools are vital to success in any job or vocation. Here at **S**upport **O**utreach **S**ervices I want to give you some tools *that will help you help yourself* in the process that is what life is all about, isn't it.

We are going to teach some (methods) & (use the tools you have) and (use analytical skills of motivation).

You should be able to analyze, compare, interpret the things you like to do, and take control in getting things done. The ability to identify, solve, and resolve problems should be a familiar in light of a person's mind-set that should not be that difficult, we have provided insightful techniques. Think in terms of problem solving that will help you face those you face on a daily basis and generate innovative solutions. Also, you will be able to effectively deal with any changes organize, and evaluate personal problems, and/or be specific in dealing with issues utilizing books, printed material, electronic or human sources in creating control out of kayos.

Given the nature and character of a person or the type of work they perform, and as they live their life. If people will learn to rely on the information provided in this study and our trust worthy methods, they will add honesty and integrity you will find these qualities are highly valued in what a person does and says.

I want discuss personal happiness and success and how happiness fits into the next chapter; I will also discuss the human aspects of living a successful productive life, as a person deals with their personal characteristics they are determined by what is right or wrong in a situation.

First, it is important to recognize and work through a person's problems as I did, that helped me feel better about the situations. The steps a person takes has it has a lot to do with their interdependence from within. The amount of determination may be relevant to the amount of successes or the degree of a failure; the most important thing is enjoying your daily experiences, day-in and day-out. I have laid a good foundation so that a person can take control and carry on no matter how bad it gets.

Secondly, the real purpose for live is living it to the fullest expectation, use good methods rather than living in self petty, anything less is usually a disappointment to a person, and it is usually reflected in losing personal joy.

The summary deals with (Recognition) - (Resiliency) - (Recovery) = being informed & using tools to *help ourselves.*

Principal 1: Personal-Attention & Care: *Who am I?* **One to One personal attention and support, evolutions, assessments and analysis, and our studies & methods:**

Knowing How to Deal With Motivation, and Control-Management

I want to close with how to deal with personal happiness and success in relation to self-discipline, self-control, self-motivation, and are you fulfilling your destiny in a positive way. I have looked at my personal disappointments and how to deal with controlling anger and controlling stress and the way to do this with methods of self-discipline.

These basic motivators of overcoming a problem works like a thermostat, preventing the **feelings** and **emotions** to escalate to the point of boiling point and overwhelming each other or causing both partners' inability to focus on the issues at-hand, but being able to cultivate a couple's **emotional level**, by enhancing their possibilities for working things out.

There should a time to make-up and that is the best part of an argument, RIGHT or the ability come to an agreement in the marriage for it to flourish, while overcoming negative thoughts and feelings, do not let them grow, or be unsolved. The truth lies somewhere between these extremes and ideas that marriages don't work.

Emotional competences in relationships:

- Is like being able to calm down (and calm down your partner)
- Empathy and by listening well
- There are "good fights" that allow a couple to discuss a problem.

We do this by sorting out the specific data that goes into the brain, my aim is to clarify the different views of an emotional situation and present them in a positive manner leaving no doubt as to where both of you stand on the differences in the disagreements. For each person there is an emotional level and the emotional level will be received and processed, looking for your true feelings in any situation and in the end that is **emotional competences** are involved in learning more about each other it will play a role as you deal with the issues. A person's mind can freeze depending on the situation like the word cancer.

In some cases doctors are not completely honest in their diagnoses until they know how the person is going to react. They want to know how they are going to react and how they are going to deal with the situation, there needs to be a rational analysis as they tell the patient at that moment and then proceed. A person can be **emotional fragile** that causes a person to be mentally unable to process the situation or because their mental capacity is limited to deal with the shock. The brain can shut down and their feelings are now based in part on the illusion something is wrong and if something is really wrong a person may not be able to respond until they get the facts, depending on their state of mind a person is vulnerable especially in the case of a severe illness that bursts their illusion of **well-being**. At that point, their world does not feel safe and secure suddenly a person feels weak, helpless, and venerable.

One of the biggest problems medical personnel has to deal with is their emotions it seems they ignore how a patient feels and reacts because they see it all the time. There comes a time when the attending physician tells a person how bad the illness has become. They may not be meeting the **emotional needs** of the patient because they feel they are going to be able to handle the situation. When they are able to deal with the illness, there should be someone to give them emotional support; it is also very true in other aspects of a person's life. How they are dealing with their feelings of helplessness or their loss of hope. The of lake of understanding for what the patient's needs does not end there, they may need reassuring information, comfort, and solace to prevent unfortunate despair. But, all too often the medical caretakers are rushed off leaving the patient in distress and their questions unanswered. Before, we go any farther there are a lot of good doctors and caregivers out there.

There is growing evidence that shows that a person's **emotional state** can play a significant role in their vulnerability in certain areas of their life, and in the course of dealing with a problem there should be a **recovery** time and that can play a major role in how well a person responds to treatment or certain kinds of problems. Beyond that argument physicians and psychologists can offer care along with cures, there are other compelling reasons to consider the psychological demeanor and the personal background of the person. They should be considered in the realm of what treatment is needed, and the many other aspects in which the treatment and care can help them as the individual deals with the healing process the same is true in our self-help studies.

We are going to show you some very good profiles that prove there is now some scientific evidence being made for more psychological and **emotional interventions** in helping people overcome their problems and in the mental health field, effective both in prevention and treatment by treating the **emotional state of mind** along with their *medical treatment*.

Yet there is an ideology in other fields, I am talking about dealing with the positive reinforcement methods of behavior modifications, I don't want a person to think they are healed or they feel they are miraculously cured overnight, some feel they are to blame for their problems or sicknesses and in some cases they are because they have been brought about by poor management of their health or addictions. The result has brought about this attitude there is a cure-all for everything this brings about a euphoric belief everything will be alright. That has brought about a wide spread misunderstanding about the extent to which an illness can be affectedly treated.

I use the statement "mind over matter" has some bearing on the healing process, others believe in healing by praying for someone and that can happen? But, perhaps even worse is when people feel guilty for having a disease or they feel they caused the problem, and in some cases neglect or an addictive behavior has caused a health problem. This can be missing leading to a degree, in the moral sense of healing and also in the spiritual realm. Because, there is a measure of truth in being happy and having a positive attitude, it can and will have an influence on the healing process. We hear of people who feel prayer is the only answer and the person or child died because they didn't get medical treatment. I believe it takes both medical treatment and prayer in most cases, not in all cases.

There is a great deal of truth as far as how much the mind has to do with healing, it has everything to do with the healing process because *every system goes through the brain*. Whether it's you or God that unlocks the

blocking force to the brain anything is possible at that point-in-time. I have spent some time making my point or some of you may think it is just a theory.

Every person must be able to look at themselves in relation to self-value. They must be able to distinguish between the physical aspects of physiology; now we are going to deal with the mental aspects the conscious and subconscious.

There may be imbalances created in the ***psychogenesis of self***, such as patterns of hostility over time and the range of hostility, and how this is manifested in a person's outward expressions of emotion of anger and self-control.

The opposite can lead to subdued inner-personal-introvertedness or inner-personal-aggressiveness. Low self-esteem and depression should consider the danger points, I believe in supporting the person is very important dynamic in helping them in the direction that is best suited to help them as a person.

The effects of motivation and drive may have a lot to do with how a person gets things done, but there are other factors to be considered, but what happens when you determine what has happened. I contend more than anything else how they feel about themselves is more important either way their self-esteem will to some degree govern how they feel as they try to solve a problem. Under reacting is another thing associated with lowered motivation and self-esteem that will drive a person to do things, which is often in the case when a person seems they can't get through the day. How a person controls their sleep and appetite cycles may affect how a person feels through the day both of these components are often a problem.

The importance of Self-Control

Self-Motivation is a reflection of an inward reality of self-control. Allow God to give you a heart transplant and not just a face-lift! Self-Control is essential to success in all areas of life.

"Whatever you set your mind to" the main thrust of this argument is doing all you can do, another point is how important is it to put your mind at ease

A strength is just another way of processing information that goes in your brain and how it processes things. A strength has to be applied towards a productive outcome, of course, you might not think you have any weaknesses, or you might see yourself as a weak person.

For example, neurotic worriers are superb at anticipating negative outcomes they often think of everything in a negative way. While this might not make them wrong in their thinking, but their natural caution plays a part in how the mind sees a potential strategy for planning in some cases. They are likely not going to jump into a business venture without thinking it through. On the other hand they are more likely to be overly cautious and not take a chance of failing.

We want you to look at how to shape your life around your strengths; maybe you're just thinking this is a waste of time what can I do to get things going. Either way, you're probably curious as to what your own strengths are allow me to cater to your intrigue, by presenting the two ways you can discover them:

Self-Reflection methods.

Each of these are big topics, I'll explain how to use *self-reflection* methods, I don't just mean sitting and thinking "Ho-Hmmm what are my strengths? Research has uncovered patterns in how people discover their strengths, and this gives you areas in which to focus your *self-reflection*. Which option would be best for people who has a high level of *self-motivation* to start a project and finish it, or people who dislike people who question their own ability in general?

The advantage of *self-reflection* is not limited to a fixed set of potential answers which can tell you which are your strengths, but it can tell you about things outside of that model. Reflection is the ability to think things through, but gives you that extra flexibility of seeing both sides of a situation.

Whatever your weakness might be it will show up again. I was determined not to make that mistake again, things seemed to happen anyway. The internal grief can be devastating to deal with how does this affect our happiness, the insight we have in our failures will help as we go into the next chapter.

ASSESSMENTS I, II, III, IV

PEACE OF MIND AND HEART, = A SMILE

Chapter 14

Conclusion

WHAT IS HAPPINESS

Which brings us to the question of what is happiness? One way to describe an emotion is by describing happiness and/or opposite emotions. Any increase in activity simulates the brain center and can bring about positive feelings and increase available energy, and in some cases it quiets down the anxiety.

There is likely going to be a physiological shift resulting in the recovery process, unless there is a shift in negative emotional and a changing of our mood in a negative sense it does not give the mind and body a chance to quieten down. The body and mind needs general rest and well-being and the way to do that is by creating some enthusiasm, striving toward vitally and being happy. The biological makeup of a person and the psychology of being happy definitely influences a person's responses to happiness, joy, love, surprise, but they also in negative way influence sadness, hurt, anger, disgust, bitterness, and last guilt and remorse.

Viewing the world as "Chicken Little" did in convincing herself and others that the sky is falling this is viewed as having a pessimistic view. Consistently putting the negative spin on life may result in paying a price in your emotional and physical well-being. But it is possible to change your way of thinking and living. These quotes and steps can help you find your way out of a pessimistic mind-set into a happier life. Do you find yourself using words like "always" and "never" when you refer to yourself? Do you say things like, "When I plan a trip it always turns out bad." How about, "I never get to do what-I-want"? Constantly referring to yourself in a negative way, that does keep pessimism firmly planted in your mind.

The next time you hear yourself thinking or saying I "never" and "always," stop and think about it. Rephrase the question in your mind, for example: "I am going somewhere" is that true or a better way to make a statement? Sure, you go places like to the store or are you over dramatizing your feelings? If you walked out the door going to work are you not going somewhere, have I made a false statement? Keep reminding yourself that negativity, or generalized negative statements keep you from reaching for the stars. It is easy to hang on to the past negative experiences by refusing to budge because if it happened once, it will happen again.

No one survives without experiencing a negative situation or hurt caused by another. People blame their parents, teachers, mentors, bosses, colleagues, spouses, friends and even siblings for their negative experiences and people put a dark spin on their lives. But, a bad experience is just that…a one-time occurrence should not affect the rest of your life. Face the demon, learn from the experience and refuse to allow the past to affect the present and future.

Life is full of good things if you look for them and take them on. You will wake up one day and discover that your world is awash out, but there is plenty of sunshine if you look for it; you must make it happen. Create a happy life for yourself by doing things that brings joy it takes a considerable effort, but the end result of seeing life on the sunny side and doing good things. Nothing makes the soul soar higher than doing something good for yourself and for another person. Instead of cowering behind the walls of pessimism, get into the world and look for ways to make it better. Volunteer on occasion at a hospital, a retirement home, for a cause or get into a group. Give blood, donate to a worthy charity or hug a kid after a race at the Special Olympics in your area. Leave a larger tip for the hard-working server, offer compliments to family, friends, colleagues, and strangers. Hold the door for someone or lighten a load by offering to help them whenever possible. Smile as you meet and greet others and usually you well get a smile or pleasant greeting in return.

When asked how you are, put a positive spin on your answer even if you are coming down-with-a-cold. Take small steps at the beginning plan to do one thing that makes you happy each day. Choose an activity from things you like to do, a good deed for someone, decide to seek counseling to overcome the negative experiences of your past make friends with the new colleague who's always put you down make them smile in return. Be who you want to be not the old you; it is never too late to begin.

There are times in life when having a pessimistic attitude is good. For example: An overly optimistic person may assure everyone (he or she is OK), and offer to drive a person after they had too many glasses of wine or beer. This kind of optimistic thinking is not dangerous, but contagious. Someone who thinks that a devastating natural disaster will never occur to them because the sun always shines on them they may not be prepared when it happens. A small dose of pessimism is good when it helps protect you and others, but a pessimistic attitude should not dominate your life. If you are more in tune with negativity, it's time to take steps toward a more joyful existence.

Are You An Optimist Or Pessimist?

We all know someone who is clearly an optimist whether it's a co-worker who bounces into the office and cheerily announces (his or her) next great plan, or your neighbor grumpily informs you of the latest depressing story from the evening news, some world views are easy to see, find out if you are openly optimist or a pessimist.

Chronic **emotional distress** in its many forms is toxic to a degree. This by no means a bad saying **positive emotions** such as **laughter** or **happiness** alone will turn the course of a serious disease, illness or bad situation, but it will help you feel better about it. There is an edge in **positive emotions** again there is a more subtle meaning when you look at the practical side in an application of what happened by using the advantages of optimism, the complex variables that effects the course of a disease, illness or bad situation. Rather than being pessimistic look at the positive aspects.

Happiness, joy, relief, contentment, bliss, delight, amusement, pride, thrill, rapture, gratification, satisfaction, euphoria, and that is best described as the far edge of mania.

There are some very important aspects to life that relate to emotional happiness starting with a zest for life and **motivation** along with **determination**. Starting from the very day a child is conceived though childhood, adolescents, teens, and adulthood right on through to their relationships, link to their emotional characteristics and genetics relate to social behaviors. To say the least the fundamentals of dealing with your feelings of joy, but how you deal with happiness is probably more important in how you feel. That relates to such things as impulses, upsets, and depressions. The **rational** and **irrational emotional feelings** that display your passions for love, joy, and happiness.

Take a love test!

This test is to see how well balanced your life and see if your relationships are in bankruptcy?

1) Are you able to love others first? Yes _____ or No _____
2) Are you able to love and for-give and even for-get? Yes _____ or No _____
3) Are you able to put things in the past? Yes _____ or No ___
4) Are you able to temper your love for others? Yes _____ or No _____
5) Are you able to love your Country, and if not why? Yes _____ or No _____
6) Are you in a bad relationship? Yes _____ or No _____
7) Have you had a history of bad relationships in the past? Yes _____ or No _____
8) Do you feel loved? Yes ___ or No _____
9) Last, do you consider yourself a loving person? Yes ___ or No _____

If you have less than 4 Yes's then your life is pretty full and blessed. Some will have more Yes answer than No's. Really when it gets down to the real truth are you loving and for-giving that really gets down to where we all live and breathe. I know I must have failed the love test in the past, but I want to be able to show my love; I'm work on being for giving.

In light of these questions did you pass the test? I want to address your **attitude, thoughts, motives,** and **feelings.** The QUESTIONS come along whether they are (**BIG** or **small**) we need to find the answers if possible we have to be able to evaluate the sincerity of our **attitude, thoughts, motives,** and **feelings** and be able to balance them in our relationships are there any hidden agendas in your relationship?

What is Happiness?
Poem Secrets to Happiness   Page 1 of 1 [18]

"Living beneath your means.
Return everything you borrow.
Stop blaming other people.

307

Admit it when to yourself when you make a mistake.

Give clothes not worn in three years to charity.

Do something nice and try not to get caught.

Listen more, talk less.

Take a 30 minute walk every day.

Strive for excellence, not perfection.

Be on time.

Don't make excuses.

Don't argue.

Get organized.

Be kind to people.

Be even kinder to unkind people.

Let someone cut ahead of you in line.

Take time to be alone.

Reread a favorite book or Scriptures.

Cultivate good manners.

Be humble.

Realize and accept that life isn't always fair.

Know when to say something.

Know when to keep your mouth shut.

Go an entire day without criticizing anyone.

Learn from the past.

Plan for the future.

Live in the present.

Don't sweat the small stuff. It's all small stuff."

http://www.gmasononline.com/SectretsToHappiness.html 2/18/05

How to become happier is having a good frame of mind

Happiness is a state of mind some people are happy only when they are unhappy, or by not letting their circumstances over whelm them.

1) They feel save in that kind of environment and don't want it change

2) They were never happy as a child

3) They feel like they deserve to be unhappy

a. because they have made bad choices
b. because they feel they are a bad person
c. because they simply don't care, live for today and don't worry about the consequences, let me qualify this statement with a conclusion.

Happiness is being happy in every circumstance a person finds themselves, no matter how bad it seems at the time. Happiness is a positive emotion that is good for the mind, body, and spirit of the person.

Become happier: Reduce anxiety and stress, Improve Self-Esteem Simple Secrets of Happiness, *The Inside Story,* **By Dianne Schilling**
[19]
Other articles **related to human resources management training:**

"While researching this article, I ran across one definition that described happiness as the 'absence of factors that contribute to unhappiness, like anxiety and pain.' Ah, the medical model! Health is the absence of disease; happiness the absence of unhappiness. I don't think so. Researchers have found that happiness and unhappiness are distinct emotional states, not polarities of a continuum. Partly nature, partly knack, happiness is emotional fallout from biological and behavioral events that you -- and only you -- can influence. It's definitely an 'inside story.'

Things that people do and don't do to influence happiness: Researchers have found that money, age, gender, income, race, education and social status don't exert much influence on happiness. Surprisingly, neither do major life events, like marriage or childbirth. After the initial high, it's back to your mind set-point. However, happy people do tend to share certain personal traits: high **self-esteem**, optimism, extroversion, and a sense of agency or control over their lives. With high **self-esteem** you believe yourself worthy of happiness, while a sense of personal agency enables you to handle life's challenges. When it comes to external factors, the only thing that appears to matter is strong social support -- in other words, friends.

If you'd like to be happier -- or happy more often -- focus on these areas:

Take Care of Your Body:

Exercise, moderate to intense aerobic exercise lifts the spirits, especially women, and is a proven antidote for mild depression and anxiety. Brain chemicals released during exercise, such as serotonin, dopamine, norepinephrine, and the beta-endorphins, are known to have strong effects on mood, and may also help to strengthen your immune system.

Eat complex carbohydrates.

Carbohydrates have a tranquilizing effect on the body by stimulating the brain's production of serotonin. (By contrast, protein has been shown to sustain alertness and mental energy.) However, with simple sugars (candy and other sweets), you get a brief boost in serotonin followed by a sharp drop; your mood crashes and your craving for sugar returns even stronger. Avoid the roller coaster ride by eating complex carbohydrates -- pasta, rice, potatoes, beans, breads, fruits and vegetables. Complex carbs are metabolized by the body more slowly and sustain serotonin levels over a longer period.

Serotonin levels are also affected by sunlight. If winters are dark where you live, try to get two or three hours of bright, artificial light each day.

Develop Self-efficacy and Resilience:

Life is twenty percent what you make it and eighty percent how you take it. Underlying that statement are the concepts of *self-efficacy* -- the belief that you have both the will and the way to accomplish your goals -- and *resilience* -- the ability to bounce back from failures and approach problems as challenges, not tragedies. Focus on your potential, rather than your limitations. Devote yourself to something you do well. Orchestrate your life so that you always have some event or activity to look forward to. Stop defining success in terms of huge breakthroughs and see it in each modicum of progress you make. Above all, break away from other people's standards and expectations.

Find Pleasure in Everyday Life:

No matter how busy or preoccupied you are, take a few minutes several times a day to be in the present moment. Wake up your senses. Discover what delights you and indulge yourself accordingly. A teacher friend takes a few moments each morning and afternoon to savor a cup of freshly brewed tea, and she refuses to drink from a mug, rotating her collection of elegant teacups from home to classroom. For you, maybe its fresh flowers, mystery novels, rummaging through antique stores, motorcycle riding or movies. Want inspiration? Read *Simple Abundance: A Daybook of Comfort and Joy* by Sarah Ban Breathnach (Warner Books, 1995).

Cultivate Friendships:

Studies have shown that having confidants and companions is a key factor in experiencing a sense of well-being. Social support boosts the immune system and improves the quality (and possibly the length) of life. Friends often see humor in tough situations, help put troubles into perspective and soften life's blows. Confiding in close friends relieves stress.

Act Happy:

Try exploiting one of social psychology's key principles: Act yourself into reality. Acting cheerful can help trigger positive emotions. Adopt the stance of being a confident, happy, successful person and you will grow into the role. A number of techniques can help: In her books and workshops, Dr. Jeannette Vos (*The Learning Revolution*, 1994) teaches people to change their 'state' using music. Start by playing music that matches your present mood and then gradually change the music to reflect the mood you desire. Color can also be used to improve mood: warm, bright, active colors help relieve depression and neutral colors tend to alleviate anxiety and tension.

Live a Meaningful Life:

Discover a greater purpose -- one strong enough to get you through minor hassles and major traumas. For a powerful exercise, try writing a personal mission statement. If you need assistance, read *Creating Your Mission Statement for Work and for Life* by Laurie Beth Jones. (You can order it online at www.amazon.com). Get clear about the values and ethics that guide your life. An excellent resource is the Josephson Institute of Ethics, a nonprofit organization dedicated to improving the ethical quality of society by teaching 'principled reasoning and ethical decision making.' Visit their website (www.charactercounts.org) and see how you measure up to the 'Six Pillars of Character.' Don't let the colorful graphics and kids' photos fool you. It's a rich site with information for all ages."

http://www.womenmedia.com/seminar-happiness. 2/18/05

The Secrets to Happiness   **Page 1 – 2** [20]
          The Secrets to Happiness

"After psychologist Steven Reiss survived a life-threatening illness, he took a new look at the meaning of life. Now, based on a survey of more than 6,000 people, Reiss offers new insights about what it really takes to be happy. (The following quotes are from Reiss' article with the above title in Psychology Today, Jan/Feb 2001, pp. 50-6.)

Happiness Defined

'Harvard social psychologist William McDougall wrote that people can be happy while in pain and unhappy while experiencing pleasure. To understand this, two kinds of happiness must be distinguished: feeling-good and value-based influences. Feeling-good is happiness and sensation-based pleasure. When we joke around and talk about or having sex, we experience and feel-good feelings of happiness. Since feel-good happiness is ruled by the law of diminishing returns, the kicks get harder to come by. This type of happiness rarely lasts longer than a few minutes or hours at a time.'

'Value-based happiness is a sense that our lives have meaning and fulfill some larger purpose. It represents a spiritual source of satisfaction, stemming from our deeper purpose and values. We experience value-based happiness when we satisfy any of the 16 basic desires---the more desires we satisfy, the more value-based happiness we experience. Since this form of happiness is not ruled by the law of diminishing returns, there is no limit to how meaningful our lives can be.'

'The 16 basic desires make us individuals. Although everybody embraces these desires, individuals prioritize them differently…you do not have to satisfy all 16 desires, only the five or six most important to you.'

'After you identify your most important desires, you need to find effective ways to satisfy them. There is a catch, however. Shortly after you satisfy a desire, it reasserts itself, motivating you to satisfy the desire all over again.'

Most people turn to relationships, careers, family, leisure and spirituality to satisfy their most important desires.

Since we have the potential to satisfy our basic desires through relationships, we can find greater happiness by finding new relationships or by improving the ones we already have. After looking at the 16 basic desires and estimating the five or six most important to you, do the same for your partner, or have your partner take the quiz. Compare the two lists---the strengths of your relationship are indicated by similar desires, and the weaknesses are indicated by disparate desires' (pp. 50, 5 2, 55).

'If you have a high desire for acceptance, for example, you need work that exposes you to little evaluation and potential criticism. If you have a high desire for order, you need work that involves minimal ambiguity and exposes you to few changes. If you are a curious person, you need a job that makes you think.

Value-based happiness is the great equalizer in life. You can find value-based happiness if you are rich or poor, smart or mentally challenged, athletic or clumsy, popular or socially awkward. Wealthy people are not necessarily happy, and poor people are not necessarily unhappy. Values, not pleasure, are what bring true happiness, and everybody has the potential to live in accordance with their values' (p. 56)."

(For more information read: WHO AM I: THE 16 BASIC DESIRES THAT MOTIVATE OUR HAPPINESS AND DEFINE OUR

PERSONALITIES, by Steven Reiss, Ph.D, published by Tarcher/Putnam: 2000.)

Rate yourself as follows: descriptions:

DESIRE	STATEMENT	RATE YOURSELF
CURIOSITY	I have a thirst for knowledge	
ACCEPTANCE	I have a hard time coping with criticism	
ORDER	It upsets me when things are out of place	
PHYSICAL ACTIVITY	Physical fitness is very important to me	
HONOR	I am a highly principled and loyal person	
POWER	I often seek leadership roles	
INDEPENDENCE	Self-reliance is essential to my happiness	
SOCIAL CONTACT	I am known as a fun-loving person	
FAMILY	My children come first	
STATUS	I am impressed by people who own expensive things	
IDEALISM	Compared with most people, I am very concerned with social causes	
VENGEANCE	It is very important to me to get even with	

	those who insult or offend me
ROMANCE	Compared with my peers, I spend much more time pursuing or having sex
EATING	I love to eat and often fantasize about food
SAVING	I hate throwing things away
TRANQUILITY	Peace of mind

http://www.mtsu.edu/~socwork/frost/crazy/happinesstest.html

2/18/05

Secrets To Happiness   **Page 1 [21]**

"The secrets to happiness and well-being is no mystery.

All it takes is the ability to do the following:

- Forget
- Apologize
- Admit errors
- Avoid mistakes
- Listen to advice
- Keep your temper
- Shoulder the blame
- Make the best of things
- Maintain high standards
- Think first and act accordingly
- Put the needs of others before your own
- Forgive Seems like a tall order?

Try slipping as many of these 'secrets of happiness' into your day as possible. You'll soon be rewarded with a more positive outlook on life! It's simple then; change your thoughts and you'll change your life forever. Right? RIGHT! The missing key to success is repetitive

consistency. Trust yourself. Create the kind of self that you will be happy
to live with all your life. Make the most of yourself by fanning the tiny,
inner sparks of possibility into flames of achievement."
    -- Foster C. Mcclellan

http://www.usaezine.com/secrets.hmtl   2/18/05

DETERMINATION

A. (**Recognition**) B. (**Resiliency**) C. (**Recovery**)
A. Life means personal **RECOGNITION** for the need for changes
B. Life means personal **RESILIENCY** is meeting the challenge
C. Life means personal **RECOVERY** is overcoming the possibilities

Support **O**utreach Services is another way we help you = **Standing in
the GAP** for others, Co-support & Co-prayer-support.

II Corinthians 10:13
"There is no temptation taken you but such as is common to man: but God
is faithful, who will not suffer you to be tempted above that ye are able;
but will with the temptation also make a way to escape, that ye may be
able to bear *it*."

Mind
Ephesians 4:17 (KJV)
V-17 "This I say therefore, and testify in the Lord, that ye henceforth walk
not as other Gentiles walk, in the vanity of their mind,"

Romans 12:2 (KJV)
V-2 "Do not be conformed to this world, but be transformed by the
renewal of your mind, that by testing you may discern what is the will of
God, what is good and acceptable and perfect."

Hebrews 8:10-11 (KJV)
V-10 "For this *is* the covenant that I will make with the house of Israel
after those days, saith the Lord; I will put my laws into their mind, and

write them in their hearts: and I will be to them a God, and they shall be to me a people:

V-11 And they shall not teach every man his neighbor, and every man his brother, saying, Know the Lord: for all shall know me, from the least to the greatest."

Hebrews 10:16-18 (KJV)

V-16 "This *is* the covenant that I will make with them after those days, saith the Lord, I will put my laws into their hearts, and in their minds will I write them;

V-17 And their sins and iniquities will I remember no more.

V-18 Now where remission of these *is, there is* no more offering for sin."

Hebrews 10:22-25 (KJV)

V-22 "Let us draw near with a true heart in full assurance of faith, having our hearts sprinkled from an evil conscience, and our bodies washed with pure water.

V-23 Let us hold fast the profession of *our* faith without wavering; (for he *is* faithful that promised;)

V-24 And let us consider one another to provoke unto love and to good works:

V-25 Not forsaking the assembling of ourselves together, as the manner of some *is*; but exhorting *one another*: and so much the more, as ye see the day approaching."

Heart
Eps. 4:16

V-16 "From whom the whole body fitly joined together and compacted by that which every joint supplieth, according to the effectual working in the measure of every part, maketh increase of the body unto the edifying of itself in love."

Eps. 4:18

V-18 "Having the understanding darkened, being alienated from the life of God through the ignorance that is in them, because of the blindness of their heart:"

Feelings
Luke 11:28

V-28 "Come to me, all who labor and are heavy laden, and I will give you rest. Take my yoke upon you, and learn from me, for I am gentle and lowly in heart, and you will find rest for your souls. For my yoke is easy, and my burden is light."

Philippians 4:6

V-6 "Do not be anxious about anything, but in everything by prayer and supplication with thanksgiving let your requests be made known to God."

1 Peter 5:7

V-7 "Casting all your anxieties on him, because he cares for you."

Accountability
I Cor 3:10-23

V-10 "Neither murmur ye, as some of them also murmured, and were destroyed of the destroyer.

V-11 Now all these things happened unto them for examples: and they are written for our admonition, upon whom the ends of the world are come.

V-12 Wherefore let him that thinketh he standeth take heed lest he fall.

V-13 There hath no temptation taken you but such as is common to man: but God is faithful, who will not suffer you to be tempted above that ye are able; but will with the temptation also make a way to escape, that ye may be able to bear it.

V-14 Wherefore, my dearly beloved, flee from idolatry.

V-15 I speak as to wise men; judge ye what I say.

V-16 The cup of blessing which we bless, is it not the communion of the blood of Christ? The bread which we break, is it not the communion of the body of Christ?

V-17 For we being many are one bread, and one body: for we are all partakers of that one bread.

V-18 Behold Israel after the flesh: are not they which eat of the sacrifices partakers of the altar?

V-19 What say I then? that the idol is anything, or that which is offered in sacrifice to idols is anything?

V-20 But I say, that the things which the Gentiles sacrifice, they sacrifice to devils, and not to God: and I would not that ye should have fellowship with devils.

V-21 Ye cannot drink the cup of the Lord, and the cup of devils: ye cannot be partakers of the Lord's table, and of the table of devils.

V-22 Do we provoke the Lord to jealousy? are we stronger than he?

V-23 All things are lawful for me, but all things are not expedient: all things are lawful for me, but all things edify not."

Responsibility
Rom 12:1-3

V-1 I "beseech you therefore, brethren, by the mercies of God, that ye present your bodies a living sacrifice, holy, acceptable unto God, which is your reasonable service.

V- 2 And be not conformed to this world: but be ye transformed by the renewing of your mind, that ye may prove what is that good, and acceptable, and perfect, will of God.

V-3 For I say, through the grace given unto me, to every man that is among you, not to think of himself more highly than he ought to think; but to think soberly, according as God hath dealt to every man the measure of faith."

Assessment I. Life is about the **RESPONSABILITY** in a person's life

Assessment II. Life is about the **ACCOUNTABILITY** in a person's life

Assessment III. Life means personal **DISCIPLINE** such as in self-correction

Assessment IV. Life means personal **MOTIVATION** in how a person lives their life

    DETERMINATION

    A. (**Recognition**) B. (**Resiliency**) C. (**Recovery**)

    A. Life means personal **RECOGNITION** is understanding the need for changes

    B. Life means personal **RESILIENCE** is meeting the challenge

C. Life means personal **RECOVERY** is overcoming the possibilities

The Lighthouse by Henry Wadsworth Longfellow
The Lighthouse
The rocky ledge runs far into the sea,
and on its outer point, some miles away,
the lighthouse lifts its massive masonry,
A pillar of fire by night, of cloud by day.
Even at this distance I can see the tides,
Upheaving, break unheard along its base,
A speechless wrath, that rises and subsides
in the white tip and tremor of the face.

And as the evening darkens, lo! how bright,
through the deep purple of the twilight air,
Beams forth the sudden radiance of its light,
with strange, unearthly splendor in the glare!

No one alone: from each projecting cape
And perilous reef along the ocean's verge,
Starts into life a dim, gigantic shape,
Holding its lantern o'er the restless surge.

Like the great giant Christopher it stands
Upon the brink of the tempestuous wave,
Wading far out among the rocks and sands,
The night o'er taken mariner to save.

And the great ships sail outward and return
Bending and bowing o'er the billowy swells,
And ever joyful, as they see it burn
They wave their silent welcome and farewells.

They come forth from the darkness, and their sails
Gleam for a moment only in the blaze,
And eager faces, as the light unveils
Gaze at the tower, and vanish while they gaze.

The mariner remembers when a child,
on his first voyage, he saw it fade and sink
And when returning from adventures wild,
He saw it rise again o'er ocean's brink.

Steadfast, serene, immovable, the same,
Year after year, through all the silent night

Burns on forevermore that quenchless flame,
Shines on that inextinguishable light!

It sees the ocean to its bosom clasp
The rocks and sea-sand with the kiss of peace:
It sees the wild winds lift it in their grasp,
And hold it up, and shake it like a fleece.

The startled waves leap over it; the storm
Smites it with all the scourges of the rain,
And steadily against its solid form
press the great shoulders of the hurricane.
The sea-bird wheeling round it, with the din
of wings and winds and solitary cries,
Blinded and maddened by the light within,
Dashes himself against the glare, and dies.

A new Prometheus, chained upon the rock,
Still grasping in his hand the fire of love,
it does not hear the cry, nor heed the shock,
but hails the mariner with words of love.

"Sail on!" it says: "sail on, ye stately ships!
And with your floating bridge the ocean span;
Be mine to guard this light from all eclipse.
Be yours to bring man neared unto man.

--Henry Wadsworth Longfellow

There are many other studies in our study guides:
Let us help you climb your Mountain.
What are the next steps in your life?

There is always our Support Outreach Services Self Help Info & Books!
Conferences - Seminars Workshops on Training Sessions & Manuals

Personal Support may help a person get past the obstacles in their life by bridging the GAPS. Guidance Answers Passion Support. In our Personal Support = One to One Care.

We will lay out some help in our outreach surveys and studies that may help a person deal with problems in their life, go to our web site to link up with these programs.

www.sosselfhelpbooks.info

SUPPORT OUTREACH SERVICES LINKS

I believe there is a bridge that will fill in the gaps in a person's life. What is a person looking for, and how do they find the missing LINKS?

1. Common Ground - A personal encounter, "One to One."
2. The Panic Button - Is Our Message Line.
3. Independent Processing Center for Materials – Self-Help Study Guides, Books, Booklets, and Services.
4. Decision Materials: Life Enhancement ABC's study guide, & Life Enhancement Stress Evaluations, Assessments, & Analysis My health & fitness program.
5. Support Center (A) Support Partner (B) Support Group (C) Support Information (D) Group Identities

CHECK THE LIST OF SUPPORT OUTREACH SERVICES AND PROGRAMS
(Please check which of these "Services and Programs," you will want)?

Regardless of your faith in God there is someone out there that will share your views. People have a common bond as they share their experiences, and that is what brings them closer together.

SOS Books

My family and my life story (book) "Facing the real me, Run John Run, the real world and me, the hurt and pain, and The real cry for help." (Book).

I would like to let you know something about our self-help books for an individual, family, organization or in a church library. Please contact me if you would like to set up a conference, and seminars based on our books. We have workshops and manuals and we will help you with these programs.

Books:

"SOS LIFE ENHANCEMENT" Who is that person in your mirror; the functions of the brain, 10 steps in behavior identification & modification; as we help you climb your mountain?

"SOS SELF IMPROVEMENTS" personal identity Self-Image, Self-Esteem relates to Self-Control, Self-Discipline, & Motivation – Self-Worth is your Core Identity Pride, Ego, and Vanity.

"SOS NEW BEGINNINGS" Study Guide on Premarital Relationships, Marriage and Children, Divorce, Single Parenting, Blended Families, & Addiction Treatments)

Book: "The Fundamentals of Christian Psychology" & the Modern Techniques of Psychology.

We believe churches and organizations might like workshops along with our training manuals on "Mentoring & Coaching; and another is "Leadership Training" on how to conduct group sessions.

You might ask what your credentials I have a B/S from Baptist Bible College and Seminary; and from Louisiana Baptist University an M/A

Thesis on Mentoring & Coaching, my PH-D Distortion "Counseling for Results".

What is your experience, I am a Clinical Christian Psychologist & Analyst, I do counseling and testing for the Master Ranch and Christian Academe, and have been doing group sessions since 2008, and I am the facilitator of Community Outreach Group Sessions.

If you want one or all of our books we will give you a break depending on how many you want. I would love to come to your church or organization based on what you can afford for our conference, seminars, and workshops. They will not need to buy any of the books for the conference, seminars; the manuals for the workshops will be a part of the workshop.

If you or your organization would like more information or references please contact me.

To participate in any of our services are free. When you order our books, and the study materials and DVD's, there is an expense:
  One book $15.00
  Two Books $25.00
  Three Books $35.00
  Study materials$10.00
  Shipping costs $ 10.00
  What you do will enable us to carry out some of these programs and services.
Our information network will give you list of study guides, newsletters are on the link, and some booklets are free. There is so much information out there and there are all kinds of help.

Support Outreach Services links:

I believe there is a bridge that will fill in the gaps in a person's life. What is a person looking for, and how do they find the missing LINKS?
  1. Common Ground - A personal encounter, "One to One."

  2. The Panic Button - Is Our Message Line.

3. Independent Processing Center for Materials – Self-Help Study Guides, Books, Booklets, DVD's, and Services.

4. Decision-Materials:

My Family Biography and my life story book: "Facing the real me, Run John Run, the real hurt and pain, the real cry for help, the real changes in my life."

Book: SOS LIFE ENHANCEMENT study guide, Stress Evaluations Assessments & Analysis My health & fitness program.

Book: SOS SELF IMPROVEMENT self-image, self-esteem, and self-worth.

Book: SOS NEW BEGINNINGS relationships, marriage & parenting. Divorce, single parenting, blended families, and addictions treatment process and recover programs.

5. Support Center (A) Support Partner (B) Support Group (C) Support Information (D) Group Identities.

6. drbarrettphd.yahoo.com / email access.

SOS Booklets
1. "Health-awareness and A Healthy Heart" and an exercise program,
2. "The No Non SENSE workout." (Booklet).
3. SOS Bible Lessons – Biblical Principals to live by - How to pray & intercessory prayer, and Spiritual Warfare. (Booklets on different Bible Subjects).

PERSONAL PROFILES, AND SHARE YOUR EXPERIENCES Newsletters.

Our newsletters are a vital link with the person. The "SOS Life Line News" is on our web site www.sosselfhelpbooks.info will have information pertaining to teens and college age young people. We will have information that adults can identify with whether they are single or married, and whatever your relationship is with your children.

The next step is to get you to respond and to participate. There are no specials because all of the services are based on what a person or organization wants. Some may want to support us along with some churches, and organizations that would be greatly appreciated and help us provide these free services. I want you to be a part of our services and programs. I don't use pressure tactics.

My hope is you will want to be a part of OUR HELP NETWORK I have a wonderful Pastor in my life, church, and class that has helped me so much in many ways they gave me the support when I really needed it. You know how my life was changed and there is a real need for the right kind of help and support in a person's life. There are inspirational speakers and I have a list of programs and services in the prefix. You can pick and choose the subjects and information that are of interest to you or your organization.

There are no membership fees or meetings to attend OUR COMMUNICATION NETWORK is set up for you. I feel that the age we live in has given us some of the best avenues available to communicate. The phone, the Internet, and our news letters are ways of meeting with you. Then you can share with us and/or partner with us. There will be special meetings conferences, and seminars you can attend if you would like. Then we will present different subjects and speakers using information from our books.

Appendix *i*
Website References

Web pictures "Being
RAY CHARLES – Blues, Jas, R&B Music –corporate Entertainment

Booking   **Pages 1 of 6 [1] P. 15**

Fanny Crosby Biographies   **Pages 1-2 [2] P. 17**
Charles Darwin, **published his initial work, The** *Origin of the Species*

years later a second work,

Charles Darwin, published his initial work, The ***Origin of the Species***
years later a second work, ***The Descent of Man Today***,

Pages 1 2 [3] P. 24

Education World Walden University   **Pages 1 – 6 [4] P.60**

"Howard Gardner's theory of multiple intelligences makes people

think 'IQ,' is about being 'smart.' The theory is changing the way

some teachers teach.

Meta cognition" An Overview   **Pages 1 of 7 [5] P. 64**
META CONGNITION OVERVIEW
© 1997 by Jennifer A. Livingston

Venture Capital Magazine   **Pages 1 - 2 [6] P. 65**
Individualism methodology cognitivism

Narcissistic Personal Disorders. Sysptoms of Disorders
Pages 1 – 4 [7] P. 106

In what ways does the brain have control over Self-Esteem"
THE TEMPORAL LOBE & LIMBIC SYSTEM
Pages 1-9 [8] P. 119

The University of Washington
People with low self-esteem less motivated to break a negative moods
Page 1 of 2 [9] **P. 140**

The Moody News Newsletter for Depression, Mania and Other Mental
Disorders
Mood disorders   **Page 1 – 15** [10] **P. 143**

Mood pages 15 -   [11] P. **152**

You may get it Wrong before you to get it Right
                         Pages 1 of 2 [12] **P. 191**
   Self improvement   "The Purpose of Life is to LIVE Ray Terris

12 Reasons Budgeting Can Improve your life   [13] **P. 199**

Steven C. Rockefeller, *John Dewey: Religious Faith* [14] **P. 200**

THE INGREDIENTS OF SELF-CONTROL Pages 2 - 10 [15]

                                P. 226

FEAR AS YOUR ALLY   **Pages 1 of 3** [16] **P. 249**

What Your Anger May Be Hiding / Psychology Today

Poem Secrets to Happiness

Become happier: Reduce anxiety and stress, Improve self Esteem

Simple Secrets of Happiness, *The Inside Story,* By Dianne Schilling

The Secrets of Happiness

Appendix *ii*

Apendix *iii*

Bible References

The Good Samaritan Christ's true example of altruism
I can't think of a better example of altruism. The setting is Christ's
teachings of the "Seventy disciples sent out," he talked with His disciples

in **Luke Chapter 10**:	P. 33
Romans 12:3	P. 38
I Cor. 8:2	P. 316
II Cor. 3:5	P. 316
Gal. 6:3	P. 316
Phi. 4:6	P. 316
II Corinthians 10:13	P. 316
Eph. 4: 16	P. 316
Eph. 4: 18	P. 316
Rom. 12:2	P. 316
Heb. 8:10,11	P. 316
Heb. 10:16-18	P. 317
Heb. 10:22-25	P. 317
Eph. 4:16	P. 317
Eph. 4:18	P. 318
Pil. 4:6	P. 318
I Peter 5:7	P. 318
I Cor. 3:10-23	P. 318
Rom. 12:1-3	P. 319

www.ingramcontent.com/pod-product-compliance
Lightning Source LLC
Chambersburg PA
CBHW051814090426
42736CB00011B/1474